Richard William Church, Mary C Church

Occasional Papers

Selected from the Guardian, the Times, and the Saturday Review / 1846-1890

Richard William Church, Mary C Church

Occasional Papers

Selected from the Guardian, the Times, and the Saturday Review / 1846-1890

ISBN/EAN: 9783744660990

Printed in Europe, USA, Canada, Australia, Japan

Cover: Foto ©Thomas Meinert / pixelio.de

More available books at **www.hansebooks.com**

OCCASIONAL PAPERS

SELECTED FROM

THE GUARDIAN, THE TIMES, AND THE SATURDAY REVIEW
1846-1890

BY THE LATE

R. W. CHURCH, M.A., D.C.L.
SOMETIME RECTOR OF WHATLEY, DEAN OF ST. PAUL'S
HONORARY FELLOW OF ORIEL COLLEGE

IN TWO VOLS.—VOL. I

London
MACMILLAN AND CO., LIMITED
NEW YORK: THE MACMILLAN COMPANY
1897

PREFACE

THE reviews, articles, and biographical sketches which are reprinted in these volumes have, with only one exception, formed part of the Dean's contributions to the newspapers whose names are given on the title-page, during a period of forty-four years, from 1846 to 1890. The Dean began writing for the *Guardian* in 1846, and continued to be a regular weekly contributor down to 1871, when he came to St. Paul's. His reviews and articles in that paper alone, judging by a list which is not even so quite a complete one, number over a thousand. For the *Saturday Review* he wrote regularly, though less frequently, between the years 1861 and 1871. No complete record remains of his contributions to the *Times*, but by permission of the Proprietors of that paper I am enabled to republish three reviews bearing the dates of 1865 and 1866. The one exception in the volume of hitherto unpublished matter will be found in the "Fragment on Elizabeth," which was written in 1889, and is included here among other papers touching on various aspects of the ecclesiastical and political history of the fifteenth and sixteenth centuries, abroad and in England.

The selection from so great a mass of material has been no easy task. I have tried to make it as far as possible representative of my father's work, and at the same time to choose those of his writings only which deal with books and matters of permanent interest. Even so, for want of space, the collection is an incomplete one; whilst much vigorous writing, which was bestowed on subjects now forgotten—on biographies which are no longer read, and travels and books of general reading now more or less superseded—has been left aside. It is almost inevitable, from the form in which the papers first appeared, that the general impression given by these volumes should be to a certain degree fragmentary and unfinished. I have tried, in some degree at least, to meet this disadvantage by grouping the various subjects together where there seemed to be any relationship of thought or subject running through them.

Up to the year 1871, in addition to his weekly review for the *Guardian*, my father wrote one or more articles for the same paper on some political question of the day. A great number of the articles on the Crimean War, the Austro-Prussian War, the Eastern Question, the Greek and Italian and Roman Questions, were from his pen. During these years, except in his reviews, he seldom wrote on purely ecclesiastical subjects. Almost the first occasion on which he wrote at any length on a Church question was at the 'time of the Purchas judgment in 1871. But these articles, like those on political matters, are too fragmentary, and deal too much with the varying aspects of the question, as they offered themselves for discussion week by week, to be suitable for republication. I need hardly mention that these papers are all of them reprinted as they stand, except for a few minute corrections. Only in three cases where certain strong terms of censure occur in the course of an article, which, justly severe as they were at the moment, I am sure that my father would have modified in any republication after the immediate cause of controversy was over, have I ventured to omit an expression as likely to mislead or to cause pain.

During my father's first years in London he still continued to write for the *Guardian*, though very irregularly. Between the years 1874 and 1880, during which time he was not in sympathy with the line taken by the *Guardian* in ecclesiastical affairs, he wrote very little, his only contributions to the paper being an occasional review. After this time he became again a more frequent contributor, writing both leading articles and reviews to within a short time of his death.

A word of explanation is perhaps needed for the insertion of so short a paper on a great subject as that entitled "The New Court," written in 1889. It is given here, because it was his last utterance on any distinctively Church question. A year and a half later, when the Archbishop of Canterbury had delivered his judgment at Lambeth, and when it would naturally have fallen to the Dean to write fully upon it in the *Guardian*, his strength had too greatly failed to make such an effort

PREFACE ix

possible. Yet he continued his work in a certain measure to the end. The two papers on "Cardinal Newman" and "Cardinal Newman's Naturalness," which were written off rapidly in the first moments of emotion, when the end of so long a friendship filled all his thoughts and threw his whole mind vividly back on the past, were written when his own health had undergone a grave decline, and he had less than four months to live. The review of "Moore's History of the Reformation," which concludes his long connection of forty-four years with the *Guardian*, was written a few weeks before his death.

MARY C. CHURCH.

CONTENTS

I

CARLYLE'S CROMWELL . . . . . . PAGE 1

II

A SEQUEL TO THE "VESTIGES" . . . 53

III

STANLEY ON THE STUDY OF ECCLESIASTICAL HISTORY . 66

IV

STANLEY'S LECTURES ON THE JEWISH CHURCH . 76

V

MERIVALE ON THE CONVERSION OF THE ROMAN EMPIRE 85

VI

EPICTETUS 99

VII

Thierry's St. Jerome   127

VIII

Ranke's "History of the Popes"   143

IX

Dean Milman's Essays   155

X

Guicciardini   167

XI

Lecky's History of Morals   209

XII

Morison's St. Bernard   230

XIII

Ignatius Loyola   238

XIV

Bossuet's Earlier Sermons   253

XV

Jansenist Expositions of Scripture   272

CONTENTS xiii

XVI
FÉNELON'S MYSTICISM — 286

XVII
LAMENNAIS — 301

XVIII
AN EIRENICON — 334

XIX
DÖLLINGER ON THE REUNION OF CHRISTENDOM — 367

XX
BREWER'S HENRY VIII. — 380

XXI
MOORE'S LECTURES ON THE REFORMATION — 392

XXII
A FRAGMENT ON ELIZABETH — 401

I

CARLYLE'S CROMWELL[1]

I

MR. CARLYLE's philosophy, whatever else it may be, is an easy one. Cynicism is hardly a deep view of human nature, but it is a broad bold view, partially undeniable and thoroughly available. Brought out smartly and with originality, the human mind is much taken with it; it is good sport, and withal seems so honest, and besides it saves trouble. Mr. Carlyle has worked it with much effect; it has helped him to popularity, not only as a clever thinker, but as a man in earnest in an age of shams. But cynicism, refine it as you will, may become wearisome. The public for a while will patiently laugh at, nay, will seriously condemn its own hollowness; it will acquiesce provisionally in the division of mankind into heroes and "flunkeys," the one all soul, the other all clothes,— the few who have no shams, and the many who are

[1] *Oliver Cromwell's Letters and Speeches: with Elucidations.* By Thomas Carlyle. *Guardian*, 21st January 1846.

nothing else. This world of ours has many sides, and this is one—an impressive one: but the world turns round, and in time shows its other phases, and then slap-dash, picturesque, undiscriminating cynicism fails, and, if it attempt to take possession of these also, is resented. It turns out that men, even in the nineteenth century, who spin cotton and make railroads, are not merely stuffed coats and breeches; and they begin to suspect a teacher of something like cant who has nothing more to tell them than this. To contemplate the heroic and to anathematise and spit upon "valet-populations" is no doubt very virtuous, but not the whole of virtue, nor even, by itself, an exceedingly healthy part of it. Cannot Mr. Carlyle manage to detect, even in the nineteenth century, at least some tendency to heroism? Cannot he give us some practical suggestions how to become heroic? not mere declamation, not mere warning against "damnabilities," not mere imaginative pictures of past heroes, but something to show that he understands and is stirred by the good of the age, as well as abhors the bad? He knows, he says, that we want direction; cannot he tell us in a plain straightforward way what he would have us do? While he sits apart, thundering on us amid mist and storm, other men risk something positive. For his own sake he also ought to try to do so. He will find it more difficult than ringing changes on the idea of cant and forging grotesque names for it; but we submit to him whether it would not be more consistent with the tone he has held to the world. A mere iconoclast, except perhaps in poetry, is a very pitiful and very useless sort of person. Men will not leave even their idols for a dreary belief in the universality of sham. Nay, may they not in time be provoked or bored into asking whether Diogenes himself, the scourge of flunkeyism, the lynx-eyed sham detector, is not a bit of a quack, and may not be parading the evils of our smug age—grievous enough in all conscience—to set off a pet hero, or his own style?

Let it be said, once for all, Mr. Carlyle's mind is not one of the deepest class. Breadth of painting not analysis, phenomena not their meaning, are his aim. All that an unusually true and vivid grouping of phenomena will explain we may trust him for, but not much more. Hence, what is so shocking in his writings, amid so much real feeling of the awfulness and mystery of our life and state, he is content to play even about Christianity. He honours it, as he honours all that is really noble, but only as an accidental form —it may be the highest the world has yet seen—of the divine in man. He knows it only as it has matched itself against the "heroisms" of the world, as projected on their plane; and all its inner life and sympathies he ignores. He seems never to have fairly confronted it. He might be a dangerous writer, but, luckily we are either too stupid or too sensible.

These thoughts occur involuntarily, as in each fresh work of Mr. Carlyle (the subject of our present remarks inclusive) the same sweeping monotonous denunciations are repeated against his own bugbear—

the cant of the day. It has now driven him upon the Puritanism of the Rebellion, and Oliver Cromwell. In it and in him he finds refuge as in the "last of all our heroisms"—the last traces of those ideas and that belief which had guided us during all preceding centuries—a "heroism" absolutely unintelligible to our unbelieving age, and frightfully smothered under its own records. A strange conjunction! sour, fanatical, strait-laced Puritanism, with its first fundamental principle of God's absolute decrees, fondled and poetised by one to whom Christianity is but the mythic expression of religion! But he shall give his account of the matter himself:—

"Few nobler Heroisms," says a well-known Writer long occupied on this subject (another phrase of Mr. Carlyle's), "at bottom perhaps no nobler Heroism ever transacted itself on this Earth; and it lies as good as lost to us; overwhelmed under such an avalanche of Human Stupidities as no Heroism before ever did. Intrinsically and extrinsically it may be considered inaccessible to these generations. Intrinsically, the spiritual purport of it has become inconceivable, incredible to the modern mind. Extrinsically, the documents and records of it, scattered waste as a shoreless chaos, are not legible. They lie there, printed, written, to the extent of tons and square miles, as shot-rubbish; unedited, unsorted, not so much as indexed; full of every conceivable confusion; yielding light to very few, yielding darkness, in several sorts, to very many. Dull Pedantry, conceited idle Dilettantism—prurient Stupidity in what shape soever—is darkness and not light! There are from

Thirty to Fifty Thousand unread Pamphlets of the Civil War in the British Museum alone: huge piles of mouldering wreck, wherein, at the rate of perhaps one pennyweight per ton, lie things memorable. They lie preserved there, waiting happier days; under present conditions they cannot, except for idle purposes, for dilettante excerpts and such like, be got examined. The Rushworths, Whitlockes, Nalsons, Thurloes; enormous folios, these and many others have been printed, and some of them again printed, but never yet edited— edited as you edit wagon-loads of broken bricks and dry mortar, simply by tumbling up the wagon! Not one of those monstrous old volumes has so much as an available Index. It is the general rule of editing on this matter. If your editor correct the press, it is an honourable distinction to him. Those dreary old records were compiled at first by Human Insight in part; and in great part by Human Stupidity withal;—but then it was by Stupidity in a laudable diligent state, and doing its best; which was something: —and alas, they have been successively elaborated by Human Stupidity in the *idle* state, falling idler and idler, and only pretending to be diligent; whereby now, for us, in these late days, they have grown very dim indeed! . .
The sound of them is not a *voice*, conveying knowledge or memorial of any earthly or heavenly thing; it is a widespread inarticulate slumberous mumblement, issuing as if from the lake of Eternal Sleep. *Craving* for oblivion, for abolition and honest silence, as a blessing in comparison!—

"This then," continues our impatient friend, "is the Elysium we English have provided for our Heroes! The Rushworthian Elysium. Dreariest continent of shot-rubbish the eye ever saw. Confusion piled on confusion to your utmost horizon's edge : obscure, in lurid twilight as of the shadow of Death ; trackless, without index, without finger-post, or mark of any human foregoer ; where your human footstep, if you are still human, echoes bodeful through the gaunt solitude, peopled only by somnambulant Pedants, Dilettants, and doleful creatures, by Phantasms, errors, inconceivabilities, by Nightmares, pasteboard Norroys, griffins, wiverns, and chimeras dire ! There, all vanquished, overwhelmed under such waste lumber-mountains, the wreck and dead ashes of some six unbelieving generations, does the Age of Cromwell and his Puritans lie hidden from us. This is what we, for our share, have been able to accomplish towards keeping our Heroic Ones in memory. By way of sacred poet they have found voluminous Dryasdust, and his Collections and Philosophical Histories."

Much-to-be-pitied heroes ! But the "Rushworthian Elysium" is of their own planting. Mr. Carlyle, if he would but take off his spectacles, would see that his pity is a good deal thrown away—that they are sufficiently at home in their abode. They dearly loved to talk and write and print ; and no more glorious mausoleum would they have coveted than a tumulus of their own "small dumpy quartos." Mr. Carlyle plainly feels that they have written and talked too much for their own character. He is afraid of the impression, and cannot trust us without a word of caution. As an initial step towards understanding their speech we must accomplish a belief that in those days, and on that side, there was nothing but manly brave veracity — no smooth oily cant, no "official or other jargon," apparently not even self-deceit. Indeed, if we will believe this, Mr. Carlyle will generously make us a present of the *quasi-*sincerity of Laud and Heylin—nay, even allow that that man of unveracious heart, Clarendon, living in veracious Puritan times, was not without some real meaning. And so believing, we shall gradually see the truth of the time :—

A practical world, based on belief in God, such as many centuries had seen before, but as never any centuries since has been privileged to see. It was the last glimpse of it in our world, this of English Puritanism ; very great, very glorious ; tragical enough to all thinking hearts that look on it from these days of ours.

He has indeed asked a hard thing of us, to believe that Puritans never canted. Believing this, we may doubtless believe his equally astonishing view of heroism in a *party*. The case certainly is without parallel ; a heroic party is a new feature in the world. We could believe it if Mr. Carlyle would show it us.

Really these poor Puritans are hardly used by their modern friend. In despite of themselves, he has, to use his own phrase, "galvanised" them into a temporary heroism. When the fit is over they will seem to have been made unfairly ridiculous. Make them heroes, and the world becomes ill-natured ; make them poor inexplicable mortals, and they will get fair play. Even in Mr. Carlyle's book, we look in vain for these Puritan heroes *en masse*, such as he speaks of in his "Anti-Dryasdust" chapter. Resolute, burly gentlemen, good fighting soldiers, preachers and Parliament men, with patience and lungs of the best,— this Mr. Carlyle does show us; for the rest we must take his word for it—that they were heroes. And of one large section he himself soon gets tired. Heroic Purged Parliament, heroic Rump, heroic "little Parliament," are not more ceremoniously treated by Mr. Carlyle than they were by the big hero of the book himself. This poetic view, applied on a large scale, breaks down. The strange and perplexed phenomena of Puritan character are not to be explained by riding wild and one-eyed through them, not by South and Hudibras wit,—neither by the "heroic hypothesis," and the "black and white surplice" antipathies of Mr. Carlyle.

The history—the epic cycle—of the Puritans is at present beyond his hopes. But in default of this, and preparatory to it, he has edited the Letters and Speeches of Cromwell. Most of them have been in print before, but dispersed in the huge collections relating to the civil wars. From far and near he has gathered and arranged all that he could find of Cromwell's, "fished them up from foul Lethean quagmires . . . washed them clean from foreign stupidities . . . washed them into something of legibility"—a necessary and very difficult business. But the book is not all Cromwell; joining and elucidating his strong homely words are jottings and sketches in Mr. Carlyle's own more elaborate style; that interweaving of schoolboy jargon and conversational familiarities, with high-pitched declamation of an antique cast, by which he is wont to bring out the blended greatness and smallness of human affairs. But the spirit and dramatic power of the scenes in the *French Revolution* are, for the most part, wanting here; partly owing to the unreal tone of sentiment which runs through the book—the mistake of forcing home-bred English Puritans into full-blown divine heroes—partly perhaps to Mr. Carlyle having written too much.

Many men have admired Oliver, but they have most of them felt doubts whether it was all fair play and above-board with him. He has been a puzzle, and they have felt it necessary to apologise. Mr. Carlyle feels no doubts and makes no apologies. Through the dim vista of the ages he makes out the dim but unquestionable form of a genuine hero, with belief, veracity, valour, insight; strong in his hatred of falsehood, impurity, injustice, and stern in his way of quelling them,—a genuine Englishman withal, rude and clumsy in speech, as Englishmen are:—

Working for long years in those unspeakable Historic Provinces, of which the reader has already had account, it becomes more and more apparent to one, That this man Oliver Cromwell was, as the popular fancy represents him, the soul of the Puritan Revolt, without whom it had never been a revolt transcendently memorable, and an Epoch in the World's History; that in fact he, more than is common in such cases, does deserve to give his name to the Period in question, and have the

Puritan Revolt considered as a *Cromwelliad*, which issue is already very visible for it. And then farther, altogether contrary to the popular fancy, it becomes apparent that this Oliver was not a man of falsehoods, but a man of truths; whose words do carry a meaning with them, and above all others of that time are worth considering. His words,—and still more his *silences*, and unconscious instincts, when you have spelt and lovingly deciphered these also out of his words,—will in several ways reward the study of an earnest man. An earnest man, I apprehend, may gather from these words of Oliver's, were there even no other evidence, that the character of Oliver and of the Affairs he worked in is much the reverse of that mad jumble of "hypocrisies," etc. etc., which at present passes current as such.

The book is composed on this view. Never once, through the whole of Oliver's difficult history, does his editor flinch from him. Oliver had enemies, and enemies tell lies, especially of heroes; at least they misunderstand them. The fact is unquestionable, and on the back of it the hero's editor rides triumphant through all kinds of evil reports. Oliver's early days are beclouded by stories of a somewhat wild youth; no great discredit to him, on at least some Puritan principles, and in spite of Mr. Carlyle, not so incredible; but woe to the unlucky scribbler who first put them about:—

The chief fountain, indeed, of all the foolish lies that have circulated about Oliver since, is the mournful brown little Book called *Flagellum, or the Life and Death of*

O. Cromwell the late Usurper, by James Heath; which was got ready so soon as possible on the back of the *Annus Mirabilis* or Glorious Restoration, and is written in such spirit as we may fancy. When restored potentates and high dignitaries had dug up "above a hundred buried corpses, and flung them in a heap in St. Margaret's Churchyard," the corpse of Admiral Blake among them, and Oliver's old Mother's corpse; and were hanging on Tyburn gallows, as some small satisfaction to themselves, the dead clay of Oliver, of Ireton, and Bradshaw; when high dignitaries and potentates were in such a humour, what could be expected of poor pamphleteers and garreteers? Heath's poor little brown, lying *Flagellum* is described by one of the moderns as a "*Flagitium*"; and Heath himself is called "*Carrion* Heath," as being "an unfortunate blasphemous dullard, and scandal to Humanity; blasphemous, I say; who, when the image of God is shining through a man, reckons it in his sordid soul to be the image of the Devil, and acts accordingly; who in fact has no soul except what saves him the expense of salt; who intrinsically is Carrion and not Humanity"; which seems hard measure to poor James Heath. "He was the son of the King's Cutler," says Wood, "and wrote pamphlets;" the best he was able, poor man. He has become a dreadfully dull individual, in addition to all! . . . From him and his *Flagellums* and scandalous Human Platitudes, let no rational soul seek knowledge.

Mark Noble fares a little better, being more thick-headed :—

Among modern Biographies, the great original is that of Mark Noble above cited, such "original" as there is;

a Book, if we must call it a Book, abounding in facts and pretended facts more than any other on this subject. Poor Noble has gone into much research of old leases, marriage-contracts, deeds of sale, and such like; he is learned in parish registers and genealogies, has consulted pedigrees "measuring eight feet by two feet four"; goes much upon heraldry; in fact has amassed a large heap of evidences and assertions, worthless and of worth, respecting Cromwell and his Connexions; from which the reader, by his own judgment, is to extract what he can. For Noble himself is a man of extreme imbecility; his judgment, for most part, seeming to lie dead asleep; and, indeed, it is worth little when broadest awake. He falls into manifold mistakes, commits and omits in all ways; plods along contented, in an element of perennial dimness, purblindness; has occasionally a helpless broad innocence of platitude which is almost interesting. A man, indeed, of extreme imbecility; to whom nevertheless let due gratitude be borne.

His Book, in fact, is not properly a Book, but rather an aggregate of bewildered jottings; a kind of Cromwellian Biographical Dictionary, *wanting* the alphabetical, or any other, arrangement or index; which latter want, much more remediable than the want of judgment, is itself a great sorrow to the reader. Such as it is, this same Dictionary without judgment and without arrangement, "bad Dictionary gone to pie," as we may call it, is the storehouse from which subsequent Biographies have all furnished themselves. The reader, with continual vigilance of suspicion, once knowing what man he has to do with, digs through it, and again through it; covers the margins of it with notes and contradictions, with references, deductions, rectifications, execrations, — in a sorrowful but not entirely unprofitable manner.

"Carrion Heath," and "my reverend imbecile friend," are used, not as authorities but as scarecrows, to deter us from believing anything against Oliver. Their asserting a thing is a guarantee of its falsehood or folly. Nor shall we find him much more respectful to authorities of greater mark. Let Whitlocke or Ludlow wag his tongue against Oliver, and forthwith one of Mr. Carlyle's choice epithets is tacked on to him, and his mouth is shut for the future. He is become an infamous witness.

So much for Mr. Carlyle himself, and his general view of the times and authorities with which he is dealing,—a necessary preliminary to considering his account of Cromwell, to which we hope to revert on a future occasion.

II [1]

WE have adverted to Mr. Carlyle's view of Cromwell. Mr. Carlyle is not a man for half measures. Other colder and more cautious biographers have respected authorities, have thought alleged facts worthy of attention, have hesitated, pondered, acquiesced at last in probabilities. Mr. Carlyle is not content with such a prosaic method, or such meagre conclusions.

[1] *Guardian*, 4th February 1846.

History, he says, is dim, even when not mendacious; the probabilities of ordinary character are no measure of a hero. With Cromwell's words and his own sympathies he is content; they tell him what Oliver *must have been.*

Puritanism was English character developed for the last time into Heroism, and Cromwell was the normal Puritan,—a union of primitive simplicity and patriarchal faith, with the keenness, intrepid recklessness about life, contempt of prescription, which were necessary to set a crooked generation to rights. Cromwell is a complete hero with a hero's attributes and claims, not to be judged by common experience, not to be charged with selfishness, insincerity, ambition. No, breathe not a suspicion against him, lest your own character suffer. Whatever be the appearance of things, whatever might have been true in an ordinary man, in Oliver, be assured that all was right. He had no interest in being great. What could it be to him, a man who loved pious retirement and his quiet home, to be in the thick of the storm; to pass from the perils of revolt and war to the blind dangers of the Protectorate; to toil for cross-grained and stupid associates, and for his reward to be misrepresented, execrated, shot at? His power was all along an act of self-sacrifice—self-sacrifice to the public good, sanctioned by an awful and imperious sense of mission. So must we think of Cromwell. We must deal with him as with a canonised person,—reverentially, lovingly, piously, with minds tuned in a heroic key to keep out vulgar thoughts.

We do not quarrel with Mr. Carlyle for his enthusiasm, if he feels it; but he really must not call people "flunkeys" and "canting persons" if they do not share it with him. He has thrown himself for the present on Oliver's own account of himself, and is content to stand by in the humble posture of direction post, or, at the highest, of showman. He shows us Oliver; an engraving of his portrait, very characteristic and striking; his letters and his speeches, equally full of character. We are left alone with the great man, to form our own judgment of him. Mr. Carlyle ought not to complain if his own interjectional bursts of rapture, and orders to love Oliver, produce less effect than the sight he presents to us.

We do not grudge Puritanism its great man any more than its temporary triumph. It earned what it won by good means as well as bad. The Puritans worked in earnest, they did not lose heart, they were vigilant and bold, they "flew high" and did not mind risks. And thus, fairly so far, the most conceited and tyrannical party that ever covered selfish ends by fair words won their game. Let their success count for what it is worth, and be measured against their utter failure in the end. And if Cromwell, contrary to the popular view, not therefore without truth and depth because rudely stated—can be shown to have been a single-minded man, let Puritanism have the benefit of it. No really great cause ought to be afraid of the fact of having had a great man for its enemy. In the mixed order of the world there is nothing wonderful in such an antagonist being matched against it. He is an overwhelming witness against a hollow cause, but not against a true one. We should not have been staggered if it *had* turned out that Cromwell was a genuine and unselfish man,—as *real* a character as his distorting Puritanism would allow, without any other ends than public ones. We could have imagined this if the *Letters and Speeches* had shown it us, but they do not. Oliver remains, after all, very much where he was—as strange a jumble as one of his own speeches—a subject, if you will, for tragedy; but not yet, at least, in a state for a flowing epic.

He begins life as a gentleman farmer at St. Ives, of strong ultra-Puritan views—a keen, shrewd, stern man, with bull-dog resolution, and a mind of hard, coarse grain, busy with itself in a wild, undisciplined Puritan way, and passing perpetually from despair to assurance. Mr. Carlyle draws a pastoral picture, imaginative and innocent, of these early days:

A studious imagination may sufficiently construct the figure of his equable life in those years. Diligent grass-farming; mowing, milking, cattle-marketing: add "hypochondria," fits of the blackness of darkness, with glances of the brightness of very Heaven; prayer, religious reading and meditation, household epochs, joys and cares;—we have a solid substantial inoffensive Farmer of St. Ives, hoping to walk with integrity and humble devout diligence through this world; and by his Maker's infinite mercy to escape destruction and find eternal salvation in wider Divine Worlds. This latter, this is the grand clause of his Life, which dwarfs all other clauses. Much wider destinies than he anticipated were appointed him on Earth; but that, in comparison to the alternative of Heaven or Hell to all Eternity, was a mighty small matter.

The lands he rented are still there, recognisable to the Tourist; gross boggy lands, fringed with willow trees, at the east end of the small Town of St. Ives, which is still noted as a cattle market in those parts.

"A modest devout man,"—such as there were many in those days of a religious squirearchy,—very amiable to their own friends, but very disagreeable to every one else; such as are to be met with among country squires even now. Cromwell's letters of this date are in the received Puritan style. Mr. Carlyle is unduly struck with them. They show nothing except that Cromwell was a Puritan. Every Puritan country gentleman who could write at all would write in the same way as the following (if we may not call it cant we must call it fashion) :—

To my beloved Cousin, Mrs. St. John, at Sir William Masham his House, called Otes, in Essex: Present these.

ELY, 13*th October* 1638.

DEAR COUSIN,—I thankfully acknowledge your love in your kind remembrance of me upon this opportunity. Alas, you do too highly prize my lines, and my company. I may be ashamed to own your expressions, considering how unprofitable I am, and the mean improvement of my talent. Yet to honour my God by declaring what He hath done for my soul, in this I am confident, and I will be so. Truly, then, this I find: That He giveth springs in a dry barren wilderness where no water is. I live, you know where, in Meshec, which, they say, signifies *Prolonging;* in Kedar, which signifies *Blackness:* yet the Lord forsaketh me not. Though He do prolong, yet He will I trust bring me to His tabernacle, to His resting-place. My soul is with the Congregation of the Firstborn, my body rests in hope ; and if here I may honour my God either by doing or by suffering, I shall be most glad.

Truly no poor creature hath more cause to put himself forth in the cause of his God than I. I have had plentiful wages beforehand ; and I am sure I shall never earn the least mite. The Lord accept me in His Son, and give me to walk in the light,—and give us to walk in the light as He is the light ! He it is that enlighteneth our blackness, our darkness. I dare not say, He hideth His Face from me. He giveth me to see light in His light. One beam in a dark place hath exceeding much refreshment in it ;—blessed be His Name for shining upon so dark a heart as mine ! You know what my manner of life hath been. Oh, I lived in and loved darkness, and hated light ; I was a chief, the chief of sinners. This is true : I hated godliness, yet God had mercy on me. O the riches of His mercy ! Praise Him for me ;—pray for me, that He who hath begun a good work perfect it in the day of Christ.

"Salute all my friends in that Family whereof you are yet a member. I am much bound unto them for their love. I bless the Lord for them; and that my Son, by their procurement, is so well. Let him have your prayers, your counsel; let me have them.

"Salute your Husband and Sister from me :—He is not a man of his word! He promised to write about Mr. Wrath of Epping; but as yet I receive no letters: put him in mind to do what with conveniency may be done for the poor Cousin I did solicit him about. Once more farewell. The Lord be with you: so prayeth your truly loving Cousin, OLIVER CROMWELL.

This letter elicits from the editor the following burst; —the touch about the old manor-house, to which the letter was sent, slightly atones for its extravagance :—

What glimpses of long-gone summers; of long-gone human beings in fringed trowser-breeches, in starched ruff, in hood and fardingale;—alive, they, within their antiquarian costumes, living men and women; instructive, very interesting to one another! Mrs. St. John came down to breakfast every morning in that summer visit of the year 1638, and Sir William said grave grace, and they spake polite devout things to one another; and they are vanished, they and their things and speeches, —all silent, like the echoes of the old nightingales that sang that season, like the blossoms of the old roses. O Death, O Time!

For the soul's furniture of these brave people is grown not less unintelligible, antiquarian, than their spanish boots and lappet caps. Reverend Mark Noble, my reverend imbecile friend, discovers in this Letter evidence that Oliver was once a very dissolute man; that Carrion Heath spake in that *Flagellum* Balderdash of his. O my reverend imbecile friend, hadst thou thyself never any moral life, but only a sensitive and digestive? Thy soul never longed towards the serene heights, all hidden from thee; and thirsted as the hart in dry places wherein no waters be? It was never a sorrow for thee that the eternal polestar had gone out, veiled itself in dark clouds; a sorrow only that this or the other noble Patron forgot thee when a living fell vacant? I have known Christians, Moslems, Methodists, —and alas, also reverend irreverent Apes by the Dead Sea!

O modern reader, dark as this Letter may seem, I will advise thee to make an attempt towards understanding it. There is in it a "tradition of humanity" worth all the rest. Indisputable certificate that man once had a soul, that man once walked with God,—his little Life a sacred island girdled with Eternities and Godhoods. Was it not a time for heroes? Heroes were then possible. I say, thou shalt understand that Letter; thou also, looking out into a too brutish world, wilt then exclaim with Oliver Cromwell,—with Hebrew David, as old Mr. Rouse of Truro, and the Presbyterian populations still sing him in the Northern Kirks:

> Woe's me that I in Meshec am
> A sojourner so long,
> Or that I in the tents do dwell
> To Kedar that belong!

Yes, there is a tone in the soul of this Oliver that holds of the Perennial. With a noble sorrow, with a noble patience, he longs towards the mark of the prize of the high calling. He, I think, has chosen the better part. The world and its wild tumults,—if they will but let him alone! Yet he too will venture, will do and suffer for God's cause, if the call come. What man with better reason? He hath had plentiful wages beforehand; snatched out of darkness into marvellous light: he will never earn the least mite. Annihilation of self; *Selbsttödtung*, as Novalis calls it; casting yourself at the footstool of God's throne, "To live or to die for ever; as Thou wilt, not as I will." Brother, hadst thou never, in any form, such moments in thy history? Thou knowest them not, even by credible rumour? Well, thy earthly path was peaceabler, I suppose. But the Highest was never in thee, the Highest will never come out of thee. Thou shalt at best abide by the stuff, as cherished house-dog guard the stuff,—perhaps with enormous gold collars and provender: but the battle, and the hero-death, and victory's fire-chariot carrying men to the Immortals, shall never be thine. I pity thee; brag not or I shall have to despise thee.

We do not doubt that Cromwell was a devout Puritan; but if this letter is an evidence of the possibility of heroes, heroes are abundantly possible still.

But with all his farming, Cromwell was early a stirring man. In the Parliament of 1628-29, amidst the grave, subtle, smooth-spoken harangues of the session, was heard an uncouth *snap* from Oliver at a certain Dr. Alablaster, who, "he had heard by relation from one Dr. Beard (his old Schoolmaster at Huntingdon), had preached flat Popery at Paul's Cross" with his Bishop's approval; and Dr. Beard was accordingly sent for to come and testify against the Bishop.

Afterwards he comes forward at public meetings at home, about the drainings of the fens, and gets the name of "Lord of the Fens." In the "Short Parliament" and the "Long Parliament" he sits for Cambridge town. When the war began he had been for fourteen years a public man.

The war came, and characters began to draw out in new forms and proportions. Out of linen-drapers and doctors, attorneys and country gentlemen, there started up a variety of captains and colonels of horse and foot, who began to flourish and blunder and skirmish in a valiant, irregular, yeomanry fashion, without doing much mischief. The ultra-Puritan gentleman farmer was in the crowd, "Captain of Troop 67"; "Colonel of a regiment of horse"; but there was little to remark about him, except that the eastern counties, where he served, were kept in very good order. Royalist gentlemen, disposed to be troublesome, felt a sharp eye upon them. The following terse epistle to an "assured" Royalist "friend" is obviously of a very quieting tendency :—

To my assured friend, Robert Barnard, Esquire : Present these.

HUNTINGDON, 23rd *January* 1642.

MR. BARNARD,—It's most true my Lieutenant, with some other soldiers of my troop were at your House. I dealt so freely as to enquire after you ; the reason was, I had heard you reported active against the proceedings of Parliament, and for those that disturb the peace of this Country and the Kingdom,—with those of this

Country who have had meetings not a few, to intents and purposes too-too full of suspect.

It's true, Sir, I know you have been wary in your carriages; be not too confident thereof. Subtlety may deceive you; integrity never will. With my heart I shall desire that your judgment may alter, and your practice. I come only to hinder men from increasing the rent,—from doing hurt; but not to hurt any man: nor shall I you; I hope you will give me no cause. If you do, I must be pardoned what my relation to the Public calls for. If your good parts be disposed that way, know me for your servant,

OLIVER CROMWELL.

Be assured fair words from me shall neither deceive you of your houses nor of your liberty.

At Edgehill, Cromwell saw Prince Rupert's charge. Edgehill was a specimen of what the war was likely to be, and for some time actually was; spirited Cavaliers and spirited Roundheads tilting bravely at each other, and taking turn about to rout and be routed; till they got tired of the novelty of the amusement, and returned to their accustomed and milder sports— fox-hunting and the Parliament-house. But the quarrel was not to die out in this way; it was to become the fiercest of all wars, a religious war. Cromwell had looked beyond his nose, and seen how it might at once be made more serious and be decided.

Long afterwards, when Parliament was offering him the crown, and he was haranguing amiably to Whitlocke and his committee, not quite knowing what to say, his thoughts wandered back to the time when his work was yet all to do :—

I did truly and plainly,—and in a way of foolish simplicity, as it was judged by very great and wise men, and good men too,—desire to make my instruments help me in that work. And I will deal plainly with you : I had a very worthy Friend then : and he was a very noble person, and I know his memory is very grateful to all,—Mr. John Hampden. At my first going out into this engagement, I saw our men were beaten at every hand. I did indeed ; and desired him that he would make some additions to my Lord Essex's Army, of some new regiments ; and I told him I would be serviceable to him in bringing such men in as I thought had a spirit that would do something in the work. This is very true that I tell you : God knows I lie not. "Your troops," said I, "are most of them old decayed serving-men, and tapsters, and such kind of fellows ; and," said I, "their troops are gentlemen's sons, younger sons and persons of quality ; do you think that the spirits of such base and mean fellows will ever be able to encounter gentlemen, that have honour and courage and resolution in them ? " Truly I did represent to him in this manner conscientiously ; and truly I did tell him : "You must get men of a spirit : and take it not ill what I say,—I know you will not,—of a spirit that is likely to go on as far as gentlemen will go, or else you will be beaten still." I told him so ; I did truly. He was a wise and worthy person ; and he did think that I talked a good notion, but an impracticable one. Truly I told him that I could do somewhat in it. I did so,—and truly I must needs say this to you, impute it to what you please,—I raised such men as had the fear of God before them, as made some conscience of what they did; and from that day forward, I must say to you, they were never beaten, and wherever they were engaged against the enemy, they beat continually. And truly this is matter of praise to God :—and it hath some instruction in it, To own men who are religious and godly.

"Truly I told him I could Do somewhat in it."— He was as good as his word,—first the *Ironsides*, then the *New Model* army, an enthusiastic military sect, springing out of prosing Genevan Puritanism, with Cromwell for their armed prophet, the very counterpart of Mahometanism and the sheiks, with scarcely more than they even of the semblance of Christian religion; all is Jewish—their mixture of unwavering faith with narrow bigotry, fierceness, obstinacy, coarseness, selfishness—their very cant is from the Old Testament;—for one phrase from the New, they had twenty from the Psalms and Prophets.

The old Puritan leaders little looked for such an apparition when they first ventured on war, and they relished it as little. A coarse, low-bred army of Anabaptists and Independents, was no congenial ally for correct, gentlemanly Presbyterianism, strong in Parliament, and believing in the spell of a resolution of the House, or a Speaker's warrant. Parliament sneered at the zealous, vulgar troopers; it tried to get rid of them, to impose upon them; it lectured, coaxed, insulted them. "Fine tricks these to mock God with," writes Oliver indignantly. The quarrel grew hot, and ended as he had foretold—"the army had to pull" their Presbyterian friends "out by the ears." Cromwell's army were become the rulers of England, and he reflects and moralises on it:—

Oh, His mercy to the whole society of saints,—despised, jeered saints! Let them mock on. Would we were all saints! The best of us are, God knows, poor weak saints;—yet saints; if not sheep, yet lambs; and must be fed. We have daily bread, and shall have it, in despite of all enemies.

Here is the pinch of Cromwell's history,—in that atmosphere of storm and darkness and confusion he moved and led. To have given a real picture of the Cromwell of those days, to have drawn out his character as a whole out of its strange, and possibly inconsistent, details; to have left us with the impression that whether we liked the man or not, *there he was;* this might have been expected of Mr. Carlyle. But though he is not fettered by party feelings, or tenderness for the liberties of Parliament, he is by his idolatry of heroes. In the French Revolution he dealt with men; he faced and portrayed realities. Here he has an ideal to reconcile with facts, and he does not succeed so well. His book labours and struggles, and leaves only impressions which counteract one another. Its parts do not adjust themselves naturally; fact pulls against commentary; elucidation falls dead upon the latter; and between them the living image of Cromwell drops through. Mr. Carlyle's own idea does not rise of itself out of his documents; he has to protect and foster it. There is a painful effort, a monotonous, impatient bluster, to keep up the reader's heroic mood. Strange to say, he will even write common-place to get himself out of a difficulty. Cromwell evaded the Self-denying Ordinance which he had so earnestly supported; his friends got a dispensation for him, and he became the real head of the army. Mr. Carlyle thinks that he would just as soon have remained at home, for "it could be no such overwhelming felicity to him to get out to be shot at, except where wanted." Mr. Carlyle must make him out to be the leading spirit of the crisis without its responsibilities; the soul of every movement, yet perfectly unconscious and careless of what the Destinies were going to make of him. A most unnaturally simple view of the case, which, whether taken by itself, or coming out among the documents of Mr. Carlyle's own book, does not commend itself as satisfactory.

Those who like Puritanism or idolise greatness may find much, no doubt, to admire in Cromwell; but they must take him as he is. When his deep and powerful character has guided a movement which tends to and finishes in his power, they must not account for the last step by some bit of special pleading, and say that he did not mean this; or when something is done by others, which he approves and uses, they must not allege or imply the silly excuse that he was not there, or did not order it. Every scene, as the history rolls on, from the Self-denying Ordinance to the Protectorate, shows Cromwell as its dominant figure; every record that remains of him shows the keen, far-sighted man, who watched hearts, and sent his influence abroad through endless channels, by hints, by condescensions, by indirect preparation, also by silence and sitting still. Mr. Carlyle seems to think that he has cleared Oliver of "fomenting the army discontents" by sweeping away at a brush all the stories of the time against him;—mere blunders, he says, of "wooden-headed Ludlow,"—lies of "red-nosed Presbyterians under the Restoration, cramming the loosely recipient Burnet over his claret." They may doubtless, as common minds do, have *imagined* instances of an influence which they saw and could not explain. Yet, after all, Mr. Carlyle makes Cromwell the army spokesman, and how Cromwell *could* work on a heart and conscience, may be seen in his letter (too long to quote here) to Colonel R. Hammond, preparing him for extreme measures against the king. It is a letter which popular opinion would ascribe to a Jesuit—to some dreaded "conspirator against the privileges of the heart." It probes conscience considerately, yet to the quick, and leaves no escape. One reads it with a kind of shrinking— its rough affectionateness and playful coaxing sympathy with "dear Robin's" perplexities, and condescending accounts of his own experience, contrasting with its real, stern, bloody business and terrible reasoning, and with the steady, keen eye which looks through "dear Robin," out of every line of it. It is, indeed, in Mr. Carlyle's own phrase, "a window into Oliver's inner man," showing something else in his way of managing his soldiers than mere "manly simplicity." It may throw some light, perhaps, on the famous three days' "prayer meeting" at Windsor in 1648, which strikes Mr. Carlyle as so wonderful; where the army met to search out what sin of theirs had made the king, the Parliament, and the Scotch, so formidable to them; where Cromwell began business by pressing on them "to see if any iniquity could be found in them, and what it was;" where, after much debating and weeping, they ended by discovering that it was their carnal conferences with the king, and by resolving unanimously that it was their duty "to call Charles Stuart, that man of blood, to an account for that blood he had shed." "This is not madness," says Mr. Carlyle to the astonished modern reader. It is not indeed. It would have been better if it had been only madness. The steps which, after this, led to the king's death, give Mr. Carlyle very little concern, though he does not give Oliver his due prominence in them. He throws himself heartily into the feelings of the army, both against the Parliament and the king. Pride's Purge is described with real zest:—

Wednesday, 6th December 1648.—" Colonel Rich's regiment of horse and Colonel Pride's regiment of foot were a guard to the Parliament; and the City Train-bands were discharged" from that employment. Yes, they were! Colonel Rich's horse stand ranked in Palace Yard, Colonel Pride's foot in Westminster Hall and at all entrances to the Commons House, this day: and in Colonel Pride's hand is a written list of names, names of the chief among the Hundred and twenty-nine; and at his side is my Lord Grey of Groby, who, as this Member after that comes up, whispers or beckons, " He is one of them: he cannot enter!" And Pride gives the word, " To the Queen's Court"; and Member after Member is marched thither, Forty-one of them this day; and kept there in a state bordering on rabidity, asking, By what Law? and ever again, By what Law? Is there a colour or faintest shadow of Law to be found in any of the Books, Yearbooks, Rolls of Parliament, Bractons, Fletas, Cokes upon Lyttleton, for this? Hugh Peters visits them, has little comfort, no light as to the Law; confesses " It is by the Law of Necessity"; truly " by the Power of the Sword."

It must be owned the Constable's baton is fairly down this day; overborne by the Power of the Sword, and a Law not to be found in any of the Books. At evening the distracted Forty-one are marched to Mr. Duke's Tavern hard by,—a " Tavern called Hell,"—and very imperfectly accommodated for the night. Sir Symonds D'Ewes, who has ceased taking notes long since; Mr. William Prynne, louder than any in the question of Law; Waller, Massey, Harley, and others of the old Eleven, are of this unlucky Forty-one; among whom too we count little Clement Walker " in his gray suit with his little stick," asking in the voice of the indomitablest terrier or Blenheim cocker, " By what Law? I ask again, By what Law?" Whom no mortal will ever be able to answer. Such is the far-famed Purging of the House by Colonel Pride.

This evening, while the Forty-one are getting lodged in Mr. Duke's, Lieutenant-General Cromwell came to Town.

And the execution of the king excites only feelings of the most enthusiastic admiration. We will do him no injustice; he shall give his reflections upon it:—

"*Tetrae belluae, ac suis molossis ferociores.* Hideous monsters, more ferocious than their own mastiffs!" shrieks Saumaise; shrieks all the world, in unmelodious soul-confusing diapason of distraction — happily at length grown very faint in our day. The truth is, no modern reader can conceive the then atrocity, ferocity, unspeakability of this fact. First, after long reading in the old dead Pamphlets does one see the magnitude of it. . . . We know it not, this atrocity of the English Regicides; shall never know it. I reckon it perhaps the most daring action any Body of Men to be met with in History ever, with clear consciousness, deliberately set themselves to do. Dread Phantoms, glaring supernal on you,—when once they are quelled, and their light snuffed out, none knows the terror of the Phantom! The Phantom is a poor paper lantern with a candle-end in it, which any whipster dare now beard. . . . This action of the English Regicides did in effect strike a damp like death through the heart of Flunkey-ism universally in this world. Whereof Flunkeyism, Cant, Cloth-worship, or whatever ugly name it have, has gone about incurably sick ever since, and is now at length, in these generations, very rapidly dying. The like of which action will not be needed for a thousand years again. Needed, alas—not till a new genuine Hero-worship has arisen, has perfected itself; and had time to degenerate into a Flunkeyism and Cloth-worship again! Which I take to be a very long date indeed.

Thus ends the Second Civil War. In Regicide, in a Commonwealth and Keepers of the Liberties of England. In punishment of Delinquents, in abolition of Cobwebs; if it be possible, in a Government of Heroism and Veracity; at lowest, of Anti-Flunkeyism, Anti-Cant, and the *endeavour* after Heroism and Veracity.

There is prudence in boldness. The end of Charles I. is not safe ground for Cromwell's sacred poet to linger upon. Let him, if he be wise, eschew prose; the subject demands a generous transcendental view, and the high inspiration of Hugh Peters. Let him not coldly excuse this heroic army and their chief, but assume their heroism. It will read well and save trouble. Who can deny that to have made "Flunkeyism incurably sick" is a good deed? Let all Lynch-law justices and Tipperary ribbonmen note it.

We shall take another opportunity of considering the new government "of heroism and veracity" which succeeded Charles I. and Presbyterianism.

III[1]

CHARLES's death was only the first step in the work which Cromwell had undertaken. He had great powers against him. Parliament and the city,—the great body of rich merchants and dogged country squires and sharp-witted lawyers and spirited nobles,—the traditions, sympathies, customs of England,—the religious feelings of the great mass of the people,—a fierce rebellion in Ireland,—an impracticable "King and Covenant party" in Scotland,—Levellers, Fifth-Monarchy men, and all monstrous forms of insubordination in his own party blazing ever and anon into furious mutiny, his own friends at last disappointed and angry,—all these were still to be overcome. And he did overcome them. He stood alone, with his small army in the midst of a disaffected nation. In all England he had no friend but those whom his terror could win for him. But to his last hour he could say that no one had ever opposed him and prospered. He stood against England, and England had to submit. Cromwell was great as a destroyer; good and evil went down together before him: what did he build up?

If Napoleon had never moved a step beyond the Rhine, he would still have left behind him a nation remoulded and stamped for generations with the

[1] *Guardian*, 25th February 1846.

impress of his own mind. The great Puritan chieftain, equally daring and energetic, and with even a more prosperous star, passed away like a dream, and left not a trace of himself in the character and serious thought of England.

He restored order and kept it by bold and merciless war, first at home and then abroad, and by a vigorous spy system, as was the custom. Order is a good thing, and was wanted in England, and Cromwell knew how to maintain it—let him have our thanks; he also saved us from otherwise inevitable Presbyterianism. But, unless the power of keeping down all opposition by main force makes a man at once a hero-governor, what is there to entitle Cromwell to a higher place than any other military tyrant? Mr. Carlyle's book shows no other. Cromwell stands out there in a solitary savage grandeur, engaged in a single-handed life-long struggle with his own friends; flattered and feared, but neither loved nor trusted; irresistible yet accomplishing nothing; summoning Parliaments, and after scattering them in his wrath, finding them next time still untamed; talking much of law reform, but without genius to reform himself or skill to find fit instruments; working out his own idea of "toleration of conscience" through the most monstrous contradictions; not understanding the people he governed, unable to touch their hearts, to mould or raise them. Were there none but fat Whitlockes, and wooden-headed Ludlows, and the Anabaptist company of "Mr. Feake and Mr. Squib" in England, none to respond to him, to recognise the true and wise ruler, and do him honour and service? This mere *bigness*, this Cyclopean one-eyed strength of character, unconquerable, yet confused—powerless when it comes to work, and for ever baffled—is but a poor kind of greatness. Gulliver in Lilliput, stung by the little people, able to crush, but not to govern, is no fit type of a great ruler of men.

Mr. Carlyle describes, with much vividness, Cromwell's victorious and terrible conflicts with "Calvinistic sans-culottism," with the Irish Rebellion, with Scotland at Dunbar, finally, with England at Worcester. His account of the Dunbar fight shall serve as a specimen. Here is the scene of the battle :—

The small Town of Dunbar stands, high and windy, looking down over its herring boats, over its grim old Castle, now much honeycombed, on one of those projecting rock promontories with which that shore of the Firth of Forth is niched and vandyked, as far as the eye can reach. A beautiful sea; good land too, now that the plougher understands his trade; a grim niched barrier of whinstone sheltering it from the chafings and tumblings of the big blue German Ocean. Seaward St. Abb's Head, of whinstone, bounds your horizon to the east, not very far off; west, close by, is the deep bay and fishy little village of Belhaven; the gloomy Bass and other rock-islets, and farther the Hills of Fife, and foreshadows of the Highlands, are visible as you look seaward. From the bottom of Belhaven bay to that of the next sea-bight St. Abb's-ward, the Town and its environs form a peninsula. Along the base of which peninsula, " not much above a mile and a half from sea to sea," Oliver Cromwell's Army, on Monday 2nd of September, 1650, stands ranked, with its tents and Town behind it,—in very forlorn circumstances. This now is all the ground that Oliver is lord of in Scotland. His ships lie in the offing, with biscuit and transport for him, but visible elsewhere in the Earth no help.

Landward as you look from the Town of Dunbar there rises, some short mile off, a dusky continent of barren heath Hills, the Lammermoor, where only mountain sheep can be at home. The crossing of *which*, by any of its boggy passes, and brawling stream-courses, no Army, hardly a solitary Scotch Packman could attempt in such weather. To the edge of these Lammermoor Heights, David Lesley has betaken himself; lies now along the outmost spur of them—a long Hill of considerable height, which the Dunbar people call the Dun or Doon. . . . There lies he since Sunday night, on the top and slope of this Doon Hill, with the impassable heath-continents behind him; embraces, as within outspread tiger-claws, the base-line of Oliver's Dunbar peninsula; waiting what Oliver will do. Cockburnspath with its ravines has been seized on Oliver's left, and made impassable; behind Oliver is the sea; in front of him Lesley, Doon Hill, and the heath-continent of Lammermoor. Lesley's force is of Three-and-twenty thousand, in spirits as of men chasing, Oliver's about half as many, in spirits as of men chased. What is to become of Oliver?

A rivulet or burn flows by the base of Doon Hill into the sea on Cromwell's left :—

The reader who would form an image to himself of the great Tuesday, 3rd of September, 1650, at Dunbar, must note well this little *Burn*. . . . Oliver's force is arranged in battle order along the left bank of this Brocksburn and its grassy glen, he is busied all Monday, he and his Officers, in ranking them there. " Before sunrise on Monday," Lesley sent down his horse from the Hill-top to occupy the other side of this Brook; "About four in the afternoon" his train came down, his whole Army gradually came down, and they are now ranking themselves on the opposite side of Brocksburn, on rather narrow ground, cornfields, but swiftly sloping upwards to the steep of Doon Hill. This goes on in the wild showers and winds of Monday, 2nd of September, 1650, on both sides of the Rivulet of Brock. Whoever will begin the attack must get across this Brook and its glen first; a thing of much disadvantage.

Cromwell resolves to cross the brook on the left before dawn next morning, and surprise the Scotch. Lambert is to lead the attack :—

And so the soldiers stand to their arms, or lie within instant reach of their arms all night; being upon an engagement very difficult indeed. The night is wild and wet; 2nd of September means 12th by our calendar; the Harvest Moon wades deep among clouds of sleet and hail. Whoever has a heart for prayer let him pray now, for the wrestle of death is at hand. Pray—and withal keep his powder dry! And be ready for extremities, and quit himself like a man! Thus they pass the night; making that Dunbar Peninsula and Brock Rivulet long memorable to me. We English have some tents, the Scots have none. The hoarse sea moans bodeful, swinging low and heavy against these whinstone bays; the sea and the tempests are abroad, all else asleep but we,—and there is One that rides on the wings of the wind.

Towards three in the morning the Scotch foot, by order of a Major-General say some, extinguish their matches, all but two in a company; cower under the corn-shocks, seeking some imperfect shelter and sleep. Be wakeful, ye English; watch and pray, and keep your powder dry. About four o'clock comes order to my pudding-headed Yorkshire friend, that his regiment must mount and march straightway; his and various other regiments march, pouring swiftly to the left to Brocksmouth House, to the Pass over the Brock. With overpowering force let us storm the Scots right wing there; beat that and all is beaten. Major Hodgson riding along, heard, he says, "a Cornet praying in the night"; a company of poor men, I think, making worship there under the void Heaven before battle joined. Major Hodgson giving his charge to a brother Officer, turned aside to listen for a minute, and worship and pray along with them; haply his last prayer on this Earth, as it might prove to be. But no: this Cornet prayed with such effusion as was wonderful; and imparted strength to my Yorkshire friend, who strengthened his men by telling them of it. And the Heavens in their mercy, I think, have opened us a way of deliverance! The Moon gleams out, hard and blue, riding among hail-clouds; and over St. Abb's Head a streak of dawn is rising.

And now is the hour when the attack should be, and no Lambert is yet here, he is ordering the line far to the right yet; and Oliver occasionally, in Hodgson's hearing, is impatient for him. The Scots too, on this wing, are awake; thinking to surprise us; there is their trumpet sounding, we heard it once; and Lambert, who was to lead the attack, is not here. The Lord General is impatient;—behold Lambert at last! The trumpets peal, shattering with fierce clangour Night's silence; the cannons awaken along all the Line: "The Lord of Hosts! The Lord of Hosts!" On, my brave ones, on!

The dispute "on this right wing was hot and stiff for three-quarters of an hour." Plenty of fire from field-pieces, snaphances, matchlocks, entertains the Scotch main battle across the Brock; poor stiffened men, roused from the corn-shocks with their matches all out! But here on the right, their horse, "with lancers in the front rank," charge desperately; drive us back across the hollow of the Rivulet;—back a little; but the Lord gives us courage, and we storm home again, horse and foot upon them, with a shock like tornado tempests; break them, beat them, drive them all adrift. "Some fled towards Copperspath, but most across their own foot." Their own poor foot, whose matches were hardly well alight yet! Poor men, it was a terrible awakening for them, field-pieces and charge of foot across the Brocksburn; and now here is their own horse in mad panic trampling them to death. Above three thousand killed upon the place: "I never saw such a charge of foot and horse," says one; nor did I. Oliver was still near to Yorkshire Hodgson when the shock succeeded; Hodgson heard him say, "They run! I profess they run!" And over St. Abb's Head and the German Ocean just then bursts the first gleam of the level sun upon us, "and I heard Noll say, in the words of the Psalmist, 'Let God arise, let His enemies be scattered,'" or in Rous' metre—

> Let God arise, and scattered,
> Let all his enemies be;
> And let all those that do him hate
> Before his presence flee.

Even so. The Scotch Army is shivered to utter ruin; rushes in tumultuous wreck, hither, thither; to Belhaven, or, in their distraction, even to Dunbar; the chase goes as far as Haddington, led by Hacker. "The Lord General made a halt," says Hodgson, "and sang the Hundred and seventeenth Psalm," till our horse could gather for the chase. Hundred and seventeenth Psalm at the foot of the Doon Hill; there we uplift it to the tune of Bangor, or some still higher score, and roll it strong and great against the sky.

After the battle of Worcester there is little known of Cromwell, says Mr. Carlyle, except what may be dimly seen in his speeches. His speeches, accordingly, he gives us in full; he has had the enthusiasm to try to make them intelligible.

His method is highly original, and not without use; he enlivens and enlightens, by creating an audience whose remarks burst out from time to time; the *hums* and *hahs* of the Parliamentary gentlemen, the "stifled" cries of Dryasdust, and the admiring, inquiring, and encouraging interjections of the editor himself, standing reverentially behind his Highness's chair. These speeches and their accompanying narrative give us Cromwell's dealings with his Parliament,—an important part of his government;

and the result is, that Cromwell, a Puritan governor, with a Puritan Parliament,—himself more powerful and better backed than any English king,—with his Parliament composed of friends nominated by himself, or chosen by none but friendly electors, sifted and winnowed in all ways, and if necessary purged,— a Parliament obsequious and cowardly,—and lastly, at no time without a large majority at his command; the result, we say, is that Cromwell could not govern with a Parliament. His dealings with them were a series of quarrels. Mr. Carlyle is in a difficulty; he began with the largest declamations about the heroism of the Puritans—men without cant, men of deep insight and lofty aims; he ends by making out—it is all he can say for Cromwell's failure to govern in concert with them — that all but Cromwell were "pedants," or self-seekers, or madmen.

That illustrious body, the Long Parliament, had long been under process of purification, it had at last been "winnowed and sifted," as Cromwell says, into the Rump. Yet this refined and purified Rump —this quintessence of heroic Puritanism,—could not get on with its heroic leader. It turns out that they are not even good men of business.

Mr. Carlyle thinks that they did not "in the least design to sit for ever, only they find a terrible difficulty in getting abdicated." The fact is unquestionable. They wanted to wait till they had reformed the law. They were three months trying without success to define an "incumbrance"; and when, at last, after endless "poking" from their army friends, they turned their thoughts to a "new representation," they made it a condition that they should be re-elected.

The army, Cromwell says, was "very tender" about them; but they could not stand this, and at length, after endless petitions, conferences, delays, they were caught one day by Cromwell in the act of trying to steal a march upon him, and were most unheroically sent about their business. "So far as I could discern," says their ruthless overthrower, "when they *were* dissolved, there was not so much as the barking of a dog, or any general or visible repining at it."

The next plan was an assembly selected and absolutely nominated by Cromwell, of his own authority as General — the "Little or Barebone's Parliament." Here is Cromwell's own account of it, with his Editor's notes :—

Truly I will now come and tell you a story of my own weakness and folly. [The Little Parliament.] And yet it was done in my simplicity, I dare avow it was; and though some of my companions — ["May dislike my mentioning the story?"—The sentence, in its haste, has no time to end.] And truly this is a story that should not be recorded, that should not be told, except when good use may be made of it. I say, It was thought then that men of our own judgment, who had fought in the Wars, and were all of a piece upon that account :— "Why, surely these men will hit it, and these men will do it to the purpose, whatever can be desired!" And truly we did think, and I did think so,—

the more blame to me. And such a Company of Men were chosen; [The Little Parliament; Convention of the Puritan Notables], and did proceed to action. And truly this was the naked truth, That the issue was not answerable to the simplicity and honesty of the design. [Poor Puritan Notables!]

The Notables would not work, select as they were. They tried Law Reform, but a sober majority were bullied by a violent minority, who would hear of nothing but the Mosaic Law, till in despair the majority met by stealth, and in a hurried instrument, each member "signing on separate bits of paper, hastily wafered together," resigned their trust. So perished the Little Parliament.

Another attempt was soon made for a Parliament, this time by way of election. But none but "active Puritans and quiet neutrals" with £200 a year, could vote or be voted for; "probably," thinks Mr. Carlyle, it was "as fair a Representative as by counting heads could well be got in England"—400 Puritan leaders. It was opened with all solemnity, and a gracious speech from his Highness, at which "all generally seemed abundantly to rejoice by extraordinary expressions and hums of approbation"; everything seemed smooth and promising. But the Parliament, his Highness having assured them that they were free, thought that they might talk as freely and interminably as in the good old days of Pym; and naturally enough they began at the beginning, and discussed how England should be governed. After many days' vigorous debating, they came one morning to the House, and found it locked. His Highness had something to say to them. From this speech of an hour and a half, exculpatory, objurgatory, and if not intelligible, very significant, we extract the practical conclusion, with the editor's running comments to assist the imagination :—

I had a thought within myself That it would not have been dishonest nor dishonourable, nor against true Liberty, no, not of Parliaments, when a Parliament was so chosen in pursuance of this Instrument of Government, and in conformity to it, and with such an approbation and consent to it,—some owning of your Call and of the Authority which brought you hither, had been required before your entrance into the House. [Deep silence in the audience.] This was declined and hath not been done, because I am persuaded scarce any man could doubt you came with contrary minds. And I have reason to believe the people that sent you least of all doubted thereof. And therefore I must deal plainly with you : what I forbore upon a just confidence at first, you necessitate me unto now ! [Paleness on some faces.] Seeing the Authority which called you is so little valued, and so much slighted,—till some such Assurance be given and made known, that the Fundamental Interest shall be settled and approved according to the proviso in the Writ of Return, and such a consent testified as will make it appear that the same is accepted, I have caused a stop to be put to your entrance into the Parliament House. [You understand that, my honourable friends ?]

I am sorry, I am sorry, and I could be sorry to the death, that there is cause for this! But there is cause; and if things be not satisfied which are reasonably demanded, I, for my part, will do that which becomes me, seeking my counsel from God. There is therefore Somewhat [A bit of written Parchment] to be offered to you; which, I hope, will answer, being understood with the qualifications I have told you, namely of reforming as to Circumstantials, and agreeing in the Substance and Fundamentals, in the Form of Government now settled, which is expressly stipulated in your Indentures. The making of your minds known in that by giving your assent and subscription to it, is the means that will let you in, to act those things as a Parliament which are for the good of the People. And this thing [the Parchment!] and signed as aforesaid, doth determine the controversy; and may give a happy progress and issue to this Parliament. [Honourable gentlemen look in one another's faces,—find general blank.]

The place where you may come thus and sign, as many as God shall make free thereunto, is in the Lobby without the Parliament Door. [My honourable friends, you know the way, don't you?]

"This Thing," as he calls it, cleared the House of the Republicans, who "went home to their countries again, their blank faces settling into *permanent grim*," and Parliament went on with its innocent functions, tormenting heretics and receiving petitions for a small advance towards coal and candle for the "godly ministers sitting in the Jerusalem chamber." Such is Mr. Carlyle's account of the doings of this first Parliament, purged of its noxious elements,—"a most poor, hide-bound, Pedant Parliament, which reckoned itself careful of the Liberties of England, and was careful only for the Sheepskin Formulas of these;" till finally his Highness got sick of them, and sent them about their business ten days before their time. Five months was their allowance; he reckoned by soldiers' months of twenty-eight days, and cheated them of the overplus. But he could not even get supplies from them, and his only satisfaction was rating them soundly in a long speech which, says Mr. Carlyle, "if read with due intensity, can be understood and believed."

A year and a half, and then another Parliament. It has been a busy interval; taxes imposed, in spite of Hampden and ship-money, by his Highness; Puritan wrath let loose, somewhat unsuccessfully, on Papist Spain; at home plots innumerable, Anabaptist and Royalist; England obliged to be kept in order by "Major-Generals" and martial law, and Royalists paying the expenses by an income tax of ten per cent. The Protector "dislikes shedding blood," says his editor, "but he has sent, and sends us by hundreds to Barbadoes, so that we have made an active verb of it —'*Barbadoes you.*'" An orderly Government, such as is said to prevail in Poland, and doubtless a very formidable Protector at home and abroad. A new Parliament may by this time know its business better than the last: it is a "hopeful" one with "official persons and friends to Government copiously elected'

—"the great body is even loyal to his Highness;" and for the turbulent ones he has, "in the present anomalous condition of the nation, silently provided an expedient." All is good humour; his Highness condescends to be jocular:—

Gentlemen, when I came hither, I did think that a duty was incumbent upon me a little to pity myself; because, this being a very extraordinary occasion, I thought I had very many things to say unto you, [and was somewhat burdened and straitened thereby.] But truly now, seeing you in such a condition as you are, I think I must turn off my pity in this, as I hope I shall in everything else;—and consider you as certainly not being able long to bear that condition and heat that you are now in.

Crowded and hot as the room is, he proceeds at great length to discourse of the state of things in general, beginning with "*that* that is the first lesson of Nature, Being and Preservation"—tells them of their dangers and their enemies, justifies the Spanish war by the Book of Revelations, "which are sure and plain things":—

Except you will deny the truth of the Scriptures, you must needs see that that State is so described in Scripture to be Papal and Antichristian. I say, with this Enemy, and upon this account, you have the quarrel with the Spaniard. And truly, he hath an interest in your bowels; he hath so. The Papists in England, they have been accounted ever since I was born, Spaniolised. There is not a man among us can hold up his face against that.

He talks of home plots, of "some little fiddling things," in the way of assassination designed against himself, and of the attempts of the Anabaptists :—

Now we would be loath to tell you of notions more seraphical! These are poor and low conceits. We have had very seraphical notions! We have had endeavours to deal between two Interests ;—one some section of that Commonwealth Interest, and another which was a notion of a Fifth-Monarchy Interest! Which [strange operation] I do not recite, nor what condition it is in, as thinking it not worthy our trouble. But *de facto* it hath been so, That there have been endeavours ;—as there were endeavours to make a reconciliation between Herod and Pilate that Christ might be put to death, so there have been endeavours of reconciliation between the Fifth-Monarchy men and the Commonwealth men that there might be union in order to an end,—no end can be so bad as that of Herod's was,—but in order to end in blood and confusion.

He justifies the Major-Generals :—

I am to tell you, by the way, a word to justify a Thing which, I hear, is much spoken of. When we knew all these Designs before mentioned, when we found that the Cavaliers would not be quiet—No quiet; "there is no peace to the wicked," saith the Scripture: "They are like the troubled sea which cannot rest" . . . they have no Peace with God in Jesus Christ to the remission of sins. They do not know what belongs to that; therefore they know not how to be at rest; therefore they can no more cease from their actions than they can cease to live—nor so easily neither! Truly when that Insurrection was, and we saw it in all the roots and grounds of it, we did find out a little poor Invention, which I hear has been much regretted. I say, there was a little thing invented, which was the erecting of your Major-Generals: To have a little inspection upon the People thus divided, thus discontented, thus dissatisfied, into divers interests—and the workings of the Popish Party.

After discoursing about Reformation and Finance, he returns to them with some vehemence:—

It hath been more effectual towards the discountenancing of Vice and settling Religion than anything done these fifty years: I will abide by it, notwithstanding the envy and slander of foolish men! [Poor Oliver, noble Oliver!] But, I say, there was a Design—I confess I speak that to you with a little vehemency—But you had not peace two months together [nothing but plot after plot]; I profess I believe it as much as ever I did anything in the world: and how instrumental *they* [these Major-Generals] have been to your peace and for your preservation, by such means,—which, we say, was Necessity. More than all instituted things in the world. . . If nothing should be done but what is [according to Law], the throat of the Nation may be cut while we send for some to make a Law! Therefore certainly it is a pitiful beastly notion to think, though it be for ordinary Government to live by law and rule, yet, to be clamoured at and blottered at. [His Highness still extremely animated: wants as if more tongues than one to speak all he feels!] When matters of Necessity come, then without guilt extraordinary remedies may not be applied? Who can be so pitiful a person?

And he winds up with quotations from the Psalms. The next proceeding is business-like :—

Speech being ended, the Honourable Members "went to the House," says Bulstrode; and in the Lobby, with considerable crowding, I think, received from the Chancery Clerk certificates in this form: for instance—

"COUNTY OF BUCKS.—These are to certify that Sir Bulstrode Whitlocke is returned by Indenture one of the Knights to serve in this present Parliament for the said County, and approved by His Highness's Council.— NATH. TAYLER, Clerk of the Commonwealth in Chancery."

Mr. Tayler has received Four hundred Indentures from Honourable Gentlemen; but he does not give out Four hundred Certificates, he only gives Three hundred and odd. Near One hundred Honourable Gentlemen can get no Certificate from Mr. Tayler,—none provided for *you;*—and without Certificate there is no admittance. Soldiers stand ranked at the door; no man enters without his Certificate! Astonishing to see. Haselrig, Scott, and the stiff Republicans, Ashley Cooper and the turbulent persons, who might have leavened this Parliament into strange fermentation, cannot, it appears, get in! No admittance here: saw Honourable Gentlemen ever the like?

The Honourable House, with an effort, swallows this injury; directs the petitioning Excluded Members to apply to the Council. The Excluded Members, or some one Excluded Member, redacts an indignant

Protest, with all the names appended: prints it, privately circulates it, "in boxes sent by carriers, a thousand copies in a box:"—and there it rests. His Highness saying nothing to it; the Honourable House and the Nation saying nothing. In this Parliament, different from the last, we trace a real desire for settlement.

Yet all they did was to offer Cromwell the Crown, and bully a mad Quaker so fiercely that his Highness interfered. The business of the "Kingship" is a severe trial to Mr. Carlyle's reverence; he puts on a grave face, but he cannot resist the obvious parallel, "*the young lady will and she will not*," till at last she defers it "from circumstances," leaving her wooer looking foolish.

The first session of this Parliament ended peaceably. Then came the attempt to construct a House of Lords, and the Republicans were let into the Commons. Immediately disturbance begins; the newcomers will only call the Lords "the other House," and Cromwell's majority cannot get the Commons to work instead of debating. The following words conclude Cromwell's dealings with his Parliament:—

It hath been not only your endeavour to pervert the Army while you have been sitting, and to draw them to state the question about a Commonwealth; but some of you have been listing of persons, by commission of Charles Stuart, to join with any insurrection that may be made. And what is like to come upon this, the Enemy being ready to invade us, but even present blood and confusion ? [The next and final sentence is partly on fire.] And if this be so, I do assign it to this cause; Your not assenting to what you did invite me to by your Petition and Advice, as that which might prove the Settlement of the Nation. And if this be the end of your sitting, and this be your carriage—[Sentence now all beautifully blazing,] I think it high time that an end be put to your sitting. And I do dissolve this Parliament. And let God be judge between you and me."

And this is all that the great Oliver has been able to do, to persuade Englishmen, even Puritan Englishmen, to be governed by him. And now we must take our leave of Mr. Carlyle. We will do him this justice,—we believe that he meant to bring out a genuinely English idea of excellence, to portray a man of rude exterior and speech, doing great things in a commonplace and unromantic way. But he must match his ideal with something better than Cromwell's distorted and unreal character, his repulsive energy, his dreary and ferocious faith, his thinly veiled and mastering selfishness.

II

A SEQUEL TO THE "VESTIGES"[1]

It is not our intention to intrude into the quarrel that is going on between the scientific world and the author of the *Vestiges of Creation;* but the appearance of his volume of *Explanations* suggests a few remarks on the general bearing of the contest.

The *Vestiges* professed to be but a popular book. It was clever; it startled and amused the public; but the aristocracy of science contented themselves with *speaking* contemptuously of it, till rapidly multiplying editions roused them, and finally brought down the Edinburgh Reviewer upon it. The mysterious author, fighting single-handed, has now delivered his fire in return against his numerous and respectable antagonists.

[1] *Explanations;* a Sequel to *Vestiges of the Natural History of Creation.* By the author of that work. *Guardian*, 18th March 1846. [*Vestiges of the Natural History of Creation* appeared in October 1844, two years before the founding of the *Guardian*. In the *Life and Letters of Dean Church* it is stated that the Dean reviewed the *Vestiges* in the *Guardian*. This is incorrect; the review referred to is the one which follows here.]

In tone and style he has the advantage. He propounds self-complacently perhaps, and ambitiously, but with calmness; he replies with dignity and temper. His opponents seem to us to have forgotten, not merely the much-vaunted philosophic virtue of indifference to consequences, but very frequently the humbler one of courtesy; his rashness and ignorance may have been provoking, but they should have been serene; they have put out too much of their strength in personalities and contradiction, and too little in the consideration and explanation of difficulties, and have exhibited some of those weaknesses and inconsistencies which they are wont to charge on politicians and theologians. With the British Association and its jokes in our mind, we scarcely expected the Edinburgh Reviewer to be shocked at the indelicacy of the *Vestiges*, or to protest against bringing the details of science before the public.

The battle will appear, we think, to the world at large to be a drawn one. The theory of the *Vestiges* is undeniably *in harmony* with the general bearing of modern science; and this the author has worked out with much skill. But his opponents have at least shown that we know far too little for a real philosophy —for anything but a mere theory. "What do I want more?" rejoins the author, who really, however, *does* want more. A theory means everything, from a vague surmise to a probability, on which men are content to live, and he has aimed, not at a mere hypothesis, but at a "new philosophy." And if he has successfully challenged his opponents to give a meaning, as he has done, to the facts of science, they have this much to say, that his *meaning* is unproved, and, so far as we at present know, unprovable.

Such seems to be the state of the question, so far as it depends on the evidence of the *facts* of science. Each party accuses the other of ignorance and misstatement; and, as far as it appears to bystanders, in the present unsettled state of our knowledge, with nearly equal justice or injustice.

Much has been said about the dangerous consequences of the book. The *Explanations* leave no doubt as to the writer's dreary Epicureanism, which he himself seems scarcely to realise. But whatever danger we may be in from this, the book itself will do little harm. Modern science has not hitherto done much to guard us; but happily we have other and better preservatives.

What strikes us about the controversy is the light that it throws upon the state of science itself. It seems to show, of some of the leaders in science, that they are not quite prepared for the contest. Brilliant in the field of experiment, they seem to fail in that of higher thought. For, however rashly, and it may be ignorantly, the author of the *Vestiges* has written,— and he plainly is a superficial man and a shallow thinker,—he shows how thought is moving. He is thinking in the line of modern science, and though his crude views are not proved, they are what modern discovery suggests; they are in the direction to which science is pointing, and *may go*. The *general fact* of a progress in animal life is certainly one of the apparent results of geology. Equally undeniable is it that every day is bringing new departments of knowledge within the domain of what we call *law*. A book like the *Vestiges* is a sign of the impression which these things are making on thinking minds. It is a call to those who lead in science to face questions which any one who reflects on the progress of science must see to be immerging on us. It raises, or at least implies, questions; most people will think, in the domain of philosophy, *fair* questions. We have seen nothing which shows that its answerers are alive to these questions; much less that they are able to grapple with them. We must confess that we see in it the revenge of moral and metaphysical science on physical. We can remember great men in the latter sporting with the fears of orthodoxy, and sneering at the dreams of scholasticism. They may want a little of both perhaps now, to help them out of some disagreeable conclusions.

The theory of the *Vestiges* is met, not on the broad principles which it involves of a higher philosophy, but in details, about which our knowledge shifts from day to day. If Mr. Weekes's galvanic pots should actually have produced the genuine *Acarus Crossii*,[1] the Edinburgh Reviewer would seem to be in a bad way.

---

[1] See *Explanations*, p. 120, and Appendix, p. 189, where a full account is given of Mr. Weeke's experiments in spontaneous

The writer's master error is his theology,—not his speculations, baseless as they may be, as to the mode in which things came into being; but that gross "shortness of thought" which in the case of the Infinite and Omnipresent makes His acting by what we call "law" the contradictory of His special and generation. They are thus commented on by the *Edinburgh Review* (July 1845, p. 6):—"'The author tells us with some detail, and great simplicity, that 'Mr. Weekes, by the action of a galvanic battery, continued for eleven months, created a multitude of insects (*Acarus Crossii*), minute and semi-transparent and furnished with long bristles.' The creatures thus created were sometimes observed to go back into the parent fluid, and occasionally they devoured each other ; and soon after they had been called to life, they were disposed to extend their species in the vulgar way ! So much for the experiment ; let us next read the comment of our author :— 'Towards the negative wire of the battery, dipped in the fluid, there gathered a quantity of gelatinous matter—a part of the process which is very striking when we mention that gelatine is one of the proximate principles, or first compounds out of which animal bodies are formed.' He cannot give up this experiment without burying his whole household ; for in truth it is the only prop on which he builds his habitation ; and the stone jelly to feed his little *larvae* is quite affecting. But in the third edition . . . he follows the lead of some hesitating critic, and adds, with graceful simplicity —' that we should require further proof to satisfy us that the matter here concerned was actually gelatine.' We tell him not to doubt at all—that a few drops of acid, properly applied, will gelatinise some of the hardest minerals—and that rock jelly floating in the *liquor silicum* is one of the most vulgar substances wrung from Nature's dugs, and in the shape of chalk infusion, has been drunk for ages by the whole race of crowing gallinaceous philosophers who were progressively developed in the central parts of our great southern capital ; nay, that the same fecundating compound has found its way to the west of Temple Bar, and created by its animating power a celestial sky-blue philosophy which is soon to fill the world with wonders."

personal acting. And his critics, though they vaguely protest against some especially gross statements, do not seem to see that this is the fatal poison which pervades his whole line of thought. They practically admit the infidel premise, and talk about acts of creation by a power superior to "vulgar nature."[1] They allow that the *idea* of a "creation by law," in the way of what we call "natural consequence," excludes the personal and special interference of God at every step and every moment, and charge themselves with the proof, on physical and historical grounds, that the course of things at the dawn of creation was not only different, but opposite to what it is now. And thus they fight at a disadvantage. Both parties, indeed, would allow that "we are not acquainted what the course of nature is upon the first peopling of worlds,"—words which it would be better perhaps if they both reflected on more seriously. But the writer who thinks that the world was evolved by orderly laws, and not made by what he calls an irregular and fitful agency, certainly appeals with ever-increasing plausibility to the *outside show* of things. If "laws of nature" he argues, prevail *anywhere*, why not *everywhere?*—if *now*, why not *at the first?* "One after another," he says, "the phenomena of nature, like so many revolted principalities, have fallen under the dominion of order or law." Small or great are nothing in nature. Why not suppose the origin of

[1] *Edinburgh Review*, July 1845, pp. 60-64, and *Explanations*, pp. 133-138.

worlds as *natural* as that, equally mysterious, of individuals? And he speaks in sympathy with the growing tendency in all provinces of thought to believe in gradual instead of abrupt transitions, to look for ordinary instead of unusual agencies and processes— a tendency which is not in itself infidel—which is so only where, in the *natural* which veils it, the *divine* which is behind is sunk and lost. The important question is, not whether in the order of external nature the Almighty working was ever in a different mode, but whether the philosophical notion of working by *laws* excludes the scriptural and popular one of real and special interference. If a man really thinks that there is any more "special exertion or fiat" of divine power in creation than in providence,—if he thinks that God is not as really present whenever rain is falling or fire ascending, as in the beginning of the world, we should tremble for his faith. But if the two notions are thought compatible, the line of argument which has been mainly taken against the *Vestiges* seems almost wasted; the true answer to its mischief is not a heap of apparent exceptions to "natural order," which further knowledge may *and is likely to* resolve, but an account of what "natural order" means. And it is not in physics or in history that we must seek for that account. The starting-point in this inquiry must be in those regions of thought in which we are often told that moralists and theologians spin dreams. Again, with respect to the theory of the *Vestiges* about "aboriginal and spontaneous generation" and transmutation of species, it seems to us that whatever becomes of the facts which it appeals to, the philosophical answers to it have been somewhat rhetorical, mixed up at any rate with appeals to feeling, and much irrelevant ridicule. Rhetoric and ingenious ridicule may hereafter prove inconvenient to *savans*, not less than to statesmen. The theory may suggest unpleasant, and to some persons, humbling and revolting ideas; but it is obvious that this, as a difficulty, ought to have no place in a philosophical discussion. And moreover, we cannot help thinking that though it would be no great credit to an ordinary person to be without these instinctive feelings, yet for a professed naturalist to allow them any weight, shows considerable narrowness of view, and want of serious reflection on the strange scene of wonders which he has chosen to contemplate. The theory of the *Vestiges* may be without evidence of fact, and have but small support from analogy; but it ought to be disposed of simply on this ground. It cannot be said to be antecedently more strange or improbable than nature generally is to the imagination of those to whom its familiar histories become more than words or sights.

There appears to us to be the same unsteadiness of view, the same want of strong and comprehensive philosophy, with respect to the question of what is called materialism. It is very well to rebuke the writer of the *Vestiges* for the confusion of thought which he doubtless shows; but we should have been glad to have seen besides more sensitiveness to the present state of facts, more precision in stating what they amount to, and more fearlessness as to the results of physical inquiry on moral truth.

The author of the *Vestiges* is quite alive to the state of the case, and turns it to account. He charges his antagonists with not keeping pace with the demands of the time. They were once in advance— the enlightened and the liberal, who took a secret pleasure in venturing on liberties with established opinions. Now they are the assailed parties, fostering prejudices, afraid of conclusions, lingering about details, and with gross inconsistency, alleges the defender of the *Vestiges*, opposing religious objections to philosophical hypotheses. The *Vestiges* affects to present a systematic theory of nature, its opponents have none; it combines and explains facts which they shrink from facing. There is much injustice and exaggeration, doubtless, in the following remarks, but they do indicate at least a partial truth.

Adverting to the fact "that nearly all the scientific men are opposed to the theory of the *Vestiges*," the author says:—

The ability of this class to give, at the present time, a true response on such a subject appears extremely challengeable. It is no discredit to them that they are, almost without exception, engaged, each in his little department of science, and able to give little or no attention to other parts of that vast field . . . doing little for comprehensive views of nature. Experiments, in however narrow a walk, facts of whatever minuteness, make reputations in scientific societies; all beyond is regarded with suspicion and distrust. The consequence is that philosophy, as it exists among us, does nothing to raise its votaries above the common ideas of their time. There can, therefore, be nothing more conclusive against our hypothesis in disfavour of the scientific class than in that of any other section of educated men. There is even less; for the position of scientific men with regard to the public is such that they are rather eager to repudiate than to embrace general views, seeing how unpopular they generally are. . . . For the very purpose of maintaining their own respect in the concessions they have to make, they naturally wish to find all possible objections to any such theory as that of progressive development—exaggerating every difficulty in its way, rejecting, wherever they can, the evidence in its favour, and extenuating what they cannot reject; in short, taking all the well-recognised means, which have been so often employed in keeping back advancing truths. If this looks like special pleading, I can only call upon the reader to bring to his remembrance the impressions which have been usually made upon him by the transactions of learned societies and the pursuits of individual men of science. Did he not always feel that while there were laudable industry and zeal, there was also an intellectual timidity rendering all the results philosophically barren! Perhaps a more lively illustration of their deficiency in the life and soul of Nature-seeking could not be presented than in the view which Sir J. Herschel gives of the uses of science, in a treatise reputed as one of the most philosophical ever produced in our country.

These uses, according to the learned knight, are strictly material—it might even be said, sordid—namely, "to show us how to avoid attempting impossibilities, to secure us from important mistakes . . . to enable us to accomplish our ends in the easiest, shortest, most economical, and most effectual manner." . . . Such results, it will be felt, may occasionally be of importance in saving a country gentleman from a hopeless mining speculation, or adding to the powers and profits of an iron foundry or cotton mill, but nothing more. When the awakened and craving mind asks what science can do for us in explaining the great ends of the Author of Nature, and our relations to Him, to good and evil, to life and to eternity, the man of science turns to his collection of shells or butterflies, to his electric machine or his retort, and is as mute as a child who, sporting on the beach, is asked what lands lie beyond the great ocean which stretches before him. The natural sense of men who do not happen to have taken a taste for the coleoptera, or the law of fluids, revolts at the sterility of such pursuits, and though fearful of some error on its own part, can hardly help condemning the whole to ridicule. Can we wonder that such, to so great an extent, is their fate in public opinion, when we read the appeal presented in their behalf by the very prince of modern philosophers? Or can we say that where such views of "the uses of divine philosophy" are entertained there could be any right preparation of mind to receive with candour, or treat with justice, a plan of nature like that presented in the *Vestiges?* No, it must be before another tribunal that this new philosophy is to be truly and righteously judged.

This is a very unfair representation of Sir John

Herschel's account of the matter, and at best it is but the natural retort of the defender of a new theory; but it is not less a call on men of science to rouse themselves from any conventionalities of argument, and adjust their opinions with greater precision and connection. We do not say that they are bound forthwith to meet theory with theory, but the appearance of a book like the *Vestiges*, and the interest it has excited, show that it is time for them to rise to something higher than that mere empirical character of mind which is one essential part, but which is far from being the whole, of the real philosopher. They must not be content with exposing the temerity of the *Vestiges ;* they must take the *initiative*, and give us views of nature—complete they cannot be, but at least real ones—adequate to our knowledge of its phenomena.

If science is to advance, it must be cultivated freely : if it is to be more than a vestibule to the workshop, it must be cultivated not merely freely but philosophically, by minds trained to appreciate harmony and greatness in system as well as arrangement in details. And if moral truths and religion are not to suffer, it must be, not by allying them with the physical sciences, but by defining with breadth and precision of thought the impassable limits between the moral and the physical ; by maintaining the substantive independence of those two incommensurables,— on the one hand, the free will and thought of men, and on the other the sequences of nature. Keep in view the great principle that belief in God does not depend upon the natural: that nature is not the real basis of religion, and we can safely afford full and free scope to science. But most certainly it is not by repeating in its old shape the starveling argument of Paley's *Natural Theology* that we shall keep out the infidel spirit that threatens to make use of science. The *Vestiges* warns us, if proof were required, of the vanity of those boasts which great men used to make, that science naturally led on to religion. It may lead beyond the experiment and the generalisation, to vast theories—visions and histories for the imagination, realities of order and law for the reason—to a *substitute* for religion. In a world of widening and self-sustained order, an Epicurean Atheism is not so difficult: something deeper than the facts of natural science is required to undercut its premises. It is the metaphysician, the abstract thinker, who is wanting in the field. It is not special pleading, or timid indecisive fighting about details, which will meet the march of that science which openly threatens to be infidel, because no one will help it to be Christian.

III

STANLEY ON THE STUDY OF ECCLESIASTICAL HISTORY[1]

IN these introductory lectures Mr. Stanley gives us the keynote of what he means to be his professorial teaching. It will be, if we are to judge from them, comprehensive, wide in its range and in its sympathies, noble and generous in its spirit, full, rich, varied, attractive,—attractive from its abundance of materials and information, from the hearty earnestness and warmth of the teacher, and from the finished elegance of his manner. On the other hand, this teaching does not promise to be distinguished by deep and searching views; it seems not unlikely to be tempted to linger on the surface by a love of the picturesque and dramatic, and by an instinctive shrinking from the thorns and pitfalls of theological controversy, and the doubts and contradictions of inward experiences; it will show, besides candour, temper, and elevation, an

[1] *Three Introductory Lectures on the Study of Ecclesiastical History*. By A. P. Stanley, Regius Professor of Ecclesiastical History. *Guardian*, 13th May 1857.

uneasy hesitation, an impulse to go to the edge checked by an unconquerable drawing back, in those inevitable questions where men have hitherto found it necessary to make up their minds; and though far from forgetting the divine and unearthly aspects of Church history, it will put out its strength and lay the stress of its results on the purely human side of that history. Mr. Stanley would be as far as possible from intending to divorce the earthly from the heavenly, the human agents from the more than human significance and importance of the actions in which they had their part. But we may expect, probably, that sometimes wisely, sometimes questionably, he will present that purely human side and significance of ecclesiastical history with a strength and exclusiveness which will be new in one of its English University chairs.

Mr. Stanley makes high claims for his special subject. The extent of its range, the greatness of its interest, the fruitfulness of its results, have never been more warmly and more largely set forth. He shows how far it reaches, and how intimately it is mixed up with the greatest and the most familiar of human concerns. He shows how what seems a skeleton may be clothed with warm flesh and blood, and made to breathe the breath of human life. He shows how it bears with a deeply practical significance on the hopes and fears and difficulties amid which our own lot is cast. His great remedy for apparent dryness and stiffness is to enlarge the points of contact with the history of the world, and to show us the men themselves. "Look at Augustinianism," he says, "as it arose in the mind of Augustine; at Lutheranism as it was conceived by Luther; at Wesleyanism as it was set forth by Wesley. It will cease to be a phantom, it will speak to us as a man; if it is an enemy, we shall slay it more easily, if a friend, we shall embrace it more warmly." And thus he claims to find interest where the men of his school are not accustomed to find much, in Creeds and Articles:—

Still more is this the case with the kindred subject of confessions and articles of faith. If we regard them merely in their cut-and-dried results, they may indeed serve many useful ends; they supply stakes to make hedges against intruders, planks to cross our enemy's trenches, faggots to burn heretics. But go to the soil from which they sprang. Watch them in their wild, native, luxuriant growth. Observe the moss which has grown over their stems, the bough rent away there and grafted in here, the branches inextricably intertwined with adjacent thickets. So regarded, they will not be less, but more of a shelter; we shall not value them the less, for understanding them better. Figure to yourselves, as you read any creeds or confessions, the lips by which they were first uttered, the hands by which they were first written. Hear the Apostles' Creed as it summed up in its few simple sentences the belief of the Roman martyrs. Watch the Nicene Bishops meeting each other, and their opponents, and the great Emperor Constantine, for the first time, on the shores of the Bithynian Lake. Listen to the triumphant war-songs of Clovis over the vanquished Arians of France and Spain, and you will catch with a clearer understanding the true significance of their echo in the old Latin hymn *Quicunque vult*, then first welcomed into Europe. Read the Articles of the English Church in their successive mutilations, excrescences, variations. Go to that most precious of collegiate libraries in the sister University, where the venerable autograph which contains them may still be seen; look at the signatures of those whose names are affixed; conceive the persons whom those names represent; imagine them as any one who has ever taken part in any council, or commission, or committee, or conclave of any kind whatever, can and must imagine them; one sacrificing, another insisting on, a favourite expression; a new turn given to one sentence, a charitable colour thrown over another; the edge of a sharp exclusion blunted by one party, the sting of a bitter sarcasm drawn by another. Start from this view, as certain as it can be made by the facts of human nature and by the facts of history, both universal and particular. Regard confessions of faith in this, their only true historical light, and in that light many a new glimpse will be obtained of their practical justice and moderation; many a harsh expression will be explained; many a superfluous scruple of honest minds will vanish away; many a foolish controversy will be extinguished for ever.

And in like manner, in the course of some good remarks as to the method of study, after advising his hearers to follow some one subject in detail, to read "great works and full works, not small works and short works," and to "study the greater events, scenes, places, and revolutions, in all the detail in which they can be represented to us," he proceeds :—

Take, for example, the General Councils of the Church. They are the pitched battles of Ecclesiastical History. Ask yourselves the same questions as you would about the battles of military history. Ask when, and where, and why they were fought. Put before your minds all the influences of the age which there were confronted and concentrated from different quarters as in one common focus. See why they were summoned to Nicæa, to Constance, to Trent ; the locality often contains here, as in actual battles, the key of their position, and easily connects the Ecclesiastical History of the age with its general history and geography. Look at the long procession as it enters the scene of assembly ; see who was present and who was absent. Let us make ourselves acquainted with the several characters there brought together, so that we may recognise them as old friends if we meet them again elsewhere. Study their decrees, as expositions of the prevailing sentiments of the time ; study them as a recent historian has advised us to study the statutes of our own ancient Parliaments ; see what evils are most condemned, and what evils are left uncondemned ; observe how far their injunctions are still obeyed, or how far set at nought, and ask in each case the reason why. Read them, as I have just now noticed, with the knowledge given to us by our own experience of all the synods of all kinds ; read them with the knowledge which each gives of every other. Do this for any one Council, and you will have made a deep hole into Ecclesiastical History.

There cannot be a doubt that this is a most important side of history, whether ecclesiastical or any other. And no man will be able to do it justice better than Mr. Stanley. But it is equally certain that it is not the only thing to be thought of in history. The scenic and dramatic, the personal and individual, however fully and precisely and brilliantly brought out, are far from exhausting what a historian has to think about. They are what give life and reality; but *that* to which they give life and reality must have a spirit and tendency and significance far deeper than that outward show of movement, which he must seek for and find if his work is to be more than a mere amusing sport and illusion. You have not told the whole story of the French Revolution when you have given most lifelike pictures of Mirabeau and the meetings of the Jacobin Club. And Mr. Macaulay's *History* would not be the book it is, if in addition to his great power of bringing back and reviving the past he had not a clear perception and a strong hold on definite political and religious principles, which give purpose to his narrative, and meaning to his minutest touches. Such a clue there must be in all treatment of history which is to attract and to instruct. Church history, like the history of a great empire or nation, requires a key; and that key is as much, in the one case, theology, as it is in the other political science. Its great controversies, its great catastrophes, its broad movements, are things above and beyond the circumstances which surround them, and the passions, the faults, the aims, the sacrifices of the actors in them. Summon up, if you will, the Nicene Bishops meeting their opponents and the great Emperor Constantine by the shores of the Bithynian Lake; hear, if history lets you, in the *Quicunque vult*, the echo of the triumphant warsongs of Clovis over the vanquished Arians; but surely, when you have grasped as vigorously as your imagination will allow, the historical origin of the two great creeds, you must be very easily satisfied if you rest in that, as a sufficient account or measure of their eventful significance, in the belief and worship of the successive generations of the Church. It is indeed to be a slave to fact and circumstance and outward impressions, to dwell on the scene or the persons or the temporary association, and to put below them the profound connection of these apparent births of accident with the religious thought and education of the world, with the shaping and strengthening of what lies deepest at the root of all that Christians rest on, and teach, and hold fast in death.

Civil history, the history of action and of social and political development, may be fairly separated from the history of philosophy, the history of purely human thought. But in ecclesiastical history this separation, if practicable, is not legitimate; ecclesiastical history must be the history of thought at least as much as of action. It is in this aspect of it, as the history of religious thought and experience and belief, that we expect Mr. Stanley to come short. The temper of his mind does not fit him for it. His inclinations and his remarkable powers point in the other direction. And the specimen which he has here given us of the way in which he proposes to teach confirms our previous anticipations.

We conclude with the following passage, the spirit of which at least has much to teach us; its dogmatic import is perhaps too vague to pronounce upon :—

A serious comparison of the actual contents of the Scriptures with the actual course of ecclesiastical events almost inevitably brings us to the conclusion that the existing materials, principles, and doctrines of the Christian religion are far greater than have ever yet been employed ; that the Christian Church, if it ever be permitted or enabled to use them, has a long lease of new life and new hope before it, such as has never yet been enjoyed. When we look at the Bible on the one hand and History on the other—when we see what are the points on which the Scriptures lay most emphatic stress —when we think how much of the best blood and life of Christendom has run to leaf and not to fruit—when we remember how constant is the protest of Scripture, and, we may add, of the best spirits of Christendom also, against preferring any cause of opinion or ceremony to justice, holiness, truth, and love—how constantly and steadily all these same intimations point to one Divine Object, and One only, as the life and essence of Christianity—can we hesitate to say that, if the Christian Church be drawing to its end, or if it continue to its end with no other objects than those which it has hitherto sought, it will end with its acknowledged resources confessedly undeveloped, its finest hopes of usefulness almost untried and unattempted ? It will have been like an ungenial spring cut short in full view of the summer —a stately vessel wrecked within the very sight of the shore.

It may be that the age for creating new forms of the Christian faith is past and gone—that no new ecclesiastical boundaries will henceforth be laid down among men. It is certain that in the use of the old forms is our best chance for the present. Use them to the utmost—use them threadbare if you will; long experience, the course of their history, their age and dignity, have made them far more elastic, far more available, than any we can invent for ourselves. But do not give up the study of the history of the Church either in disgust at what has been, or in despair of what may be. The history of the Christian Church, no less than of the Jewish, bears witness to its own incompleteness. The words which describe its thoughts constantly betray their deflection from the original ideas they were meant to express—"Church," "Gospel," "Catholic," "Evangelical," the very word "Ecclesiastical"—are now too often mere shadows, sometimes even the exact opposites, of their ancient, orthodox, scriptural meaning. We need only trace the steps of their gradual descent to their present signification, in order to see how far they, and we with them, have to ascend again before we can reach the point from which they started, the point to which we have still to attain. Read, too, the expressions of the best and wisest Christians in their best and wisest moments. Take them, not in the passion of youth, not in the heat of controversy, not in the idleness of speculation, but in the presence of some great calamity, or in the calmness of age, or in the approach of death. Take that admirable summary of mature Christian experience which ought to be in the hands of every student of Ecclesiastical History—one might well add, of every student of theology, of every English minister of religion —which is contained in Baxter's review of his own narrative of his life and times. See how he there corrects the narrowness, the sectarianism, the dogmatism, of his youth, by the comprehensive wisdom acquired in long years of persecution, of labour, and devotion. Let us hope that what he has expressed as the result of his individual experience, we may find and appropriate in the collective experience of the old age of the Church.

IV

STANLEY'S LECTURES ON THE JEWISH CHURCH[1]

As there is much that is of great interest and value in these Lectures, it ought to be said at starting that between Dr. Stanley's view of the Bible history and its authority, and that taken by ordinary readers of the Bible in England, there is a great interval. He would be the last to deny it; and he would only say that we were wrong, and that he hoped that in time we should come to know better. But as there is a great deal that we may learn from him about the Bible and its history, it is desirable to say at once what it is useless to conceal or evade. Ordinary readers of the Bible do see in it the record of a history more supernatural, more interwoven with miracle than he, fully believing the providential character of the whole history and the miraculous character of certain parts, is prepared to admit. Ordinary readers suppose it to tell of an immediate

[1] *Lectures on the History of the Jewish Church.* By A. P. Stanley, D.D. *Guardian*, 1st April 1863.

presence and interposition of God, where he shrinks from venturing so to interpret the narrative. It would be absolutely unfair to say that he does not see the hand of God in the Jewish history; for it is his purpose to trace it continuously and throughout. But it is to be remembered that he conceives of its manner of working in a way very different from the common way, and hardly intelligible to most of those who accept the Bible as a Divine and inspired book, the result of a history unlike any other in the world, from the part which God directly took in it, disclosing, at the time, that He was taking part in it.

The history of the Old Testament wears a different aspect according as it is simply looked at in itself, or as it is connected with the Incarnation and Resurrection of the Son of God. These were, in the highest and fullest sense, which nothing can get over, miracles; events utterly different from anything else that we know of in the world or in history. A course of things which was a preparation for and part of such events as these, as it confessedly runs on into miracles without parallel and analogy, is on a different level from any other history in the world. A different scale of probability, a different standard of judgment in many important particulars, may be expected to apply to it. It is a question of fact and evidence, of course, in each case, not to be settled *a priori*, of what nature its records are, what they really say, what really happened, how God chose that the occurrences of that preparatory time should be understood and transmitted,—how much, in fact, we are permitted to know of that early history. But, as God dealt with the world differently from all the ordinary ways of His dealing with it when the Son of God was made flesh and rose from the dead, the mind, impressed with these miracles, is not surprised to find the whole precedent history pervaded with the supernatural, and marked with the assumption of the miraculous. It is this that ordinary readers are impressed with in the Old Testament history. The Call of Abraham and the miracles of Moses do not stand alone as separate alleged instances of Divine interposition; they are felt as steps and links in that train of working which went on till "the Word was made flesh," and the Crucified arose from the dead. They belong to a system of things of which these last wonders are a part. On them is reflected from these latter a Divine character which separates them from all other things which could happen to men, or have been done by men, not thus linked with the coming of God into the world. Dim, vague, featureless, they may be to our modern eye; "formal," we are afraid Dr. Stanley would call the common simple aspects of the history; but the essential thing, that which gives them meaning and glory, is that they are felt to be memorials and instances of the Divine presence, as the Divine presence afterwards made itself known, when the Lord came to visit us. It seems to us that the look and significance which are thrown on the character of Jewish history by the Incarnation and Resurrection of our Lord — occurrences so absolutely unique and unlike all other things that have been known in the world, and bringing with them the presumption of having been led up to by events as extraordinary—are lost sight of by Dr. Stanley. The hand of God was not in the background or many steps off,—it was in the front place when Christ came; and why should it not have been so in what confessedly prepared for Christ? Fully and most reverently recognising that hand, Dr. Stanley for the most part declines to localise it; to say that in this place or that it wrought differently in its perceptible manner of working, from its ordinary working in human affairs. If in any given case it cannot be localised, be it so; but the record says that in certain cases it did make itself seen and known; and so great a fact, if a fact, seems to us to transcend in interest all that, however great and wonderful, is merely of a likeness to the transactions and events of the history of our common experience. To turn away our eyes from this feature of the sacred story, whatever else that turning them away enables us to see more clearly, is like taking the spring out of the year. The Bible history may doubtless be made of the deepest interest merely as a human history; but the great interest of all about it is that it claims to be something more. It claims, besides all that is human about it, to be a dispensation of God's government, an order of dealing with human character, actions, and fortunes, as singular and unique as the unexampled event in which it culminated is unique, amidst all that we know of God's ways. This element we feel to be missing when we follow the course of Old Testament history under Dr. Stanley's guidance. We repeat emphatically that he by no means denies its presence. In certain instances he distinctly acknowledges it; and he is always under the sense of the mysterious awfulness of the history. But to the ordinary reader of the Bible, the difference between its history and all other history is the predominant thought. In Dr. Stanley's mind the great source of interest is the similarity which he traces between the Bible history and all human history. The effect of this with him is, it is true, to lift up to a higher level the things of earth, and the importance and significance of what has gone on and passes still in the political and social changes of the world. But that, valuable as it is, is not enough, if the Bible and its history really belongs, as the general belief of Christendom supposes it to belong, to a sphere above and diviner than that of our common experience. This, the source not merely of great moral influences and lessons, but of great doctrinal aspects of the ways of God and the relations of man to Him, and still more of deep devotional aspirations and outpourings of the spiritual mind, is—not denied, not ignored—but left in the background by Dr. Stanley. He dwells often on the fearlessness and force with which the *Christian Year* brings forward the human and natural side of the Bible history, and "blends together the natural and the supernatural in that union which is at once most Biblical and most philosophical." But if, in its author's mind, the subordination of the two elements and their relative prominence had been the same as in his own view, the *Christian Year* would never have been written; at least we should never have had its deeper thoughts, its devotional tone, and all that has made it the echo of religious feeling in the modern English Church.

It may be said that the ruling thought of these Lectures is the indefiniteness of the Divine side of the Bible, and that their ruling purpose is to exhibit the religious value of this indefiniteness; to show how it is compatible with the fullest and deepest belief in the reality of the Divine working, and admits all that is most positive and substantial in religious thought and feeling. Not only is it wiser, truer, safer, Dr. Stanley would say, to be content with indefinite views and statements in the matters which the Bible history brings before us, but it gives to these subjects an infinitely increased solemnity of interest. It is doubtless true that there are coarse gross ways of understanding the Divine dealings, and that very often it is more religious and more reverent to abstain from precise assertions when we are speaking of the ways and works of God. But there are limits to this. The Call of Abraham would have been equally a Divine work, if it had been like the call which summons a missionary of the modern world to devote his life to carrying truth to strange lands; but it is idle to say that it makes no difference to our thoughts whether the Call of Abraham was something more than this, something *unlike* all our experience. The Decalogue would have been as binding on the conscience of man even if it had not been given on Sinai; it would have been almost as wonderful if it had been the code produced by the enlightenment and elevation of the leader of a desert tribe of those days; but it is unreasonable to say that, if it is indeed the monument of a direct communication between God and man, it is the same thing in interest and importance as if it had been something thought out by the spirit of man under the influence, as we know it now, of the Author of all goodness and wisdom. And so with other things. Parts of the Bible history may have been read and understood as supernatural, which are either purely natural or what we now call providential. But the great hinges of it are more than this. No arguments in favour of indefinite rather than too limited and literal views, no warnings against narrow and human conceptions of God's ways, can get rid of the presence of the miraculous. Not only is it interwoven with the very sense and reason of the history, but it is indissolubly linked with that of which the life of our Lord was the climax. Let us learn where we were wrong in supposing a miracle. But it is not philosophical nor religious to shrink from the miraculous, as such, if it really comes before us; to be content to subordinate it to the providential, or to hold up the providential so as to obscure it. If God did not teach men as He is described in the Bible to have taught them, we must be content with what our increased knowledge, depriving us of what we have hitherto relied upon, now makes us aware of; but if He did, it is not a thing to be put into the background, or to explain away, or to make slight account of.

What Dr. Stanley has done, and done well, is to represent in its full force and truth the human side of the history. It must have had its human side. It is the history of men like ourselves, and, in most ways, things must have happened as they ordinarily happen among men. There must have been a certain actual way in which things came to pass, and, for the most part, it was probably in some such way as he supposes. The surrounding relations and conditions of life must have been of some certain kind, must have had a certain outward reality of fact, and these Dr. Stanley undertakes to revive and call up before our minds. To do this successfully is no inconsiderable work. To make us feel and understand the times in which—the real men among whom—the events related in the Bible took place, is a service next in importance to that of making us fully understand the purport of the events themselves. If in this latter aspect Dr. Stanley comes short, he renders us great help in the former. The criticism to be made on the Lectures may be expected from our knowledge of Dr. Stanley's other works. There are passages where his imagination seems to require control, and where a colour almost unnaturally romantic is thrown over transactions where the original narrative can hardly be said to invite it. And again, his vast knowledge, his love of associating things together which seem far apart, his power of seeing analogies and likenesses, sometimes appear to us to spoil the simplicity and truthfulness of his representations. In superficial likenesses he sometimes overlooks deeper and more important differences; and his power of illustration tempts him to overload and refine. It strikes us sometimes that where we need, and looked for, thought, we find ourselves only in the midst of brilliant rhetoric. But Dr. Stanley always teaches us a lesson in the breadth and elevation with which he is sure to treat the subject in which he feels interest. In his closing lectures on the Prophetical Office and the Prophets he does not, we think, tell us all that is to be said about them; but as far as he goes, and especially in the last lecture, he brings before us the characteristics of the Jewish Prophets with a power and with a height of feeling which are very striking and noble. We do not accept many of his conclusions; but we believe that he is right in the general calm and patient temper in which he reasons on the questions before him. The danger of such writing as his is this—that it presents some temptation to slide into a vague and misty way of looking at great subjects, a way in which feeling takes the place of thought; some risk of losing our sense of the Divine in the interest excited by the human side of the history; some risk of acquiescing in what we feel to be short of the whole truth.

V

MERIVALE ON THE CONVERSION OF THE ROMAN EMPIRE[1]

A CHANGE such as that which we call the conversion of the Roman Empire—a change so vast, so gradual, consisting of so many parts, spread over such a long tract of years, involving in a common transformation, by the action of influences adapted to each, the very dissimilar and sharply contrasted portions of society which, locally and morally separated from one another, were embraced within the Empire—eludes the grasp of the mind which tries to penetrate and embrace it with accuracy and distinctness. The historian finds it hard to comprehend in one survey its manifold and constantly shifting aspects, to measure the rate and the depth of its progress, to ascertain its conditions and causes, and to exhibit their joint concurrence and play upon one another, in that completeness which alone gives the true account of their effective force.

[1] *The Conversion of the Roman Empire. The Boyle Lectures for* 1864. By C. Merivale, B.D. *Saturday Review*, 3rd December 1864.

It is a light thing to say that the history of this change never has been fully written; it never can be written. "Subtilitas naturæ subtilitatem sensus et intellectus multis partibus superat." The infinite workings of mind and feeling, of thought and wish, of fear and hope, amid infinitely differing circumstances of education and temperament, of worldly condition and social habits, of recollections, prejudices, moral standards, and amid a constantly varying spectacle of outward things and events—which contributed to the supplanting, among the most intelligent and highly civilised of mankind, of all their native and long-accustomed beliefs by the most obscure in its origin of Oriental religions—defy the powers of imagination and thought adequately to explore, to analyse, to co-ordinate them, and to construct a representation of the process at all answering to the reality.

We see its broad features, but we cannot but know that there must have been much of at least equal importance going on which has passed for ever beyond our reach. We have probably some of the best writings of the time, giving us the impressions of the thinkers and observers who reflected it and influenced it; and these help us to understand the public, the avowed, the palpable movements in the great struggle. But they fail us when we want to know more of what was taking place in its hidden depths—of those obscure and complicated and fugitive transactions which were, perhaps, deciding more than was decided by the decrees of Emperors, or the keen and eloquent words of philosophers or Fathers. Of the growth and conflict of opinions and ideas, the ebb and flow of old or new, among nameless thousands, in the various gradations of society, in the meditations or debates that went on in palaces and villas among the thoughtful and refined, in the confused ferment of crowded suburbs or obscure hovels, in private families, among women, among slaves, among traders or soldiers, in the daily market talk of great cities, in the business or festival meetings of innumerable municipalities— of the varying effects on countless neighbourhoods of the presence, the moral character and ability, the ministrations, the discussions, the fortunes, of a Christian congregation—of all this, whatever we may imagine or conjecture, we can know but little.

From the language of individual writers we can only guess, more or less safely, at the real thoughts and views of the mixed crowds who were the subjects of the change. We assume certain general forms of opinion and feeling among certain classes of heathens, on the strength of the words of representatives like Seneca or Lucian, and we attribute to the body of Christians the belief and the general way of speaking of which we have evidence in Justin or Tertullian. But we know from our own experience that living society is not fully represented by even the greatest of contemporary writers. We can compare broadly the great outlines of doctrine and argument which confronted each other in the struggle. But how rarely and how indistinctly can we ever catch sight of the actual point of meeting and contact where, in real life and under the present feeling of great questions at stake, the two encountered and tried their strength against one another. And while such important and critical portions of the whole great change—a change which began from the bottom of society, and of which the early stages were necessarily obscure—passed without any one capable of noticing and recording them, or thinking it worth while to do so; while so much in its developments depended on what it is impossible for us now to ascertain; the evidence about it which does remain, though it is abundant and valuable, is yet capriciously and provokingly irregular—very satisfactory in one part, interrupted by hopeless gaps and blanks in another. Yet, though the very progress of our knowledge shows us more and more that about much of the inquiry the only wise thing is to recognise distinctly the evident limits of our power to know, there are few subjects which, after all the learning and ability already devoted to it, would better reward the student. It is a long history of many parts, spread over a wide range. There are tracts in it which are still unexplored, aspects of it which have yet to be considered, masses of facts which have been passed over as too entangled or too unconnected, but which a closer and more comprehensive examination may unravel and arrange; there are questions, old or newly arising, which continue unanswered, but which do not discourage the inquirer. It is a field into which we should suppose that no one has ventured who has not been strongly attracted to return to it.

Mr. Merivale, with his great knowledge of the period, and his thorough appreciation of both sides in the struggle, is qualified as few men are to write instructively about it. The *Boyle Lectures* are not history, and they rather make us wish for history instead. With the advantage of suggesting and justifying the gathering up and representation of its phenomena in broad and generalised forms, traced with strong and bold lines, they combine the disadvantage of being an inconvenient form for exhibiting and commenting on the facts on which assertions rest. But we must take them as Mr. Merivale himself presents them to us, as partial illustrations of particular aspects of the subject, or as suggestions for inquiry. So far as they enter into the question, they do so with great freshness of view, great appreciation of the surrounding state of things, great honesty, much largeness of mind and generosity of sentiment. They are powerfully and eloquently written. It is an eloquence which, in its florid richness and its novel forms, recalls sometimes rather the later than the earlier and severer models, and it is kept up all through, with a want of relaxation and relief, at a high pitch which has something monotonous in it. But it is the eloquence of true feeling, and it rests upon a substantial foundation of vigorous thought, accurate knowledge, and wide sympathies.

Mr. Merivale confines himself almost entirely to

one part of the inquiry into the causes of the conversion of the Empire—the internal correspondence of the moral and religious doctrines of Christianity to the condition and wants of the society which it leavened. His way of giving a measure of the change produced is to bid us imagine what must have come to pass, what an extraordinary revolution of habitual thoughts and feelings must have taken place, in the interval between two memorable assemblies of the authorities of the Roman State—the one, the debate in the Roman Senate on the punishment of Catiline's associates, in which it was distinctly assumed as the ground of argument, without rebuke or protest, that there was no future state or judgment; the other, three centuries afterwards, when the chief magistrate of the Empire presided over the solemn settlement and definition of the Christian creed at Nicæa. Between these two points, those at the head of the Roman government had passed "from the denial of the first principle of positive belief to the assertion of an entire system of revealed religion." In that space the step had been taken—a step so enormous as to make the characteristic difference between the old and the modern world—to a view of human life in which a future state of immortality is assumed as a matter of course, and in which all the earliest prepossessions and most common habits of thought imply it, from one in which, as naturally and of course, the presumption and the customary suppositions were all the other way. The state of religious belief which preceded this change has been delineated with much ability and force by Mr. Merivale, and it forms the most important feature of his book. What was at the bottom of the religious sentiment of Heathenism, considered apart from the confused multitude of objects of worship to which it was uncertainly and restlessly directed, was a profound belief in a Divine Providence, with no belief in a future life. Men were sure that this world was guided by the unseen Powers, but they could imagine the reality of no other world. It is the existence of the one element without the other which, to our habits of thought, so necessarily and inseparably goes with it— of faith in an unseen and almighty Providence, without the expectation of a future life—which Mr. Merivale brings out in describing the ground of religious ideas on which Christianity had to work. He insists on the fact, however difficult it may be to us to "divorce these two ideas," that the fundamental element of religious faith and hope and obligation—the belief that "He *is*, and that He is a rewarder of them that diligently seek Him"—did control life and actuate duty, though neither in popular opinion, nor among the intelligent, was the thought of a future existence seriously entertained. This natural belief in Providence without futurity was, on the one hand, spoilt and degraded, not merely by Polytheism, but by the local ideas of Divine patronage which were at the bottom of Roman, as of all other ancient religions —the favouritism of the unseen Powers for a single race. On the other hand, before it came in contact with Christianity, it had been corrected and enlarged by the growth of opinion and the teaching of great historical events. The unity and equality of the whole human race "in its claims on God and man"—the truth to us so familiar, but which to believers in the fundamental idea of heathen religion, the exclusive direction of the Divine government to the destinies of a privileged race, was so inconceivable—gradually made its way through the barriers of opposing religious and national antipathies, and, with the necessarily wider scope thus given to the natural persuasion of a Providence, and the altered aspects of the relations of individual men to the Supreme Being, had made a deep impression, not only on thinking men, but on the popular mind.

Various causes co-operated to this result. The wider views of God, and of man's place in the world, had been timidly and inconsistently suggested, and then recalled as untenable, by Greek philosophy. But after Plato and Aristotle, the great facts of the Macedonian conquest, with the civilisation which it spread, the intercourse which it opened, and the new centres at which it united the world together, were a practical test and confirmation of what had been but a speculative guess, and brought daily custom and experience to reconcile the imagination to the novel thought which the philosophers had cautiously shrunk from as a paradox contrary to nature. To the Stoics, after the results of Alexander's empire, it was easy to carry out what Plato nad half taught, about the government of the world and the destination of mankind, with much more firmness and consistency. Then, upon the teachings of the Stoics, familiarising men with universal conceptions of Providence and of the common nature and duties of man, supervened the equalising influences of the Roman law—that law which had grown, under the practical necessities of empire, from a collection of the narrowest municipal usages into a code of jurisprudence for the world; which, in its aim at expediency and convenience, had overridden that jealous religion of race and family in which it had its first beginnings; which had gradually been "refined and modified into the expression of universal reason on the great principles of equity and legal use"; and which, in creating the new conception of a law of nations—"the image, to the Roman, of the mind of God Himself"—brought with it also the fundamental equality of all who are amenable to that law, and their equal right and interest in all that man can look for at the hands of Providence. Mr. Merivale brings out with great force and feeling, and with no more than justice, the refinement and expansion of religious ideas, the manifest progress from lower and coarser to higher and worthier ones, in the heathen world before Christianity. Views of religion which raised it from a political tradition and badge to a personal relation towards God and towards other men, and which led on to a presentiment of futurity— an "almost belief in immortality"—had been reached, and earnestly insisted on, by some of the most powerful of those whose thoughts led and formed their time. They were, doubtless, indistinct and limited views. The immortality of the Stoics only had interest for an "aristocracy" of elect souls; their conceptions of the Highest fluctuated between a Person and a Fate. But the working of thought in the schools of philosophy had already broken down the strength of national credulity and superstition, and they had found a response in the conscience and good sense of the multitudes.

Nor were these advances in religious thought unpractical speculations. The contrast is a familiar one between the inquisitiveness, the freshness of impression, the sanguine audacity of pure inquiry, in the earlier schools of philosophy, and the sober ethical lessons about life and practice which occupy the later ones; but no one has done so much justice as Mr. Merivale to the serious greatness of the function which the philosophers of the Empire discharged to the society of their time. He bids us remark that they were the comforters and preachers of a sad and anxious time, and that they fulfilled their calling in no unworthy spirit. He calls attention to the deep sadness which pervades the atmosphere of the New Testament, and bids us observe that the gloom was even greater which reigns over the contemporary secular history. "St. Paul is sad and St. John is pensive; but the Christian St. Paul is not so sad as the philosopher Seneca, the Christian St. John is not so pensive as the philosopher Aurelius." And then he calls us to notice with what feeling and what earnestness the philosophers set themselves to meet the circumstances of their times. In the philosophy of the Empire, "we open on an era of preaching instead of discussion." The philosopher, unconsciously to himself, anticipates, in a society which was not yet Christian, the place and the familiar offices of the Christian minister. He is "no longer a logician with an essay, or a sophist with a declamation; he is a master, a preacher, a confessor, a director of souls; not a speculator inquiring into truth, but a witness of God bearing testimony to the Divine law, and charged with the cure of souls entrusted to his teaching." Epictetus and his brethren were the "spiritual advisers," the "directors of conscience," the "physicians of the soul," in the bitter trials and emergencies of life; they "spent their lives in teaching men to sympathise with their fellows"; "the whole world they felt to be akin to them, and to the whole world they went forth to teach and preach a message, self-imposed, of love and pity"; "not to make themselves wiser, but to make men better and happier." Mr. Merivale does not shrink from the parallel which his words suggest. "Christian preaching found its shadow in heathen preaching," and philosophers as well as apostles were persecuted from city to city. "The spirit of prayer had gone abroad among the heathen." Christian Fathers and heathen teachers were bent in different ways on the same great ends; they answer to one another, though they write against one another. "The face is not the same; not one, but like, as that of brethren should be." And the result was not in vain. "Viewed on every side," he says, "there is no period of history, as it seems to me, when men were more in earnest about spiritual hopes and fears than in the third century of our era." He thinks that the justice which the fellow-labourers themselves, in what was at bottom the same cause, were not able, from their necessary rivalry, to do to one another, may at length be rendered by the disciples of those whose work turned out right and was successful towards those whose methods were inadequate and mistaken, but whose earnestness is beyond doubt.

The force and main interest of Mr. Merivale's book seem to us to lie in his just and vivid account of the religious development of heathenism; of that condition of spiritual enlightenment and moral education to which heathen society had in fact attained before Christianity, and which was the foundation on which Christianity was built. The next step of the inquiry is to see what it was which, among so many competitors, gave to Christianity the victory; what were the special adaptations to the wants and ideas of heathen society which enabled Christianity to do for it what rival systems, which had started in the race for influence with equal or greater apparent chances of success, failed to do. In this part of the subject Mr. Merivale is not so successful. What he has to say is compressed into two lectures; and he hardly appears so much at home in discussing with precision and freshness what Christianity brought to meet the state of thought among the heathen, as in discussing this heathen state of thought itself. He says very truly:—

But for this revelation of God's personality, announced distinctly and characteristically in Jesus Christ, the religion of the Christian would have run just the same vicious courses as all human creeds and philosophies before it. No purity of morals, no holiness of ideas, no conviction of miraculous gifts, no assurance of an indwelling Spirit, would have saved it; for all these elements may be found in more or less force among the heathen systems; the salt of Christianity has been the dogmatic belief in the incarnation of the Divine, in the personal manifestation of God in Jesus Christ the Son of God, Himself God, issuing from God and returning to God.

The distinction and the admission are of the utmost importance, and are not always borne in mind. But Mr. Merivale has hardly done justice to his own view of the matter, in working it out in a rather meagre lecture on the correspondence of the great Christian doctrines to the questions and thoughts and needs of those to whom they were presented. It seems to us that we miss the grasp and freedom and sense of familiarity in handling theology which are manifest in his handling of heathen history and thought.

A good deal more seems to be wanted than perhaps, in his confined framework, was possible to Mr. Merivale, of precise distinction, of assignment to their proper periods or places of particular steps and phases of the movement described. The variations of religious ideas, through many centuries and in societies remote from one another, are difficult to bring together under large generalisations without falling into over-statement and looseness. What perhaps justly applies to one part of a period and may be a convenient characteristic by which to stamp our impression of the whole, yet may want much subsequent qualification to be equally exact. Some of Mr. Merivale's illustrations will appear to many to be fanciful and open to question, as, for instance, what he says of the influence of Roman legal ideas on the language of St. Paul—an influence which, if it ultimately made its way into theology, it seems rather forced to recognise in writings like his. And before a cautious reader can always accept the summary which is put before him of a doctrine or state of opinion, the history of its transformation, or the appreciation of a character or a life, he may have to allow for the scale on which the work proceeds, and ought to bear in mind the corrections and discrimination which he may presume were intended to be applied. But the contribution which Mr. Merivale has made to the subject which he treats is a very important one. He has endeavoured, with much success, to enable a Christian reader to enter, with sympathy and real respect, into what the religious thought and earnestness of heathenism did for the reception of that Divine system which was to overthrow it and take its place.

VI

EPICTETUS[1]

I

IF ancient Stoicism, in its effect on individual character, is seen to best advantage in the *Meditations* of M. Antoninus, it is best seen, as a discipline and system of moral teaching, in the abstracts which Arrian has preserved of the conversational lessons of Epictetus. The reports want the brilliancy and genius, as well as the philosophical reach and depth, of Plato, and they want the clearness and easy flow of Xenophon. But they have all the appearance of being thoroughly genuine and faithful in representing, not only the thoughts and main drift of the teacher, but his favourite ways of speaking, his favourite ways of handling an argument or directing the course of discussion, his humour, the things that made him angry and scornful, his characteristic modes of showing his

[1] *The Works of Epictetus.* A Translation from the Greek, based on that of Mrs. Elizabeth Carter. By T. W. Higginson. *Saturday Review*, 27th October 1866.

anger, his characteristic retorts and rejoinders. Arrian may be believed when he says that he wrote them down as notes and memoranda for his own use, and not for publication. They are often obscure, the threads of connection in them get sometimes broken or entangled, and they abound with repetitions; but they also abound with passages of vigorous and animated language, clear and direct in expression, full of the life and force of earnest conviction, and rising at times into masculine and unsought eloquence. Mr. Higginson, who on the return of peace in America exchanged the command of coloured troops in the civil war for the study of Epictetus, has given us a "translation based on that of Mrs. Carter." We hardly know what the expression implies, for we have not had an opportunity of comparing the two translations; but the present one, though rendering Epictetus on the whole with fidelity and spirit, is not to be depended upon in debatable passages. Mr. Higginson says that he has allowed himself, in order to popularise his version, a terminology "more pliant and varied" than Mrs. Carter's. But in translating a philosophical work the terminology ought to be accurate. "Self-conceit," whatever may be said for it on etymological grounds, is not the fair equivalent for οἴησις, and the use of it confounds intellectual shallowness with a moral fault not implied in the Greek term. "What is right and what is wrong" is not what Epictetus meant by τί μοι ἔξεστιν, καὶ τί μοι οὐκ ἔξεστιν (I. 1). "Dealing wisely with the phenomena of existence" is a very loose way of turning προαίρεσις τῶν φαντασιῶν; and τὸ συνημμένον has a distinct technical sense in the Stoical logic, which is not that of "a process of reasoning." A translator of Epictetus, if he gives due warning, may choose the most intelligible equivalents he can find for such technical terms; but he ought not to slur them over as if they were not there.

It is a curious and characteristic mark of the time that a Phrygian slave like Epictetus, who had passed his early years in such a household and service as that of Epaphroditus, Nero's freedman and confidential agent, should have become known and recognised in a society like that of the Empire, not merely as one of that very varied class called philosophers, but as the weightiest and most practical moral teacher of his day. It shows how oddly high and low were mixed and shaken up together, and how, in spite of all that was thought and felt about slaves, contempt and the stigma of social position gave way completely before personal qualities. The lame old slave, with nothing but his character as a thoroughgoing and real guide in moral improvement, retired, after he had been made free, to a provincial town, and discoursed, to all who cared to hear, about the subject which interested him; and his school or lecture-room at Nicopolis became, as appears from many incidental notices in Arrian's book, a fashionable place of resort to learners from Rome. He only spoke, and did not write; and, as has been observed by a recent French critic, M. Martha, he approaches as closely to the character of a great heathen preacher as was possible for any one in those days. If in their form his instructions were more like those of the professor, in their spirit and aim they are most like what we call sermons—short, popular, earnest, and to the point. The investigation of scientific and speculative truth is not their object. They profess no originality of inquiry or discovery. They have the most direct and immediate reference to practice; they are founded, to an extent which to many people would at first sight appear incredible in a heathen, on religion and on the ever active belief in God; and they were intended to be, in the sense in which Latimer's or Wesley's addresses were intended to be, real and sharp attacks on the hearers' consciences. Unbounded everywhere in his scorn for talkers and purposeless idlers of all sorts, he reserves his severest sarcasms for his brethren who lecture to be praised. It is quite in the spirit of early Methodism that he says, "The school of a philosopher, my friends, is a surgery; you are not to go out of it with pleasure, but with pain; for you come to me sick, one with one illness, one with another, and am I to sit and talk to you in epigrams and pretty speeches for you to go away full of my praises, and each one with his headache, or broken arm, or abscess, just as he came?" To much the same effect he quotes his own master, Rufus Musonius, who used to say, "If you are at leisure to praise me, I speak to no purpose"; and who indeed, adds his scholar, used to speak in such a manner, that each of us, as we sat and listened, supposed that some person had been telling tales of us to him; so exactly did he hit the real facts, and set the sore places of each before each one's eyes.

"Tell me," he goes on, after a sarcastic description—which might do for a modern popular chapel—of a philosopher's school, with its thousand benches, and the orator in his fine gown going up into his pulpit to make his address—"tell me, who that hears your lecturing is brought to feel 'concern' (ἠγωνίασεν) about himself, or has turned his thoughts inwards? Who, as he goes out, says, 'The philosopher hit me hard there; I must give up these things'?" Epictetus himself, according to his disciple Arrian, succeeded in impressing his hearers with his own earnestness and seriousness. At any rate, while he spoke, "his audience," says Arrian, "could not help being affected in the very manner he intended that they should be." Another touch which brings before us the zealous and importunate witness for religion, well known in later times, but whom we should not expect to meet with, except in one obscure body of men, under the Caesars, occurs in the following passage. He is speaking of the guides and directors of men, and of the patience, temper, and clearness of head required in them:—

This is no very safe affair now, and especially at Rome. For he who does it must not do it in a corner; but must go to some rich consular senator, for instance, and question him. "Pray, sir, will you tell me to whom you intrust your horses?" [And then follows a string of questions about the people whom he trusts with his money and his clothes and his health, etc., such as are sometimes urged as an argument in favour of "spiritual direction" of conscience. Then he goes on.] "Have you anything better than these?" "You mean the soul?" "Yes; can you show us how far you have taken care of this soul; for it is not likely that you, so wise and high, would carelessly let the best thing you have be neglected and lost?" "Of course not." "Then do you take care of it yourself? And by the advice of another, or by your own ability?" Here comes the danger; first, he may say, "Pray, my good sir, what business is that of yours? What are you to me?" Next, if you go on troubling him, he may lift up his hand, and give you a box on the ear. I was myself once a great admirer of this method of instruction, till I fell into adventures of this kind. (II. 12.)

Epictetus is called, and indeed calls himself, a Stoic. But he was a Stoic in much the same general sense as we sometimes speak of a Puritan or a Jansenist —a sense expressing a general tendency of character and principles, rather than the clear and exclusive adoption of the theory and methods of a school. Stoicism was the "straitest sect" of Roman morality, and, like other "straitest sects," it had a looser as well as a more restricted and exact meaning. Besides having its true philosophical adherents, who were chiefly interested by its speculative questions and doctrines, Stoicism was the fashionable and rather vague profession at Rome of most men who aspired to elevation,

dignity, and purity of mind; of numbers of men of
narrow earnestness, who prided themselves on pushing
everything they held to extravagant and impracticable
consequences; and it was professed, further, by a
crowd of impostors who declaimed against the flesh
and the world in order to secure for themselves a
larger share of the enjoyments of both. Epictetus
called himself a Stoic because religious belief and
moral sensibility were strong in him, and he realised
keenly the mysterious greatness and weakness of
human life, the power of will and character, and the
limited extent to which man is master of the conditions
of his course and fate; and because persons with
strong convictions on these points naturally went to
Stoical schools, read Stoical books, adopted Stoical
formulae, and talked in Stoical language. But his real
models and philosophical heroes were not Zeno and
Chrysippus, but Socrates and Diogenes. The Stoical
philosophy, in its various branches, was a very elaborate, comprehensive, and positive one; and its genuine
disciples took great pride in their achievements, and
spared no pains to fortify and develop their system.
But there is not a trace of this enthusiasm for a theory,
or for scientific speculation and research as such, in
Epictetus. Chrysippus is all very well, with his
immense literary activity and his six or nine books
devoted to the elucidation of a famous logical puzzle.
In their place Epictetus thinks these things useful
enough, as instruments for securing accuracy of
thought and expression, and for exercising the mind

in the difficult task of sifting and distinguishing. He is indeed very careful against seeming to undervalue them; but he thinks that people read a great deal more of these things than they understand, and understand more than they can make any use of. What he takes from the Stoics are their technical expressions for what seem to him the broad, undeniable, primary facts of our experience of the world and the human mind. He adopts their terminology—the divisions by which they had mapped out the provinces of human knowledge and classified its materials and methods, their fundamental doctrines about the system and government of the world, their classification of objects and faculties, their general conceptions and phraseology about morality, duty, and the end of human life. But he adopts it because it is ready to his hand, and, of all the philosophies within his reach, the most congenial and the most convenient for his purpose. There is no appearance that he had thought out independently the scientific conclusions of Stoicism, or that he entered heartily into the purely intellectual and scientific side of the Stoical system. He had no care for physics, and not much in reality for logic, though he talks a good deal about it, lays stress on its importance in its proper place, and draws illustrations, not always very happy ones, from the logical theories and debates which were the rage in the Stoical schools. But man as a moral agent, the work and care of God, the " spectator and interpreter of God's works," in danger of going wrong, but capable of unlimited improvement, was the only real object of his interest; and his interest in man was not that of the student and inquirer, not the speculative interest of the numberless investigators of human nature, but the directly practical interest of a moral teacher who wants to produce real effects. His business is to apply the leading doctrines of Stoicism—too true, in his view, and too obviously in accordance with nature and fact to be seriously disputed—to the actual formation of character and conduct of life in individuals. But with the practical result of the Stoic schools he is deeply dissatisfied. With bitter irony, he says, arguing with an Epicurean whom he is trying to involve in an argumentative contradiction :—

Otherwise [if you do not follow your principles to certain logical conclusions] you will not differ from us Stoics. For we, too, say one thing and do another; we talk well and act ill; but you will be perverse in a contrary way, teaching bad principles and acting well. (III. 7.)

And in another place he breaks out with almost fiery passion :—

Show me a Stoic, if you have one? Where? or how should you? You can show, indeed, a thousand who can repeat the Stoic reasonings. But do they repeat the Epicurean less well? Are they not just as perfect in the Peripatetic? Who then is a Stoic? . . . Show me some one person formed according to the principles he professes. Show me one who is sick, and happy; in danger, and happy; dying, and happy; exiled, and happy; disgraced, and happy. Show him to me; for, by Heaven, I long to see a Stoic. But you have not one fully developed? Show me one then who is developing; one who is approaching towards this character. Do me this favour. Do not refuse an old man a sight which he has never seen. . . . Show him to me. But you cannot. Why then do you impose upon yourselves, and play tricks with others? Why do you put on a dress which is not your own, and walk about with it, mere thieves and pilferers of names and things which do not belong to you? I am now your preceptor, and you come to be instructed by me. And, indeed, my aim is to secure you from being restrained, compelled, hindered; to make you free, prosperous, happy; looking to God upon every occasion, great or small. And you come to learn. . . . Why then do not you finish your work? . . . It must be your fault, or mine, or more truly the fault of both. Well, then, shall we at length begin to carry such an aim with us? Let us lay aside all that is past. Let us begin. Only believe me, and you shall see. (II. 19.)

It would be too much to call Epictetus a great moral reformer, any more than a great philosopher. For both characters, he wants power, enthusiasm, wide sympathies. the capacity for large plans and thoughts —the adventurous, hopeful, imaginative spirit which carries men to great enterprises, both in the world of intellect and among mankind. He had little hope for the multitude; and it is difficult to conceive the contagion of ideas spreading widely from his teaching. But to the circle which collected round him he showed the example of a man not content with thinking and talking about a high ideal of duty, but setting infinitely more value on any attempt to realise it, and bent on doing so in a common-sense, straightforward, unpretending sort of way, appealing to nothing abstruse or recondite, but to familiar and current ideas about what was right and becoming among men, and to the common appreciation of consistency between profession and conduct. His weakness is his theoretical philosophy; he moves somewhat encumbered with it, as by something worn from custom rather than from any sense of its value. His strength is in the handling of those common topics of which all feel the force and the weight—the reasons why men should be manly, fearless, high-souled, real; why they should set the true value on what they are, and on things round them; why they should govern and correct themselves, and make their life agree with their judgments and their words. There are far greater thinkers than he in antiquity. It would be difficult to point to so earnest and so impressive a moral teacher.

Epictetus, though he has probably had many readers, has had them mostly among people who do not write and quote. The rambling way in which his conversations have been recorded and put together might not repel persons bent on self-improvement; but it would stand in the way of the popularity of the book. He has had, however, at least three remarkable readers who have transmitted his influence through their own writings. The discourses of Epictetus contributed largely to form the character of the Emperor Marcus Antoninus. Epictetus was one of the writers whom Pascal, who did not read much, read with the deepest sympathy; and he wavers between the feeling that Epictetus "would deserve to be adored" if only he acknowledged human weakness as he points out human duty, and aversion for what seemed to the Augustinian Portroyalist "the diabolical pride" of his self-reliance. And he influenced deeply, both in substance and form, the speculations of Butler. We do not know much of Butler's reading; he quotes, as far as we remember, "Arrian's Epictetus" only once; but he must have been very familiar with the "Discourses," and must have made them to a great degree part of his own thoughts. The ideas on which Epictetus dwells as the foundation of all his teaching—the ideas of the world as a great constitution, of a moral government by self-acting pleasures and punishments, of the coincidence of the good of the individual with the good of the whole, and of the supreme approving and disapproving faculty in man—are those which in a more developed and systematic shape are the basis of Butler's moral doctrines. Less essentially significant, but equally observable, is the likeness between the two writers in their impatient severity towards mere show and unreality of profession, and their preference for direct and homely forms of expression. Butler's invective against lazy reading and disinclination to the trouble of forming judgments—against the "prodigious" absence of curiosity in readers "to see what is true," and his condemnation of those "who come abroad in disorder which they ought to be dissatisfied to find themselves in at home"—recall the indignation of Epictetus against the readers and talkers of the philosophic schools. And the quaint sentences with which Butler likes to point his argument—"Everything is what it is, and not another thing," "a man is not to form or accommodate, but to state things as he finds them"—have their counterpart in Epictetus when he bids us train ourselves, "not with a view to change the constitution of things, a gift neither practicable nor desirable, but that, things being as they are with regard to us, we may have our mind accommodated to the facts"; and to use our eyes, "not persuading them to show us one object rather than another, but receiving such as they present to us"; or when he asks us whether, in our desire for impossibilities, we wish "vice not to be vice, but something else?" θέλεις τὴν κακίαν μὴ εἶναι κακίαν ἀλλ' ἄλλο τι;

Among the readers of Epictetus we ought not to omit a remarkable student of his writings mentioned by Mr. Higginson. This was Toussaint L'Ouverture, the "great exemplar of coloured soldiers, who made the works of this his fellow-slave a favourite manual." As the works of Epictetus, in whole or in part, were a chosen subject with French translators—the *Biographie Universelle* enumerates nineteen French translations previously to the beginning of this century—the statement is possible. But Epictetus had an odd, and hardly a very obedient, disciple in the great negro chief.

II[1]

IN a former article we made some remarks on Epictetus as a moral teacher. We will add a few words on some of the points which strike a reader of Arrian's reports of his teaching. There is a curious mixture in him of largeness and narrowness. He has the widest theoretical views of human brotherhood; men are all "sons of God," citizens of God's great city, the world; yet, after enforcing this strongly and eloquently, he seems incapable of making his sympathies expand with his theory. The various interests and infinite goings on of human society are out of the range of his vision. It was very well to point out that, as we cannot get rid of sickness and death, it is reasonable to meet them with fortitude, as parts of our natural condition; but the instinct to know and to improve is just as little to be got rid of, and just as reasonably to be viewed as part of the great plan; and of this he takes no account. His having been a slave may have contributed to his stern and earnest directness; and of course it is one of his points that it makes no difference to a true man whether he is bond or free; but he seems to show signs of the exaggerated undervaluing by a slave of the advantages to a man of

[1] *Saturday Review*, 10th November 1866.

having always lived as a free man among free men. One of these signs is a tendency to confine his thoughts and efforts within the walls of his school. He has nothing to say to the political and social world without. Its ways are not his, and he cares not to see what place they may have in the great scheme of things. He has no future; posterity seems never to cross his thoughts. He is too kindly-natured and too honest to rail or call names; and, except when he is challenged or defied, he is not defiant and scornful. But though Epictetus cared for nothing in the world except for men, vast and important sides of human nature were to him as if they did not exist. He had boundless faith in individual power of improvement; "be assured," he says, "there is nothing more tractable than the human mind; you need but will, and it is done, it is set right." But he never really thought that this was applicable on a large scale. He contemplated a few in his mind, and none beyond them. He had no very wide horizon. He had no high notions of human nature in the mass. His great anxiety was that those who had high qualities should not misdirect or throw them away, but educate them to the highest perfection. This is his hope for the world—the saving and turning to full account of its choicest and noblest natures. "You," he says to some one who is supposed to shrink from manly duty—

you have nothing to care for, but how to be like the rest of mankind, as one thread desires not to be distinguished from the others, in the many which make up the piece.

But I would be the purple one, that small and brilliant part which gives a lustre and beauty to the rest. Why do you bid me resemble the multitude then? at that rate, how shall I be the purple?

And, going on to quote an example of a man who had sacrificed his life to his idea of duty, he asks :—

What good, then, did Priscus do, who was but a single person? Why, what good does the purple do to the garment? What but to be beautiful in itself, and to set a good example to the rest? (I. 2.)

It is to these choice specimens of human nature that he addresses himself; whose gifts at once are their own witness and proof, and impose their own heavy responsibilities.

Did Socrates prevail on all who came to him to take care of themselves? Not upon the thousandth part; but being, as he declares, divinely appointed to such a post, he never deserted it. . . . "Why, who are you?" Here one ought nobly to say, "I am he who ought to take care of mankind." For it is not every little paltry heifer that dares resist the lion; but if the bull should resist him, would you say, "Who are you? What business is it of yours?" . . . Do not say to whatever excels, "Who are you?" If you do, it will somehow or other find a voice to tell you, "I am like the purple thread in a garment. Do not expect me to be like the rest, nor find fault with my nature, which has distinguished me from others." "What then" [asks his pupil], "am I such a one?" Indeed, are you such a one as to be able to bear the truth? I wish you were.

But as I am condemned to wear a gray beard and a cloak, and you come to me as a philosopher, I will not treat you cruelly, nor as if I despaired of you; but will ask you, "Who is it, young man, whom you would render beautiful? Know, first, who you are; and then adorn yourself accordingly." (III. 1.)

The multitude must go its own way; not being allowed to drag down those who know better to its own level, but at the same time treated with patience and good humour by men who feel themselves superior to it, and aim higher:—

"Well; but can these things be explained to the multitude?" To what purpose? Is it not sufficient to be convinced oneself? When children come to us clapping their hands, and saying, "To-morrow is the good feast of Saturn," do we tell them that good doth not consist in such things? By no means; but we clap our hands also. Thus, when you are unable to convince any one, consider him as a child, and clap your hands with him; or, if you will not do that, at least hold your tongue. (I. 29.)

He describes with some humour the unfortunate attempts of philosophers to communicate their wisdom, and the occasional loss of temper which follows on the ill-success of their instructions:—

We are altogether unpractised in the application of what we have been taught. Only give to any of us an uneducated person for an antagonist; and he will not find out how to treat him. But when he has a little moved the man, if he happens to answer at cross-purposes, the questioner knows not how to deal with him any further, but either reviles or laughs at him, and says, "He is an illiterate fellow, there is no making anything of him." . . . There are phrases, repulsive and obscure to the illiterate, which yet we cannot dispense with. But we have no capacity at all to move them by such arguments as might lead them, in following the methods of their own minds, to admit or abandon any position. And, from a consciousness of this incapacity, those of us who have any modesty give up the matter entirely; but the greater part, rashly entering on these debates, mutually confound and are confounded; and at last, reviling and reviled, walk off. (II. 12.)

But to those who have the power to understand their own nature and position, to see things as they really are, and to draw the right inference from what they see, Epictetus is exacting and unsparing in his demands; and to them he addresses himself, returning to the charge again and again with the earnestness and importunity of a zealous preacher. His thoughts revolve very much in the same round. He impresses by his force, intense conviction, and carelessness of show or study. A limited number of ideas, noble and elevated ones, are his stock; and his discourses are variations on these chosen themes. His energy and seriousness, and withal an occasional vein of almost Horatian humour, with touches of indignant scorn for cowardice, laziness, and baseness, give plenty of life to his addresses. But there is a want of variety in them. The inevitable "tyrant" and "beautiful woman" are ever recurring to express the different temptations of human life; the quotations about Anytus and Melitus, or about the conducting superintendence of Zeus and Destiny, are continually doing service, and "writing Dion's name" is for ever standing for an instance of the deliberate exercise of an art or faculty. He hammers with vigour and effect, but his method is hammering. There is a want in him of the higher and more fascinating gifts of the teacher and thinker—a want of subtlety, of play, of range, a feeble sense of the variety of character and working. In his philosophy he leaves out the immense, unceasing, inexhaustible activity of human life, its infinitely changing aspects, functions, and ends, the enlarging hopes and prospects ever opening to it He has indeed the idea and outline of a great system of the universe, but he peoples it with details but narrowly and poorly. And so he has a certain kind of advice to give which is very valuable, but, beyond the somewhat limited sphere in which he views human life and duty, he has not much to say. His power consists in his strong hold of a few great and elementary truths, and in the thorough reality of feeling and expression with which he insists on them.

As Epictetus was both a Stoic and a preacher—both of them professions naturally tending to paradox and the saying of more than is meant, and liable to tempt a man into one-sided over-statement—it is the more deserving of notice that, though he does not escape the snares of extreme and extravagant assertion, his natural common sense and good judgment impose an habitual and strong restraint on him. He cannot always get through a discourse about the things "in our power" and things "not in our power" without running on, in the vehemence of his thoroughgoing earnestness, into consequences which raise a smile at the result in which he lands his pupils. But he is generally on his guard. He is absolutely free from the pretension of thinking himself a perfect example of his own teaching. Nothing can be more hearty than his disavowals of all pretensions for himself, and his warnings against them to others. "Don't let us talk," he says to his hearers, "of doing anything perfectly and profitably, since we are both of us far enough from anything of that kind." He protests against the attempt to carry moral training beyond nature and reason; "for thus we who call ourselves philosophers shall not differ from jugglers." "Rope-dancing is no doubt both difficult and dangerous; but this is no reason for learning it." There is a curious protest in one place in favour of cleanliness, and against the affected untidiness of the stricter philosophers. He insists on the duty of intellectual vigilance and exertion, bids his hearers "practice intellectual assent and doubt," and indignantly draws pictures of the mental sloth and apathy of mankind, "yawning and slumbering over our poor neglected reason, imposed upon by every appearance, and not knowing the mischief done"; "nodding over that work within on which ruin or recovery depends." His discourses are full of sharp sarcasms against people who read books, or practise their reasoning powers, or study philosophy, for show or mere amusement. He is continually bringing up for pitiless ridicule the man who had read all Chrysippus through, and declared that he understood him and could pass an examination in his books; "as if I should say to a wrestler, Show me your muscle, and he should answer me, See my dumb-bells. Your dumb-bells are your own affair; I want to see the effect of them." "This is but the measure, you unfortunate," he says to the pupil who piques himself on his syllogisms, "and not the thing measured." But at the same time there is no fanatical undervaluing of learning, or cultivation, or the gifts of reason and language. For each function and power in its own place, and in its proper subordination to higher ones, he argues earnestly, and always resists the commonplace inference that, because a thing has been overvalued, it may be assumed by those who are wiser to be worthless. Thus, of eloquence :—

A book will always be read with more pleasure and ease if it be written in fair characters. . . . It ought not to be said then that there is no such thing as the faculty of eloquence, for this is at once the part of an impious and a timid man. Impious, because he dishonours God's gifts; just as if he were to deny any use in sight, or hearing, or speech itself. . . . And not only ungrateful, but cowardly too. For such a person seems to me to be afraid that, if there be such a faculty, he may on occasion be compelled to respect it. . . . These are the foolish, clownish notions of those who are ignorant of the nature of things, and afraid that whoever perceives such a difference must presently be carried away and overcome. But the great point is to leave to each thing its own faculty, and then see what the value of the faculty is; to learn what is the principal thing, and always to follow that; to consider other things as trifling in comparison with that, and yet, so far as we are able, not to neglect even these. (II. 23.)

Perhaps the most remarkable thing about Epictetus is the degree in which the religious element becomes prominent in his teaching, and the way in which his morality is combined with it and grows out of it. The Stoical schools had been the founders of what we call natural theology—the attempt to ascertain and establish the grounds in reason for religious belief. But in Epictetus the belief has become an energetic practical principle of the most pervading kind. His whole teaching rests on the idea of the great system and constitution of things, governed by the wisdom and goodness of God, in which each man fills his part, and in which he is watched and helped by God his Father. No Christian teacher could be more penetrated with this thought, or could have it more constantly present to his mind; and it is expressed by Epictetus in words which, for their devout earnestness and faith, it is not easy to read for the first time without wonder. Thus he exhorts to the praise of God :—

Are these the only works of Providence with regard to us? And what speech can fitly celebrate their praise? For, if we had any understanding, ought we not, both in public and in private, incessantly to sing and praise the Deity, and rehearse His benefits? Ought we not, whether we dig, or plough, or eat, to sing this hymn to God? Great is God, who has supplied us with these instruments to till the ground; great is God, who has given us hands, and organs of digestion; who has given us to grow insensibly, to breathe in sleep. These things ought we for ever to celebrate; but to make it the theme of the greatest and divinest hymn, that He has given us the power to appreciate these gifts and to use them well. But because some of you are blind and insensible, there must be some one to fill this station, and lead, in behalf of all men, the hymn to God; for what else can I do, a lame old man, but sing hymns to God? Were I a nightingale, I would act the part of a nightingale; were I a swan, I would act the part of a swan. But since I am a reasonable creature, it is my duty to praise God. This is my business. I do it. Nor will I ever desert this post so long as it is permitted me; and I call on you to join in the same song. (I. 16.)

So he represents morality as an offering of the whole man to God:—

Boldly make a desperate push, man, as the saying is, for prosperity, for freedom, for magnanimity. Lift up your head at last, as being free from slavery. Dare to look up to God, and say, "Make use of me for the future as Thou wilt. I am of the same mind. I am one with Thee. I refuse nothing that seems good to Thee. Lead me whither Thou wilt. Clothe me in what dress Thou wilt. Is it Thy will that I should be in a public or a private condition; dwell here, or be banished; be poor or rich? Under all these circumstances I will testify unto Thee before men. (II. 16.)

Does any good man fear that food should fail him? It does not fail the blind; it does not fail the lame. Shall it fail the good man? Is God so negligent of His own institutions, of His servants, of His witnesses? . . . What, then, if God does not bestow food? What else than that, like a good general, He hath made me a signal of retreat? I obey, I follow; speaking well of my leader, praising His works. For I came when it seemed good to Him, and again, when it seems good to Him, I depart; and in life it was my business to praise God within myself, and to every auditor, and to the world. Doth He grant me but few things? Doth He refuse me affluence? It is not His pleasure. He did not grant it to Hercules, His own son. (III. 26.)

His language is equally impressive when he looks forward to the end of life, and describes the temper in which it should find men :—

At what employment would you have death find you? For my part, I would have it be some humane, beneficent, public-spirited, noble action. But if I cannot be found doing any such great things, yet at least I would be doing what I cannot be restrained from, what is given me to do—correcting myself, improving that faculty which makes use of the phenomena of existence to procure tranquillity, and render to the several relations of life their due; and if I am so fortunate, advancing still further in the security of judging right. If death overtakes me in such a situation, it is enough for me if I can stretch out my hands to God and say, "The opportunities I have received from Thee of comprehending and obeying Thy administration I have not neglected. As far as in me lay, I have not dishonoured Thee. See how I have used my perceptions; how, my convictions. Have I at any time found fault with Thee? Have I been discontented at Thy dispensations, or wished them otherwise? Have I transgressed the relations of life? I thank Thee that Thou hast brought me into being. I am satisfied with the time that I have enjoyed the things Thou hast given me. Receive them back again; and distribute them as Thou wilt. For they were all Thine, and Thou gavest them me." (IV. 10.)

I would be found studying this, that I may be able to say to God, "Have I transgressed Thy commands? Have I perverted the powers, the senses, the instincts which Thou hast given me? Have I ever accused Thee, or censured Thy dispensations? I have been sick, because it was Thy pleasure, like others; but I willingly. I have been poor, it being Thy will; but with joy. I have not been in power, because it was not Thy will; and power I have never desired. Hast Thou ever seen me saddened because of this? Have I not always approached Thee with a cheerful countenance; prepared to execute Thy commands, and the indications of Thy will? Is it Thy pleasure that I should depart from this assembly? I depart. I give Thee all thanks that Thou hast thought me worthy to have a share in it with Thee; to behold Thy works, and to join with Thee in comprehending Thy government." Let death overtake me while I am thinking, while I am writing, while I am reading such things as these. (III. 5.)

We cannot read Epictetus without being continually struck with the coincidence of his thoughts, and even phrases, with many of the sayings which we are familiar with in the New Testament. The coincidence is not such as to suggest the least ground for surmising any connection on his part with Christian teachers, or any knowledge of their doctrines; it is only a further proof that Christianity, besides the strong repulsion and antagonism presented to it by heathen society, found also deep and unsuspected affinities within it. He is, it need not be said, widely separated from Christianity; but his thoughts, though at a distance, move constantly in the same direction, and fall into forms which irresistibly recall its great maxims. For example, men ought to think of themselves as the "witnesses of God" in the world, "testifying of Him" to others; they ought to "follow God as their pattern"; they ought "to have no will but the will of God"; their "one pleasure ought to be the consciousness that they are obeying God," "as free yet as the servants of God"; God gives His gifts to be used under the sense of responsibility, and a man's great concern ought to be as to how he has employed the powers and opportunities committed to his trust and charge; God takes care of His "faithful servants," and afflicts them—"not that He hates them; God forbid —but to exercise them and use them as His witnesses to others," and gives the hardest tasks to those He loves best. Again, men should not want any one to see their efforts but God; they ought to be ready to resign what God has given—"they were all Thine, and Thou gavest them me"; it is a mistake, when "we might give all our care to *one* thing, to prefer entangling ourselves with *many*"; "nothing is to be had for nothing"; we "must lose our own, if we want what is not our own"; we ought to think "of the exchange" we are making, "how much for how much"; "two trades cannot be combined," and if we are busy about one we must give up, or be hindered in, the other. People familiar with this kind of language in Epictetus—and he does not say these things as anything new or unfamiliar, but as the forgotten or neglected dictates of the common sense to which he can appeal in all—would recognise something to which they were not altogether unaccustomed when they heard the same sort of things in the Sermon on the Mount and St. Paul; such sayings as that "one thing is needful," "no man can serve two masters," "what shall a man give in exchange for his soul?" "take no thought"; or when life was represented as a use of "talents" entrusted to men, or as the service of God, itself perfect freedom. The contrast of "the flesh" and the higher principle; the comparison of the body and members, some with higher, some with lower offices; the similitudes, drawn from the games, of men training themselves and striving for the mastery; even the analogy between the man with high aims and duties, and the soldier giving up innocent and natural ties that he may serve "without distraction," are as common in Epictetus as they are in St. Paul.

Epictetus shows most instructively how far the

ideas of serious men, who thought more of self-improvement and trying to do right than of anything else in the world, had advanced in the civilised society of the Empire; how far their high and simple religious feeling, combined with a common-sense consideration of the facts and illusions of life, had approached to the Christian point of view. He shows, too, in our opinion, where such noble attempts failed. Epictetus wants sympathies, and can give no sufficient motive for them; and it need not be said what is involved in that want. Again, there is frequently an appearance of paradox and artificial speaking in Epictetus which does not show itself in St. Paul; that is to say, the language of the New Testament becomes natural, because of its enlarged horizon of the other world. Epictetus seems as if he had come after or before his time; too late for philosophy, too early for religion. We are tempted continually to apply to his system the hackneyed phrase, — it is magnificent, but it is not philosophy. It is too one-sided and careless of knowledge for its own sake; and it is not religion—it is inadequate, and wants a basis. Yet for all this, as long as men appreciate elevated thought, in direct and genuine language, about human duties and human improvement, Epictetus will have much to teach those who know more than he did both of philosophy and religion. It is no wonder that he kindled the enthusiasm of Pascal, or fed the thought of Butler.

VII

THIERRY'S ST. JEROME[1]

M. AMÉDÉE THIERRY has chosen in St. Jerome a subject well suited to his method of representing a period by a set of pictures in detail, but his treatment seems to us to fail in two points. He is too prolix; as, for instance, when he thinks it necessary or interesting to follow Jerome and his company of lady travellers step by step through their journeys in Syria and Palestine, sketching what he supposed they saw, and imagining what he supposed they felt. A more serious shortcoming is that he fails, as it appears to us, to form, or at any rate to express, with force and comprehensiveness a distinct picture of St. Jerome's character as a whole. This is the more material because it is what he professedly undertakes to do, and what he remarks upon as wanting in the works of preceding writers. But though he may have taken a different point of view from them, he does not seem to us to have hit

[1] *Saint Jérôme. La Société Chrétienne à Rome, et l'Émigration Romaine en Terre Sainte.* Par M. Amédée Thierry, Sénateur et Membre de l'Institut. *Saturday Review*, 29th June 1867.

what he aimed at. He exhibits particular sides of the character which he depicts with clearness and attention to historical evidence. But we still miss the complete living man, painted really from life, and not from a conventional notion of him. M. Thierry seems to write of him timidly, as if he felt bound to treat with all respect a rather strange saint, whom at the same time he could not at bottom quite make out: and he writes of him apparently with not the faintest sense of humour. No doubt St. Jerome is a Father of the Church; and his great works impress our imagination with a sense of their importance which is by no means out of proportion with their intrinsic value. But, in spite of the idea which we derive of him from famous pictures, where he is represented as a venerable recluse with his legendary lion, or as receiving his last communion, St. Jerome is one of whom it is impossible to write with reality and justice unless plenty of room is made for his ruggedness, irritability, and coarseness, and for the odd and ludicrous contrasts between the ideal of saintliness and the matter-of-fact outbursts of his ultra-Johnsonian roughness and impetuosity of temper. It is easy to write of him as a high saint whom it is irreverent to criticise; it is easy also to write of him with any amount of sarcasm and abuse. But what is wanted is to do real justice to a very remarkable man —remarkable in his self-dedication to religion and study, and remarkable also in his fierce energy, and coarse loves and hates; to be sensible of his ungovernable rudeness and extravagance, and of its abundant grotesqueness and frequent repulsiveness, yet to be alive also to the strength and unselfish laboriousness of that robust and indefatigable nature. But of all this combination M. Thierry is, as far as we can see, only partially conscious. He never ventures to be amused with St. Jerome; and a man who can write about St. Jerome without being at least sometimes amused at him cannot, we think, be said to have taken his measure.

Jerome, the Romanised Provincial, the harsh and violent Dalmatian in blood, the Roman in artificial culture, but utterly without taste or justice or moderation, one of those products of the contact of high civilisation with ambitious and aspiring barbarism so common in his day and not unknown in our own, was a combination of the ascetic, the student and critic, the satirist and pamphleteer, and the director and guide of aristocratic religious ladies. When all these characters were grafted on a nature in the highest degree passionate, enthusiastic, inexhaustible in its rough vigour, self-confident, and without the faintest notion of checking and restraining itself, the result is at any rate not a commonplace one. And no writer of the same class, not even St. Augustine or Tertullian, has told us so much about himself, and impressed the stamp of his personal character so curiously on his writings. There must be plenty to say about such a man; but M. Thierry seems to us to have missed the true way of conceiving him, and to have been led astray by a formula. Jerome, he says, was above everything "a man of action." It is in action that the unity of his character emerges out of the various partial and inadequate aspects of him; it is by action that he was so powerful among his contemporaries, and that he is immortal in history. "Jerome," we are told, "has done more than he has written, and for the most part, he wrote only with an eye to immediate action." His works were works for the occasion, thrown off at a heat on the spur of a real emergency. And more than any of his contemporaries he was "a man of the fourth century"; he was *pars magna* of all that marked the time; he cannot be understood without thoroughly understanding the "opinions, wants, passions, prejudices of that period." Therefore, says M. Thierry, "il faut devenir avec lui homme de son temps." The conclusion is unexceptionable, only unluckily it is one of those things which are more easily said than done; but we do not agree with the statement on which it rests. It seems to us mere exaggeration to talk of Jerome's greatness in action, or indeed to talk of his "power" among his contemporaries. He was great by the peculiar and rare character of his literary activity, and by the results, in their value inestimable, and manifest to all the world, which were their fruit and imperishable monument. What we understand by a man's greatness being in action is such a career as that of Athanasius, or, in another way, Augustine. But it is sheer over-statement to say that Jerome played a part such as theirs. What M. Thierry means is that, student and critic as he was, Jerome had a large correspondence, and imprinted his own personality, his life, his adventures, his loves, his hates, his quarrels, his passing humour and moods, on his commentaries and theological treatises. The man is always before us; he contrives to interweave notices of what was passing round him, and references to real men and his own experience of them, with everything that he writes; and he lets us into his opinions and feelings with a vigour and unreserve which certainly give great animation to his writings. It is true, also, as M. Thierry says, that some of his most considerable works were begun, not simply for the sake of their subject, but to satisfy the wish or the needs of a friend. Or else some question or some tendency stirred and alarmed him, and he straight wrote off a pamphlet or an invective. All this contributes to connect his writings with a real life, and to fill them with touches which disclose character and feeling. It enables us to see Jerome as a living man, acting and feeling; but it is not enough to justify us in talking of him as eminently a "man of action."

Further, M. Thierry has followed a method of writing which undoubtedly saves a good deal of trouble and is convenient for vivid and picturesque representation, but which is not so favourable to exact truth, and does not command a reader's confidence. He seems to make it his rule simply to accept Jerome's points of view and his statements.

Jerome's letters, and polemical pamphlets and prefaces, are a perfect mine of forcible and precise narrative, and of pointed and epigrammatic commentary. M. Thierry seems to think that a biographer may safely take them all as the well-weighed words of an informant thoroughly to be depended upon. It seems to us that it is impossible to read twenty lines, either of Jerome's eulogy or of his abuse, without feeling that he was one of the most passionate and exaggerated of writers. If ever strong language gave warning to the reader that it needed to be sifted and taken with large allowance, it is Jerome's. But M. Thierry scarcely seems sensible that he is dealing with a writer given to strong language, apt to speak vehemently on first impressions, equally undiscriminating in his admiration and his hostility, and obviously delighting in the exercise of his talents for strong and coarse sarcasm.

Considering that Jerome was generally in the thick of a good quarrel, it is not safe for his biographer to be so trusting. In his controversies Jerome may have been in the right; but something more than his own word ought to be shown for it. And in all that he says of the Roman ladies, on whom he exercised so remarkable an influence, and for whom, amid the dangers and at last fall of the city and the miseries of the perishing Empire, he found a refuge in the convent of Bethlehem, what we wish for is that the real facts could be separated from his obviously extravagant and often fulsome rhetoric

about them. But in this we get no help from M.
Thierry. He accepts it all, merely translating it into
elegant and graceful French, and softening down the
coarsest and most offensive portions. And while he
scarcely seems to appreciate what is so often brutal
and unjust in Jerome's abuse of his opponents, he is
almost as severe as Jerome himself upon their mis-
behaviour and bad motives. He gives an account of
Jerome's quarrel with the Bishop of Jerusalem, which
began about the doctrines of Origen, and ended in
Jerome's estrangement from his old friend Rufinus.
It is a quarrel about which, if anything is clear, it is
that it was a most disagreeable exhibition of the
temper and motives of all the persons concerned in
it, and it is made more repulsive by its connection
with one of the most odious and detestable episodes
in the history of the fourth century—the policy and
proceedings of Theophilus of Alexandria with respect
to Origen's followers and opinions. We have our
knowledge of it mainly from Jerome's version of it,
and it is impossible to read his account without seeing
how he and every one else deceived themselves into
thinking that a fierce and unscrupulous indulgence of
personal jealousies and dislikes was really a controversy about theological truth. But M. Thierry is
blind to everything except the bad passions and bad
behaviour of those on the opposite side to Jerome.
We do not say that he is not right in preferring
Jerome to Rufinus. Perhaps Rufinus was cold,
selfish, ungrateful, envious. Perhaps Jerome's former

affection for him was misplaced and ill-repaid. Perhaps the enthusiastic Melania of the convent on Olivet looked with a jealous eye on the enthusiastic Paula and Eustochium at Bethlehem, and caused a coldness between old friends. But we think that a distinguished French historian, writing about them in cold blood in our days, ought to have shown us some better reason for thinking so than that it was Jerome's way of looking at the matter. He has no words hard enough for Rufinus; there is no measure of malignant and artful hostility against Jerome which he does not impute to him. His was not a common jealousy—he was a *ténébreux hypocrite ;* he was suspected of enriching himself at the expense of the poor; many people thought him *un malhonnête homme ;* he was conceited, affected, pompous, and a stammerer. All means of attacking Jerome came equally well to his hand, and he "*ramassait*" all that he could find anywhere of spiteful scribblers and contemptible sectaries, a "*meute retentissante,*" to annoy and calumniate his great adversary. Yet every word of this rests simply on the bitter invectives of Jerome himself, of whom an equally bad character, though not quite so mercilessly ferocious, might be extracted from the writings of Rufinus. M. Thierry actually seems to think that it tells against Rufinus that Jerome called him "Grunnius," and a "Chimaera." So, again, who would not think, for instance, in reading the following, that M. Thierry had some plausible grounds for thus contrasting the pride and ambition of the patrician lady who was *against* Jerome with the humility and modesty of her who was *for* him? And yet it is simply his assumption, because one is praised by Jerome, and the other had forfeited his favour. And who would not suppose, too, that M. Thierry thought Jerome's fashion of revenging himself, on the whole, to be one worthy of admiration, for its ingenuity and completeness, while it was fully justified by the wrongs which provoked it:—

La fastueuse humilité d'une patricienne d'époque récente [Melania] n'imposait plus à côté de l'abnégation de deux filles des Scipions [Paula et Eustochium], offrant en holocauste, devant l'étable du Christ, le plus grand nom de l'histoire romaine. Les douces vertus de Paula, son savoir modeste, sa vie saintement cachée, ne contrastaient pas moins avec l'humeur altière et l'agitation bruyante de Mélanie; mais ce qui dut blesser celle-ci sur toute chose ce fut de voir l'homme à la renommée duquel elle avait cru jusqu'à y attacher la sienne [Rufinus], amoindri, effacé, devant l'incomparable gloire de Jérôme. De ces plaies de l'orgueil et de la jalousie, il s'était formé dans son cœur un ulcère qui le rongeait. Irrité de tant de persécutions, où l'odieux se mêlait à l'injustice, Jérôme s'en vengea avec éclat, et, dans l'ordre de sentiments, qui avaient prise sur son ennemie, sa vengeance fut complète. Il retrancha de ses livres les éloges qu'il lui avait donnés jadis et qui l'avait fait connaître dans le monde. Le passage de sa chronique où il la proclamait la plus illustre des femmes chrétiennes et une seconde Thécle, fut impitoyablement supprimé. Il évita dès lors de la nommer dans ses lettres, ou il ne le fit plus qu'avec amertume. Comme Mélanie, en Grec, signifiait *noire*, il disait que " Son nom était l'image vivante de son âme."

By this obvious want of just insight M. Thierry has spoiled what is really the interesting part of his book, his picture of the Roman Faubourg St. Germain in the fourth century. Jerome's writings supply the materials for a picture, very curious and lifelike, even if it be in some points overcharged, of the high and fashionable society at Rome as it was affected by the two new and eventful conditions of that age. These two conditions were, one of them, the progress of Christianity among the rich and important families of the capital; the other, the disastrous and dreary prospect of things in the Empire, which year by year was becoming more hopeless till men's worst fears were realised in the sack of Rome by Alaric. Christianity acted, as it was natural that it should act, especially when it was still so new to the world, in two ways. It had become a fresh and novel road to wealth, to power, to worldly enjoyments, and it attracted of course crowds of votaries who made no scruple of using to the full the advantages which were thus opened to them; and, on the other hand, the really earnest people who embraced it for itself, for its truths, its hopes, and its rules of life, interpreted it in the most extreme and uncompromising way of which it was capable. On one side, Rome was full of priests, monks, and devotees, sleek, fashionable, easy-going, masters of all the arts of getting money and enjoying it, whom Jerome describes with a zest and force which would do no discredit to Juvenal; and the Bishopric of Rome had become a post which men, considered respectable, put themselves at the head of armed factions to gain, and won at the price of riot, bloodshed, and executions. On the other side, the more serious minds thought that the only way in which they could show their belief and interest in Christianity was by doing their best to break up and discredit the life of the family, hopelessly tainted, as they thought, by the vices of heathenism, and by scattering all their possessions broadcast to those who wanted and to those who asked. Rome was Babylon, and the only place for Christians was in those Eastern solitudes where men divested themselves of every tie to this life and lived only to pray, or at least to remain in some retirement from society where they might be entirely separate from a world doomed and visibly on its way to ruin. This was the sort of people with whom Jerome early became connected, and among whom he played his part; the fine-lady world of Rome, which had turned from the extreme of luxury and delicate living to a degree of severity and self-renunciation that never seemed hard and absolute enough, which in its fierce reaction against the long-licensed voluptuousness of heathen civilisation was barely willing to spare marriage, and made a point of doing everything to discourage and disturb it. It was a social revolution which without question elicited a high degree of strength and noble effort from natures which otherwise would have been wasted and would have perished in the break up of that degenerate time; but which was accompanied with all that might be expected of overstrained exaltation of feeling and temper, of recklessness and harshness, and in no small measure with the self-deceit and half-heartedness, issuing in inconsistency and juggling trickery, which weak minds always bring into austere and exacting movements that carry them helplessly away in their overpowering swing. This rush of the rich and high-born and delicate into poverty and hardship, and into the stern opinions which were then accounted of the essence of religion, is a hard subject to judge fairly about under greatly changed conditions of society. Seen closely and in detail, there is much that is most objectionable —objectionable on the best and most solid grounds. Yet when we look at it at a distance and in the long run, in connection with the circumstances around it, if it was mischievous, it was also fruitful in high and beneficial influences. It helped to elevate the level of feeling about women, as well as the general standard of what men might and ought to do to aid and console one another; it helped also to redeem a decayed society, and get out of it the best, probably, that it was capable of yielding. The tendency to harsh extremes which belongs to the condition of a religion which is in form a sect was still powerful in Christianity. That was in the nature of things, and could not be helped. Given the existing conditions of the world as between what Jerome represented and

what was represented by his antagonists Jovinian and
Vigilantius, we can have little doubt about our preference. Both were extreme, and both were coarse
and unreasonable; but, at least, Jerome on the whole
had a high purpose. Probably it was best under the
circumstances that Jerome should be, as M. Thierry
describes him, the leader of high society at Rome.
Only it ought to be remembered that what was the
best thing under such circumstances need not be
very admirable in itself, or an example to be held
up with sympathy and eulogistic colouring to other
times.

M. Thierry seems rather carried away by his admiration for Marcella's house for devout ladies on the
Aventine, and for the patrician colony—the "emigration" as he calls it—which followed Jerome to Palestine, and settled with him in the convents of Bethlehem, under the government of Paula and Eustochium.
But his picture of the whole of this society, with its
high-spirited and strong-minded leaders, its contrasts
and foils among the Pagans and the worldly Christians
of the same set, its passion for Biblical learning and
for the sacred languages, its deep and romantic
interest in the scenes of sacred history, its resolute
and unflinching perseverance in its purpose of the
austerest religion, is well put together. What it wants
is that qualifying caution and measure which most
conveys the impression that a man feels what he is
talking about to be real; and, what belongs to the
same attitude of mind, fair and even dealing among

the various personages of the story, who sometimes in their actual career came into collision. M. Thierry seems to us to form his idea of ladies like Paula and her companions from the ideas he has got of the religious duchesses and countesses of Paris. Now of course it is legitimate to make one set of people help you to imagine their counterparts of another age; but it is necessary to be careful not to confound the two, and not to lose the real characteristics of the one in a too hasty assumption of their likeness. And further, as we have noticed before, he is not even-handed. Why in the world is the unlucky Melania to be always spoken of with disparaging epithets, while Paula is always honoured with the most reverential language? Why is Melania called regularly "orgueilleuse," a "terrible fanatic," the "victim of mysticism," a "millenarian prophetess," and so forth, for doing neither more nor less than Paula, who is always held up as a wonderful combination of the sternest austerity, with the greatest humility and modesty? The reason is, and there is no other to be given, that Melania had Rufinus for her director, and therefore must have shown the bad side of the religious fervour of the time—a good reason for a legend writer or a dealer in stories, but one against which a writer like M. Thierry ought to have been on his guard.

But the value of his book altogether, vivid and full of matter as it is, is greatly diminished by that spirit of exaggeration which mistakes the true proportion and place of what is really great and important. It needs no exaggeration to state truly the importance of a life like Jerome's. He was a man of real genius and lofty aims. His association with Roman ladies like Paula and her family, and their community with him in his studies and great works, throws a touch of the romantic over the ruggedness of the monk and the scholar, and we can perhaps hardly estimate the benefits which his spirit of criticism, and his acquaintance with Oriental learning, rude and imperfect as it may seem to us now, wrought for the Western Church. The Latins, stiff, ignorant, self-satisfied, and presumptuous, had already got far into the groove of traditional and customary blunders when Jerome began; and he had a hard matter, as it was, to persuade them that there was anything for them to learn and to correct. He was the link between Eastern learning and Latin prejudice and conservatism; and he was the only man probably, for Augustine wanted critical scholarship, who could have saved the Latin Church from perpetuating and consecrating more mistakes with respect to the Bible than it did. But M. Thierry is really absurd in his rhetorical flourishes about him. "Le plus grand théologien qui fût au monde," "le grand justicier des mœurs," "jamais les oracles de la Grèce païenne ne reçurent autant de députations à leurs portes," are some of the extravagant exaggerations which M. Thierry falls into from forgetting that there were other people besides his hero in the world. And this tendency to rhetoric tempts him at times to misread his texts. Here is an instance. Sophronius, he says, translated Jerome's Latin version of the Hebrew Scriptures into Greek, and he proceeds :—

L'Occident eut le rare et suprême honneur de voir une interprétation grecque de la Bible, puisée chez un auteur latin, remplacer dans beaucoup d'Églises d'Asie le texte consacré des Septante.

An honour, indeed, if it were so; and we look with curiosity, as Jerome does often say unexpected things, for the authority for this remarkable statement. Jerome, however, says nothing about "churches," or about his text taking the place of any other. He simply observes :—

Me putabam bene mereri de Latinis meis [in translating from the Hebrew], et nostrorum ad discendum animos concitare, quod etiam Graeci versum de latino, post tot interpretes, non fastidiunt. — In Ruf. II. No. 24.

We cannot find in Jerome's modest statement any authority for M. Thierry's singularly improbable one.

VIII

RANKE'S "HISTORY OF THE POPES"[1]

RANKE'S *History of the Popes of the Sixteenth and Seventeenth Centuries* is a book which has produced a permanent effect on opinion in England. The Dean of St. Paul's, in a short preface to the fourth edition of Mrs. Austin's excellent translation, relates how he was impressed with the value and importance of the work when first published in Germany in 1834-1836, and how he introduced it to the notice of English readers in two articles in the *Quarterly*. "I believe," he continues, "that I may safely assert that, mainly in consequence of those articles, the translation of the book was undertaken by Mrs. Austin." Mrs. Austin succeeded in the difficult task of making a translation of German prose read like an original English work; and as she was in communication with Ranke, she had the advantage of being able to refer to the writer himself on all points of doubt and question. The book itself, for its subject, its novelty, and the unusual skill

[1] *The Popes of Rome.* By Leopold Ranke. Translated by Sarah Austin. *Saturday Review*, 15th December 1866.

displayed in translating it, would have been sure to engage the interest of English readers; and it was followed up by Lord Macaulay's article, which gathered up its lessons and pointed out its significance at a moment when a great and unlooked-for theological movement of opinion gave the subject more than even its historical importance, and connected it with the conflicts of great parties and living men. The history of the Papacy and of the Roman Church since the Reformation was felt to be treated in a way in which no one had before thought of treating it. Immense learning had been accumulated by preceding writers to illustrate it, and a series of events which had so stirred and divided mankind could not fail to call out abundance of keen and just observation on all sides. It had afforded an inexhaustible theme for theological advocacy or attack, for political comment, for literary panegyric, and, it need not be said, for the most extravagant flattery and the bitterest sarcasm. And, if all sides did not seem equally genuine and sincere when they praised, there could be no doubt of their sincerity when they hated and denounced. But no one had yet attempted to look at this history from two sides, instead of only from one; to look at it as a whole, instead of confining all interest and giving all right to one of the two great conflicting parties.

To do this seems to us now a very simple and obvious thing. But it was such books as Ranke's which really taught us how to do it. In his own subject he is the first who thought of doing it, and he made a great step towards doing what he had conceived. And it is obvious that, if the book had remained buried to the mass of English readers in its original German, or had been less fortunate in its English translator, its effect here would have been much more limited. The translator in this case has been almost as important a person as the writer.

It is of course superfluous to criticise or praise so well-known a work. But the oldest book may suggest fresh reflections when we read it again after some interval; and the appearance of a new edition tempts to a few remarks which occur to us on renewing our acquaintance with the *History of the Popes*. Ranke's industry, keen insight, conscientiousness, and largeness of view, certainly do not appear less striking or less real on a second reading. His power of doing justice, of keeping two different sides of a subject present to his mind, of entering into ideas and motives which he does not share, gives him a great advantage in describing and judging the furious and eventful conflicts which followed the Reformation. And he combines remarkably the power of seeing great movements in their large outlines and complete developments, at once with sobriety and self-restraint in generalisation, and with critical exactness in dealing with evidence, and a strong sympathy for the details of character and feeling which light up all history. We cannot read him without feeling that he is a man who means to get to the bottom of his subject, who has real knowledge and the faculty of thinking powerfully about it. But as a book to be read, we must confess that we lay it down with the feeling that it is short of what a history like this ought to be. As a work of historical art and skill it fails to satisfy us, both in its form and its substance. As to its form, it is one of the most uncomfortable books to read that we know. We are carried on, not continuously, but by a series of jerks. At one moment we are reading general European history, then we are thrown into a chapter of abstract speculation, and thence we pass into the minute and curious intrigues of a conclave, or the domestic habits of a Pope. We have the *disjecta membra* of a deeply interesting history; but reading Ranke is like reading the *excerpta*, and most important passages of a course of philosophical lectures, of which the connecting form and arrangement have been dropped; or, rather, it is like having the separate parts of a great machine lying before us, but not put together so as to make up the machine and enable it to work. Of course, in the question between form and substance, form is the least important part. But it is important, nevertheless, and an historical inquirer and discoverer ought to remember that the world has examples of great historical compositions in which the utmost care for form has not involved any sacrifice of substance; and he ought not to think it beneath him to pay attention to arrangement, proportion, disposition, and connection of parts, and all that turns a set of fragmentary notes into a complete work with the unity and the perfection of a whole. With Gibbon before him, no historian has a right to think that his subject is too vast or too full of detail to admit of being put into shape, and made convenient and agreeable to read; and if he thinks that his matter is so valuable that he need not trouble himself about the undress in which it comes from his commonplace book or his oral lecture, he must not be surprised if readers complain of clumsiness.

Nor are Ranke's defects only those of form. His book is not properly so much a history of the Popes, as a series of philosophical comments on the connection of their policy and history with the progress of European history. This is perhaps more convenient for the writer than for the reader. It is a way of writing which enables the writer to say what he wants as the thoughts occur to him; but it does not always suit the reader, who wants to know the story, its facts and its links, as well as his teacher's reflections on it. And it all along seems as if Ranke had never firmly made up his mind what sort of book he was going to write. He gives an immense deal of history, new and curious history; and he gives a great deal of generalisation, pointing out the drift and significance of the history as it goes forward. One element interferes with the other. The philosophising reduces the purely historical portion to mere sketches—doubtless with many vigorous touches, but still mere incomplete sketches—with some features elaborately worked out, and others, equally real, totally unnoticed and left blank; and it is also apt to displace inconveniently the different portions of the work. Thus, for instance, we are deep in the eventful policy of Urban VIII. before we are told who Urban VIII. was. Then, as to the exposition of general causes and movements, there is a good deal that is loose and hazy in expression, and in which facts seem hastily assumed, and rather arbitrarily invested with a meaning, or made to bear a conclusion. Ranke of course is right in the leading idea of his work—the great and astonishing fact, never before him so fully recognised or so strongly brought into life, of the reconquest by the Papacy of an empire which seemed hopelessly at an end; of its extraordinary resuscitation to a moral vigour greater in some respects than it had shown in the Middle Ages; of the wonderful power of a triumphant reaction, able, by an unexampled combination of unflinching secular violence and boundless spiritual self-devotion, to roll back the strongest and most natural tendencies of an age which seemed to have conquered its freedom; till the impulse yielded, not to the strength of opposition without, but to the old inevitable slackening within, and the Papacy subsided from the aggressive and formidable attitude which it had assumed for a time, to a self-defensive conservatism and a worldliness supposed to be decent. In his tracing of the course and fortunes of this great struggle it need not be said how much is masterly, comprehensive, and full of truth and evidence. But the details are unequal. There is often a looseness and want of precision and authority in the way in which facts are stated. General assertions are made, or accepted from others, of which it is obvious to remark that they are of a nature to suggest questions and to need explanation rather than to be the basis of historical argument. And Ranke has a way occasionally of making an oracular enunciation or aphorism— or, still more, some *mot* or trait of character—do duty for something more solid and matter-of-fact in confirmation of what he puts before us. We must add that when he comes to handle theological controversies, and attempts to get to the bottom of them, and to disengage their essential and deeper principles and meaning, he seems to be unable to deal with them in anything more than their superficial aspect. His account of the theological debates at Trent, his contrast between the Lutheran and Tridentine doctrines, and, later on, his representations of the Jesuist casuistry, and of the theology and development of Jansenism, seem to us quite unworthy of such a work as his aspires to be; they are confused, slovenly, and inadequate. No doubt such abstract and complicated disputes are hard to exhibit at once in an accurate and a popular summary. But to do so is part of the duty of one who writes of the greatest theological movement the world has ever known.

Besides the merit of the main idea of his work, the great revival and second decline of the Papacy, and the force and distinctness, if we cannot say vividness, with which he keeps before us the real impulses of this revival, its instruments and conditions, and the ultimate causes of its failure—there are two things which Ranke usually does very well. His personal sketches of the Popes are distinct and suggestive. As we have said before, we think them inadequate for his work. He ought to have told us a good deal more at least of many of the number than he has done; and what he gives is often disproportionately full of detail in one place, while the rest of the portrait is left untouched. But as mere sketches, they certainly bring back to our imagination the men whom they represent in a shape which makes us remember them. The procession which passes before us in his pages of old ecclesiastics, with such a family likeness, yet all individually different—fierce or smooth, devout or diplomatic, fanatics or men of the world, public-spirited or self-indulgent, yet all equally bound by inflexible necessities and understandings, absolute in theory but the most helpless of slaves, trying to realise the highest religious pretensions, which only recoiled on them more and more in the shape of the most undeniable facts of moral and social degeneration and misfortune—is at once a very curious and a very solemn one.

The other point in which it appears to us that Ranke is excellent is in the way in which he concentrates a great variety of facts from all kinds of sources, so as to exhibit the course and effect of some great movement or change on a large scale. As an instance, we may mention his astonishing account of the way in which the returning wave of Catholicism swept over Germany after the Council of Trent; the force with which he makes us see that there was a time when Austria, Bavaria, and the Lower Rhine really seemed as strongly and hopelessly Protestant as any other part of Germany, and yet how, in the course of a generation or two, this was entirely and permanently changed. So, again, with the reconquest to Romanism of Poland and Hungary, and the very near reconquest of Sweden. He makes it clear, in general, that this success rested on three chief things—on the activity of the Jesuits in conversion and education, and the extraordinary power of a rigid method in the hands of very ordinary but resolute men ; on the Erastian ideas of the power of governments, developed by the Protestants, and turned by the Catholics against them ; and on the strong backing of the Pope and Spain. Only, we repeat, while we read the facts on which Ranke's account rests, we cannot refrain often from a secret doubt as to the foundation or the real explanation of some of them. When he represents Germany in the middle of the sixteenth century as almost wholly Protestant, with not more than a tenth of the population adhering to the old religion, with the champions of Roman theology dead, and none to take their place, with the nobles and chapters mainly on the side of the Confession of Augsburg, with all the schools and universities in the hands of the Protestants—and when he then goes on to represent all this as in a few years reversed, education falling into the hands of the Jesuit teachers, who were mostly foreigners, and princes and bishops able to prohibit and root out Protestantism with no extraordinary effort—we cannot help asking what the previous estimate of the strength of Protestantism was really worth. We want to know how far the facts cited were typical and characteristic, or exceptional; and to what extent the alleged acceptance of Protestantism was real or apparent, the estimate of men's hopes or fears, of their rhetoric of alarm or triumph, rather than of their knowledge and belief. Ranke's array of facts is striking; but they would have carried more weight if explanation and verification had accompanied them more distinctly.

We can believe that the progress of historical inquiry will alter a good many of Ranke's estimates of men and events. We must own to a sense of insecurity in following his representations, at least in detail. We are often surprised and struck, but we feel that we have not the key. But nothing can alter the value of two features of his work. One is his resolute and pertinacious determination to leave no true side of a subject out of his account. Even if he can only bring in his qualification clumsily, even if the addition of a fact on the other side appears not far from a contradiction of his own conclusion, he never fails to remind his readers of it. The example of an historian who is ready to sacrifice convenience, symmetry, the look of consistency, to the paramount claim of evidence to which he will not shut his eyes, even though he cannot adjust it to his view, is invaluable. The other thing to be noticed is his accumulation of material. Ranke was one of the first who pointed out the vast store of unknown and unsuspected information contained in the State Papers of Venice, and his work is very much based on the judgments formed at the time by the Venetian agents and diplomatists. Since he first wrote, we have learned a good deal about them; but he deserves the credit of having impressed us with their importance. Indeed, his appendix, which contains accounts of a number of these contemporary documents — and not only Venetian ones—and also copious extracts from them, is not the least interesting portion of the book. When we remember what the Popes even of the seventeenth century were in theory and claim, and compare it with what is reported by not unfriendly but sharp-eyed and calm observers at the time, of their ways, their families, and their government, it would not be easy to find elsewhere an instance to match the contrast which thus arises between the ideal and the matter of fact. One part of this contrast is of special interest at this moment, when we are watching the fortunes of the temporal power, and hearing such strong assertions of its sacredness and exceptional rights. In Ranke we read the process of its formation, as to the largest part of it, and also the way in which from the first it was governed. Its growth and formation went on long after the Papacy had come to its senses, and awoke from the wild intoxication or moral insensibility of the Borgias, Rovere, and Medici; and it went on in the ordinary way in which Italian territory, principalities and cities, changed masters. The conquest of Ferrara, the escheat of Urbino, belong not to the days of the unreformed Papacy of Julius II. or Paul III., but to the reformed and decorous Papacy of the next century. It was the reformed Papacy which went on extending its limits as an Italian principality, just by the same means, neither better nor worse, as those used by its neighbours—by legal claims and pretexts enforced by cannon against weak heirs or pretenders. It seems wonderful that even Ultramontanists should not admit that a kingdom won by the sword must take the chances which attend all earthly conquests.

IX

DEAN MILMAN'S ESSAYS[1]

DEAN MILMAN was a frequent contributor to the *Quarterly Review*, and much of the work of his *History of Latin Christianity* was first sketched and prepared in the shape of articles. Where these articles have in substance reappeared in their proper place, and with their final revision, in the History, it would have been superfluous to republish them. But Dean Milman carried his study of Latin Christianity beyond the limits where his History ends, the middle of the fifteenth century. Had time and strength been allowed him, we might have had a continuation of it to Tridentine and post-Tridentine times, not inferior in interest and value to the earlier portion. But this was not to be. He had, however, begun to collect his thoughts and shape his judgments on the religious history of Europe which succeeded to that of the Middle Ages, and to throw into outline his conception of some of its principal characters.

[1] *Savonarola, Erasmus, and other Essays.* By H. H. Milman, D.D., Dean of St. Paul's. *Saturday Review*, 13th May 1871.

These fragments, which first appeared in the *Quarterly*, are now collected and republished. The essays on Savonarola, on Erasmus, on the Popes of the sixteenth and seventeenth centuries, and on the fall of the Jesuits, form an imperfect continuation of the great completed History, but they bear the stamp of the same remarkable qualities which distinguish it from all ecclesiastical history that we are acquainted with. Besides these there are two essays on some of the questions, both of theory and practice, raised by the speculations and the progress of the Oxford movement, in which Dean Milman could only see an attempted revival of that mediaeval religion with which he was familiar. The last paper in the volume is the last article contributed by him to the *Quarterly*, an article on "Pagan and Christian Sepulchres," occasioned by De Rossi's investigations at Rome, and inspired by the strong interest which a personal visit and a sight of these solemn memorials almost invariably creates.

The historical fragments make us regret that the finished picture which might have embodied them was never completed. Dean Milman's great and rare qualities were even perhaps more suited for the later history of the Church than for the earlier; and though we should be sorry to be without much of what he has done for the Middle Ages, we are not sure that we would not exchange it for the same amount of work on the time from the fifteenth to the eighteenth century. An English history of the Re formation, its causes and its consequences, has yet to be written. Reminded as we are daily, and in all kinds of ways, of its good and its evil results, and sensible, as we cannot help being, of its overwhelming eventfulness, we yet fail to rise to the height of the historical phenomenon itself, and we see it treated on every side in ways which, either for eulogy or condemnation, narrow, vulgarise, and impoverish our ideas of it. Dean Milman's imagination and insight, his fearless courage, and his unusual combination of the strongest feelings about right and wrong with the largest equity, would have enabled him to handle this perplexed and difficult history in a manner in which no English writer has yet treated it. We do not say that he could be expected to be entirely successful. He wanted, what many of our most eminent teachers of the present day want, a due appreciation of the reality and depth of those eternal problems of religious thought and feeling which have made theology. Impatient, sometimes unduly so, of the attempted solutions, and keenly alive to the strange and grotesque look which they frequently presented side by side with the visible course and show of the world and life, he contemplated them without interest; and deeply stirred as he was by all that the strife about them brought out in the temper and character of the human agents, all that for the sake of them men did and felt and suffered, yet he instinctively turned away as much as he could from adventuring his thoughts very far into the perplexed debates themselves. Of course a history of religion which inadequately understands and estimates religious belief and doctrine, and the earnestness which desires above all things that it should be complete and true, cannot be a perfect one; an account, however excellent, of what is outward in the fortunes and conduct of a religious body, cannot make up for the neglect or superficial understanding of those inward and spiritual ideas and efforts which are its soul and life. Dean Milman would have been more at home with the men and the events of the Reformation than with the philosophy and theology of its disputes. The German, Italian, and English divines, the Popes and Cardinals and Jesuits, who met them in the "world's debate," would have risen before him as men, with their hopes and fears, their temptations and their policies, their greatness and their crimes, much more easily and much more really than he could have entered into the significance of the battles of their day about Justification or the Sacraments. A man must be able to do both, before the history of that great crisis in the fortunes of the world is duly set forth; but to have done the first as Dean Milman would have done it, so loftily, so intelligently, so fearlessly, so justly, would have given us a book which for the present we want. We must content ourselves with imagining the book he would have written from the sketches he has left us.

A sort of measure of Dean Milman's qualifications for dealing with religious history is given in these essays. He writes of Savonarola, of Erasmus, and then of the Popes, from those of the Riario and Borgia type to those of the Lambertini and Ganganelli order. They are all vigorous and brilliant studies, full of knowledge, full of historical grasp and intelligence, full of noble sympathy and noble scorn, full of regulated humour of all the shades from amused and compassionate playfulness to indignant sarcasm; kindling, as Dean Milman's wont was, from a style of often careless roughness into passages of powerful and finished eloquence. But he had to deal in them with subjects which were in unequal degrees congenial to him, and for which he was, and probably felt himself, unequally adapted. Savonarola was a subject which, if the character was to be treated with sympathy at all, needed, it seems to us, a subtler and more delicate power of entering into the mysterious conditions and experiences of the spiritual side of human life than the historian ever gave evidence of possessing. He opens his essay with the question, What was Savonarola? — "hypocritical impostor? self-deluded fanatic? holy, single-minded Christian preacher? heaven-commissioned prophet? wonder-working saint, all but canonised martyr? priestly demagogue? enlightened lover of liberty? rude Iconoclast? purifier and elevator of art?" "Had he more of St. Bernard, of Arnold of Brescia, of Gerson or of Wycliffe? was he the forerunner of Luther or of Loyola, of Knox or of S. Philippo Neri, even of John of Leyden or our Fifth-monarchy men?" These are pertinent and inevitable questions, and questions which, if we only choose and keep one point of view, and pass by what interferes with it, it is not difficult to answer. It is as easy to make a case for Savonarola's profound Catholicism, or for his affinity to the Reformers, as it is to conclude with Bayle that he was an impostor, or with Roscoe that he was a disgusting fanatic. But the question, what was he in fact—in all the complexity of that real assemblage of qualities which his character and actions present—still remains for those who are not satisfied, in the presence of strange and difficult phenomena, with partial solutions of them.

Dean Milman has marked the reality of the question, but we cannot say that he satisfies us that he has mastered the answer. The outward look of the scenes in which Savonarola moved, the words and deeds by which he disclosed himself among the men and circumstances of his time, are done full justice to; and so, too, is justice done to his heroic greatness, his moral purity, his genius, even his Catholic orthodoxy. "He died because he was a preacher of righteousness, in an age and Church at the very depths of unrighteousness." But his aim was "a monkish reformation" of a "Church which still professed monasticism to be the perfection of Christianity." If the Dean had said a "Puritan" reformation, he would have been nearer the mark; but then what is involved in the idea, in its widest sense, for which our most available word is "Puritanism"? Savonarola's monkery was an accident of his time; his Puritanism, no doubt, was of the essence of his mind and soul. It betrays an inadequate power of entering into Savonarola's strange and awful personality when a writer merely puts him before us as a great preacher of righteousness, spoiled by monastic Christianity; and the justice, insight, and sympathy with which part of the picture is rendered show that it was a defect of faculty and insight, not want of will, that hindered the execution of the rest.

Turn from Savonarola to Erasmus, and there we find at once that the writer is far more at home. Dean Milman has given perhaps the best and truest portrait that has ever been presented of a man who was even a more important person in the history of his time than Savonarola. Erasmus is indeed a "representative man"; the pattern and sample of those who, in days of impending change, sympathise deeply with what is new, while they are honestly and reasonably still as deeply attached to what is old. And Erasmus, in his division of interest between the old religion and the new learning—in his distraction of feeling between the intolerable abuses, which no one had branded so mercilessly as himself, of the old system, and the tremendous and unfathomable dangers which seemed to be revealing themselves in the changes which were at hand—in his vast and astonishing learning and his equally perfect and unfailing wit—in his daring courage and his cowardice—in his noble standard and aims, and the noble use to which he put his life, and in the strange mixture of self-indulgence and love of comfort —Erasmus, in his strength and his weakness, in his achievements and in his perplexities and miscarriages, is put before us with a most just, and yet very generous feeling, by Dean Milman. And he is successful, because here he is able to put before us his subject as a whole. It is its completeness which satisfies and interests us. We feel that there is no part which is beyond the writer's range of view, and no part which he has left out of account. It is a conception, thoroughly understood and powerfully grasped, of a character which has been much oftener either superficially celebrated or superficially disparaged.

If Dean Milman had attempted to write of Luther, or Ignatius Loyola, or even of Calvin, his success probably would have been more like his appreciation of Savonarola than of Erasmus. To the outward, stirring, visible facts of their career he would have been in the highest degree equal; but he would have failed to enter into the inward trials and struggles and dim ideas which bore fruit in the doctrine of Justification and the Company of Jesus, and he would probably have looked away in amused disgust from the metaphysics of Calvin. But when he comes to deal on a large scale with the results on the outward world of the silent and secret meditations of these mighty thinkers, on the forces which they set in array, not only in schools and pulpits but in cabinets and battle-fields, on their effects on the councils and policies of Popes and emperors and kings, on the way in which they remodelled Europe and directed the course of the world for ever, then all his aptitudes come into play. He will not allow either of the partisan views of these great religious conflicts and transformations. He looks at the whole field and its varying fortunes from a higher and more comprehensive point of view. He finds and points out, as much to the Protestant as to the Roman Catholic, a subject of the deepest interest in the wonderful and strangely mixed history of the Popes since the sixteenth century. He has given, for English readers, life and order and consecutiveness to what are to most of us the rather dry bones of Ranke. His three sketchy and rapid essays, based on the great German History of the Popes—for a great work it is in spite of its uninviting form—show us what a book we might have had from Dean Milman, to enlarge our ignorant and confined notions of religious history abroad, and to bring light into regions where prejudice and delusion reign supreme.

We would almost venture to say that if the truth had been better and more generally known in England about the modern religious history of the Roman Church, if the Popes had been known to us as Ranke has shown them, as men, often interesting men, with their human good and evil, instead of as vague general impersonations of some ill-defined but shocking wickedness, we should not have had so much stupid fanaticism about Popery, but neither could the dream have arisen and taken root in intelligent minds that at Rome there was a divine and supernatural system, different from all earthly ruling and statesmanship in its purity of purpose and its heavenly wisdom, which made the communion which it governed an exception to all the ordinary rules of human experience. If people had duly learned that the Popes of Rome were, as statesmen, not very different from the lay statesmen with whom they contended or allied themselves, and, as ecclesiastical authorities, not worse than the great ecclesiastical authorities of the same period in England or Scotland, it would not have been so easy to fly round to the opposite extravagance, that they are something infinitely better, and belonging to a different order of things.

These historical fragments are the most important portions of the volume. The essay on Pagan and Christian Sepulchres is interesting, but from Dean Milman we should almost have expected it to be more so. The other two papers are controversial. One is a criticism of Dr. Newman's Essay on Development; the other is a warning, derived from the apparent results of the French Church system, against supposed Anglican attempts to introduce or imitate it at home, especially in the matter of confession. They are marked by the writer's ability, acuteness, and breadth of view; they fail, it seems to us, as it is likely they would fail, in really getting to the bottom of the questions they treat. The obvious difficulties of Dr. Newman's argument, the obvious dangers and evils attending on any discipline involving confidential relations between clergy and people, the indefensible absurdities of some of the disciples of the Oxford movement, especially when in their transition state, are strongly and not uncandidly put; but the subtleties of

Dr. Newman's view, which perplexed himself even when he was most sensible to its apparent charms and attractions, elude Dean Milman's grasp; and it is not all religious minds which would be satisfied with the standard of religious thought, affection, or effort with which the Dean himself would probably have been content.

Both the essays, though there are passages in them of great force and permanent interest, carry us back many years, to 1845 and 1846. It is curious, in one of them which is based on Michelet's book on the Priest and the Family, to notice the observations of a well-informed man at that time on French morality and French prospects. Michelet had written that the Family was the only hope of France, and that the Family was in danger from priestly influence. Dean Milman draws attention to his allegations and his fears; states what seemed the then condition and character of France; and leaves it to the future to cast light on the influences then at work. "For the first time," he notices, "in later French history (must we not ascend almost to St. Louis for an earlier precedent of this moral phenomenon?) the Court of France has set the high example of domestic virtue." He remarks that "if statesmen whom he could name as examples of every amiable, as well as of every high and honourable virtue, may not represent their whole class, yet at least they are not represented by the Richelieus" of Louis XV.'s time, and that domestic virtue has greatly improved both in the upper class and in the bourgeoisie, at that time the actual rulers of France. What then might be looked for as the result? Was the reign of order beginning?

That this revolution should not continue; that the future history of France should not be like that which Louis Blanc has written—or rather that which Louis Blanc would wish to write—not a succession of republican abortions, of wild conspiracies against all order and government, of St. Simonianism, of Fourrierism, and every other strange scheme for the complete regeneration of society; nay, still worse, of actual convulsion and sanguinary strife . . . not an eternal anarchy, a chronic state of dissolution, till the weary world yearns for the peace of some strong despotism—the one guarantee for all this, under God, is the Family.

This was the prospect and the problem in 1845. Dean Milman himself, and we still more, have seen what has been the reality. To what is it attributable? Were Michelet's complaints of the disintegrating influence of the French clergy on families and households really borne out by facts? Or have family truth and purity been mined and dissolved by another set of forces very different from anything wielded by the clergy? Perhaps the *Univers*, and soberer and wiser people than those whom the *Univers* represents, would have some sharp recriminations on Michelet himself. But after all that has happened, under the Empire and since its fall, we note with increased interest the anxieties felt as far back as 1845, by competent observers, about the dangers and weakness of French family life.

X

GUICCIARDINI[1]

I

THE collection of Guicciardini's unpublished papers, which has been given to the world by his family and has been edited by a learned Italian professor, is one of great value and interest. It has long been known that the family archives contained a great variety of important documents—Guicciardini's correspondence, and other productions of his indefatigable pen; and fragments from time to time have made their appearance. But we now have the bulk of these remains set before us. The editing appears to have been intelligently and carefully done, though it does not come up to the exact precision with which, by good English or French or German editors, the reader is put in full possession of everything relating to the

[1] *Opere inedite di Francesco Guicciardini*, illustrate da G. Canestrini. 10 vols. Firenze. *Saturday Review*, 13th February 1869.

papers before him, and is told, not only what is given to him, and its relation to what has been published before, but also what is withheld from him, what is imperfect, and what is not to be found. We should have preferred a little more of this critical information to Professor Canestrini's prolix though not uninstructive prefaces, in which there is no want of knowledge or of shrewdness and good sense, but in which the knowledge and the good sense are wrapped up in an amplitude of academic full dress which is trying to business-like readers who want to get on with their work and deal with facts. In his fear, too, of unnecessary notes, the editor is rather sparing of desirable elucidation. A foreign reader is perhaps no judge of what is wanted by Italians in illustration of the allusions in the letters to Italian things or persons; but even an Italian might not know who was that "Marchese di Orqueta" who, in Henry VIII.'s time (1512), so curiously attempted to anticipate the policy of later days by attacking France from the Peninsula by the passes of the Pyrenees at Fuentarabia and St. Jean de Luz, or where was that place—called, if Guicciardini remembers rightly, Verruiche — near which the King of Scotland was said to be encamped. An Italian reader might very reasonably ask to be reminded that Guicciardini, who like most of his contemporaries is apt to stumble at foreign names, and expresses Avignon and Valladolid by "Vignone" and "Vagliadulit," was trying to represent the way in which the Spaniards pronounced the outlandish

English names of the Marquis of Dorset and the town of Berwick.

A few dates may be convenient in reference to Guicciardini. He was born in 1482; he studied law at Florence, at Ferrara, and at Padua, from 1498 to 1505. In that year he returned to Florence, where he combined the functions of a professor or reader of law with those of an advocate, becoming the standing counsel, as the custom was, of a number of guilds, monasteries, and towns. In 1506 he connected himself by a marriage treaty with the powerful family of the Salviati, a house which always leaned to "close government," and practically to the Medici interest. He was sent in 1512 to Spain, to represent the Republic at the Court of Ferdinand of Aragon, where he remained till the following year—an embassy which did not prevent the surprise and overthrow of the free Government of Florence, and the bloody sack of Prato in a time of peace by the Spanish Viceroy in Italy, and the re-establishment of the Medici. In 1513 he returned home, and joined the party of the Medici; from 1516 to 1523 he was Leo X.'s Governor of the "Emilia," the province containing Modena, Reggio, and Parma. From 1524 to 1527 he served the second Medicean Pope, Clement VII., as President of the Romagna. In 1527 came the sack of Rome, followed by the imprisonment of the Pope; in 1530, the final overthrow of Florentine liberty by the allied powers of Pope and Emperor, which was followed by the rule of the revived Medici dynasty.

Guicciardini gave his services both to Alessandro and Cosimo, but his part in active life became gradually more limited. Busy with his pen, and a watchful but hopeless observer of the course of the world, he died in 1540. Thus he was ten years old at the accession of Borgia as Pope Alexander VI. (1492), twelve years old at the time of the great French invasion under Charles VIII. (1494) and the revolution which expelled the first Medici and restored the republic. His boyhood was passed in the midst of the feverish and short-lived enthusiasm which the religious republicanism of the great Frate called forth, and of the fierce and deadly hatreds which it provoked. He set himself to study law in the autumn of the year in the early summer of which Savonarola had perished (1498). While he was growing up, and following University lectures at Ferrara and Padua, it was the palmy days of the Borgia triumphs (1500-1503), succeeded by the first openings of the political game of Julius II. Pope Julius, Ferdinand of Aragon, Maximilian, and Louis XII. were filling the world with dismay at their boundless perfidy, and with admiration for their ambition and power, when the young lawyer was starting in public life at Florence; he was setting up house, and bringing his wife home during the month which preceded the League of Cambrai, 10th December 1508; he made his last arrangements about his marriage settlement a few days after it was signed. Such were the events and circumstances amid which he grew up, and first became acquainted with the world and the ways of men. When he was thirty he heard in Spain of the terrible battle of Ravenna, and of the sacrifice of the last free State on the mainland of Italy to the necessities and ambition of the great contending Powers (1512). He returned home, hopeless of free government, deeply impressed with the vast chances of the Pope, as the one native power in Italy, in the varying and perilous struggle. A Pope to him was simply a temporal prince, in a thin but most convenient disguise, who would as often gain as lose in the political game, who had just as much right to play high in it as a king of Spain or of France, and to play it as cunningly and as remorselessly as they, and who was the only one of the players who represented distinctly, and with sufficient power, Italian interests. When he came home from Spain he had made up his mind. He threw himself on what seemed to him the rising tide of the age. He accepted the Medici at Florence; he devoted himself without reserve to the service of the Popes, who were also Medici. It may be added that he lived to see to what extent the forecasts of his subtle and cautious mind were made good by the event. He was right in a great deal; he proved wrong in much more. With all his keenness and sagacity, he had not detected the ruling tendencies of the time or the deeper movements which were to shape the future.

Guicciardini's fame as a writer is an ambiguous one. His *History of Italy* takes rank, conventionally and in libraries, among the great modern examples of classical writing and historical art. From its first appearance it has been read and weighed by men of thought and men of action, and has undoubtedly influenced their minds. It quickened, and partly perhaps shaped, their own reflections on the policy and the nature of man. It stamped upon literature and general opinion its aspect of the ruin of Italy and the crimes of the Popes. It set up a standard of composition which unconsciously perhaps stimulated and regulated the efforts of men so different in their ways and so original as De Thou, Davila, and Lord Clarendon. And there are many reasons why it should be considered a great work. It is grave, full, impartial, judicious. The subject is handled in a large and elevated way. It is full of sagacity and power—sagacity calm and always conscious both of its penetration and its limits; power never baffled, nor failing in discrimination and clearness, before the more complicated phenomena of character. No one can wonder at the fame of a work of such massive proportions and strength. Yet it is one of the classics which we respect but do not love. Before our own times readers found it dull. The prolixity of the narrative and the artificial array of the ponderous and intricately woven sentences have long been felt as severe trials. The joke of the criminal who, when offered his choice between the galleys and reading Guicciardini, broke down hopelessly at the war of Pisa, if it was intelligible when first made, is much more intelligible to readers of Lord Macaulay. Its moral tone, too, its cold passionless recognition of the facts of boundless wickedness, repelled or perplexed. Montaigne, of all men, professed himself to be shocked at the way in which Guicciardini writes as if religion and conscience were things no longer in the world, and tracks with relentless suspicion what seem the finest actions to their hidden springs of selfishness or corruption.

The judgments which we form of Guicciardini from his History are considerably modified by an acquaintance with his other writings. The History was his latest work; and Guicciardini, we suspect, was one of those men who do not improve as writers as they get older. Their knowledge and experience grow, and perhaps their ideas; but not, in the same proportion, their power and spring of mind. They turn solemn, diffuse, formal. In their caution and fear of mistakes, they entangle and overload themselves with details and qualifications which they have not strength and liveliness enough to throw into their proper places. They become slaves to artificial rules of correctness and propriety, both in the plan and the treatment of their subject, in what they think due to its importance and dignity, and in making their language correspond to this dignity. In their fear of what is bold, and their distrust of what is natural and simple, they become dry, thin, and wooden in their writing, or, what is worse, elaborately pompous. When Guicciardini sat down to write his *History of Italy*, he remembered that he had a reputation to sustain, great models to rival or excel, posterity to impress; his work rose before his mind on a large and imposing scale; it was to prove his familiarity with courts, with letters, with men and affairs; it was to be the monument of his political wisdom, it was to shine with reflections and sagacious remarks and classical sentences. The work came out not unworthy of its theme, full of authentic statement, full of keen thought; but life and play and easy movement had disappeared before the courtier's notions of what was decorous and stately, and the scholar's notions of what was elaborate and ample in style. He had great success in constructing astonishing sentences in which everything relating to the main subject was remembered, contrasted, balanced, qualified; people admired them, but the strain and effort were too obvious and too continuous, and readers soon got tired of them.

But these hitherto unpublished remains show that this manner of writing was a studied and artificial one. In this voluminous collection we may see distinctly how Guicciardini broke himself in for the style of his History; he appears like a rhetorician of the schools under the Roman Empire, composing set orations, deliberative, judicial, and so forth, on various questions of the time, in which a vast amount of windy declamation is curiously mixed up with interesting notices of fact, and real insight into affairs. Among them, for instance, is a long and elaborate speech against himself, in which a supposed accuser alleges and heightens with circumstantial detail and passionate invective Guicciardini's offences against the State in his public life, and sets forth the reasons why he should be punished with the utmost severity; and this is followed by a reply in defence. But he did not always write in this forced and pedantic fashion. The collection contains a great quantity of business letters of great interest for the history of the time; his correspondence, public and private, from the Court of Ferdinand of Aragon in 1512-1513; his correspondence as the Papal representative in the Romagna under Leo X., and again under Clement VII. when the Constable of Bourbon was marching through his province on Rome; and these letters are those of an able, keen-sighted, and energetic officer, alive to emergency, and with his powers strung to meet it—plain, clear, exact, and forcible in all that he writes. The collection contains also the interesting fragment of Florentine history from the Government of the first Cosimo de' Medici to the League of Cambrai (1433-1508), written in his youth, when Soderini was still Gonfaloniere, and in the midst of the men who had been active in the Republican Government, and had followed or opposed Savonarola, whom Guicciardini, a boy of twelve, had probably seen die. It contains also a series of detached thoughts on the political and moral phenomena of the day, and various notes and memoranda about his family and life. In all these papers Guicciardini writes like a man who thinks more of his subject than of the grandeur and skill of his sentences—a man full of family affection and household interest; full of shrewd appreciation of all things round him, keenly observant and not easily deceived, with few illusions and no very high standard or hope, but with much considerateness, an evident wish to do justice broadly and substantially, and, along with an undisguised desire to advance himself, with very genuine public spirit and interest in the greatness and welfare of his famous city.

The papers about his family and his own life have in them much that is interesting. They were written solely for the eyes of members of his house, who were in the most solemn way enjoined to allow no copy of them to get abroad, nor even to permit them to be seen by strangers—an injunction which his present descendants have wisely not thought themselves bound to comply with. They are written, he says, only for the instruction of his descendants: "Io l' ho scritte solamente a quello fine, come quello che desidero due cose al mondo più che alcuna altra: l' una la esaltazione perpetua di questa Città e della libertà sua; l' altra la gloria di casa nostra, non solo vivendo io, ma in perpetuo." His family for several generations had produced a line of busy citizens and successful traders, men with a watchful eye to their own interests, hearty haters of disorder, enthusiasm, and popular ignorance and blundering, with much public spirit and a keen relish of the pleasures of life. His biographical accounts of his ancestors for the century before him give a vivid and lifelike picture of varieties of the well-to-do Florentine burgher, men of weight and activity in the affairs of the city, but not reaching the first rank. They were public officers, commissaries, captains of galleys, ambassadors, *Cavalieri, Gonfalonieri di Giustizia;* fifteen times, he says, this last honour came to their house, and only five other families could boast of having had it oftener. They made money; they had shops; they went the voyage to England or the Levant. In the factions of Florence the family was represented on both sides; and, in the alternations of fortune, the Guicciardini who was on the winning side took care of the Guicciardini on the losing side. Thus, when Cosimo de' Medici was banished, Giovanni befriended Cosimo's partisan Piero; and when Cosimo returned, Piero's interest saved Giovanni. But, on the whole, the family took the Medici side; several of its members were leading supporters of Cosimo, and his son and grandson. Yet there was some reserve; when the Medici fell, the Guicciardini do not appear to have suffered, and when the Medici came back, the Guicciardini were at hand with their service. They had constant employment, without doing anything conspicuous or being very successful. Their descendant, with a curious mixture of family feeling and outspoken candour, notes their characteristic traits, and balances their faults and their good qualities. They were a very handsome race; they were hot-tempered men, as the historian himself appears from his letters to have been considered to be; and he is particular to record, and does so without scruple, that they were almost all men of pleasure; but they were fair dealers in money matters. A family likeness runs through most of them to the portrait here drawn:—

Fu uomo animoso [he is speaking of Luigi, his great-uncle] e di buono cervello, ma un poco furioso e volenteroso nelle cose sue, che fu causa di fargli pigliare molte imprese, di che riuscì con poco onore. Nelle cose dello Stato, fu partigiano de' Medici, e per loro si sarebbe assai adoperato, massime innanzi agli ultimi tempi, ne' quali non si tenne molto bene contento di Lorenzo. Circa alla conscienza, fu netto dei fatti della roba di altri, e veddesene lo effetto,—che benchè avessi quattro mogli, non avessi figliuoli legittimi, avessi lo stato grande e assai fattorie che erano di più utile che oggi, e godessi etiam molti anni le entrate del figliuolo prete; non di meno lasciò poche sustanzie. . . . Fu uomo di corpo bello, statura grande, e bianco e gentile aria, e di complessione molto robusta, che si vedde e in tutta la vita che fu savissimo, e nella morte, che benchè fussi di ottanta anni, morì con grandissima fatica e passione come se fusse giovane. Fu libidinosissimo etiam vecchio circa le femmine, e sarebbesi posto a scherzare colle sue fanti, e a motteggiare etiam per la via con qualche vile donna avessi riscontro, sanza rispetto alcuno o della età o della degnità sua.

One of them incurs his descendant's very marked contempt. He had let himself be driven out of the Palace, when chief magistrate, by a mob, and was much blamed for his cowardice. There is something delightful in the gravity with which Guicciardini distinguishes in the matter, and, acquitting his ancestor of all blame for running away to save his life, points out that the mean-spirited stupidity was in not taking care beforehand, by crushing his enemies, that he should not have to run away:—

Tutti coloro che hanno scritto questo movimento danno carico grande alla Signoria, e massime al Gonfaloniere per esserne capo, e biasimangli come uomini vili e da pochi, che non dovevano mai abbandonare il palagio. Io non intendo ora giustificare particularmente questa accusa, ma la conclusione è che ogni uomo savio non avrebbe fatto altrimente; perchè avevano la moltitudine inimica e gli Otto della guerra, i quali gli tradirono; erano abbandonati da' Collegi e da' buoni cittadini, in modo che quel partito fu necessario, e furonne ancora confortati e pregati da' Collegi per minore male. Perchè e' non è dubbio se avessino voluto fare resistenza, ne sarebbono usciti in ogni modo con qualche detrimento loro grande di morte o di altro, e con più danno della Città; perchè la moltitudine si mitigò alquanto vedendogli cedere in qualche cosa. Ma la verità è ben questa, che e' meritano di essere biasimati in due cose: l'una che non punirono rigidamente, o per misericordia o per poco animo, quegli che avevano sostenuti, e spezialmente Messer Salvestro [de' Medici]; il che, se avessino fatto, sarebbe suto facile cosa che la moltitudine spaventata e vedutasi tôrre i capi, si fussi quietata: l'altra che quando ebbono notizia di quello che apparecchiavano i Ciompi, non fecions i rimedii potettono, e di levare su i cittadini che gli avrebbono favoriti, che tutti poi stettono fermi, e di fare venire fanterie di fuora che era loro facile. Ma fidaronsi degli Otto e rapportaronsi a' preparamenti loro, i quali gli tradirono; sì che il Gonfaloniere non merita di essere biasimato di avere a ultimo abbandonato il Palagio, perchè questa deliberazione fu necessaria, e di meno danno alla Città che se violentemente ne fussi stato cavato e morto. Ma bene può essere caricato di essergli mancato l' animo, o vero abbondato la misericordia, che è spezie di dapocaggine, a punire i tristi, e così d' avere avuta troppa fede in chi non doveva.

But, with a contemptuous fairness, he gives this unworthy ancestor his due :—

Secondo posso ritrarre, fu uomo *che ebbe un poco la lingua lunga*, e dovette essere di poco animo : e non credo anche fussi il più savio cittadino del mondo, ma dovette essere ordinario uomo, massime nelle cose dello Stato. Può bene essere che nelle mercatanzie fussi valente, e gli effetti la dimostrano : perchè quando il padre morì, ebbe a restituire tanto che non gli avanzò molta roba, e non di meno fu poi ricchissimo : e la ricchezza, e lo essere uomo di buona natura e si buona casa, e credo liberale, gli dettono riputazione anche nello Stato.

He is careful to record that there was a bishop in the family; that he was a bastard, and gained his bishopric by simony; and that, though he had plenty of brains and a wonderful memory, he was otherwise very like the laymen of the family :—

Fu uomo di cervello e ingegno assai con modo, ma furioso e mutabile, e di poco animo : ebbe una memoria profonda, colla quale teneva a mente tutti i fatti e le cose sua, benchè non ne scrivessi nessuno. Furono i costumi sua cattivi, perchè e' fu dedito assai alla lussuria, nel quale vizio fu notato pubblicamente e ebbene carico grandissimo non solo da giovane, ma da vecchio e insino al tempo che morì. Nella gola seguitò l' uso degli altri preti che si stanno a Firenze a poltroneggiare, che il pensare a mangiare è una delle maggiori faccende che abbino. Circa allo spendere fu liberale e magnifico in vestire, in tenere buono e onorevole corte, in convitare spesso e bene ; ma avaro nel distribuire le sue entrate secondo le opere della pietà, così in tutto quello che tornassi utile a parenti, co' quali volle sempre vedere le cose minutamente, in modo che nè in vita, nè in morte, non giovò mai loro. Così fu anco avaro co' sua servidori. . . . Fu di natura molto collerico tanto che era quasi intollerabile. La vita sua fu molto prospera, perchè essendo bastardo, e non avendo lettere o virtù, conseguì tanti benefici e tante dignità. . . . Fu di corpo bellissimo, perchè era grande di statura, bianco e bell'aria: fu sanissimo e gagliardissimo. Ebbe alla morte tutti i sacramenti della Chiesa ; non so già con che disposizione gli pigliassi, ma aveva gran paura e dolore della morte. Morì essendo di anni 54, e visse talmente che io n' ho fatto menzione più tosto per fare memoria di quella dignità che ebbe (che innanzi a lui non solo non fu mai vescovo in casa, ma nè ancora forse prete alcuno), che per tenere conto delle qualità e costumi sua.

A pleasanter picture is this of an old Florentine gentlewoman, Guicciardini's grandmother, whose only fault was that she was so timid :—

Non solo ebbe compiutamente tutte quelle parti che

si aspettano a una donna, e di forma che fu più che mediocre, e di governo di casa in che fu eccellente ; ma ancora ebbe ottimo ingegno e giudicio in quelle cose che si aspettano agli uomini. Lei sapeva giuocare comodamente a scacchi e sbaraglino ; leggere benissimo : non era sì forte di abaco, ma che datogli un poco di tempo non avessi fatto, non colle regole ordinarie della aritmetica e che si insegnano per le scuole, ma col cervello suo. Ebbe buona notizia delle cose dello Stato, e tale che molti uomini che vi sono drento adoperati non hanno forse tanta, e volontieri parlava e udiva parlare di tutte quelle cose che sono proprio ragionamento di uomini : ebbevi accompagnata la bontà in modo che visse e morì santamente. Alle parti sopradette se si fussi aggiunto uno animo conveniente, sarebbe stata da ogni banda eccellentissima ; ma la fu più timida ancora che non si aspetta a una donna. Honne voluto fare menzione, perchè rispetto a queste virtù io sono affezionatissimo alla memoria sua : l' ho amata assai mentre era in vita, sendo io ancora fanciullo, perchè la morì nel 1498, e più l' amò così morta, perchè l' età mi fa più gustare le sue virtù.

Of his father Guicciardini speaks always with great tenderness and affection. It is curious, in the letters between him and his brothers, to see the familiar way in which the father is always spoken of by his Christian name, Piero, as if he were one of themselves, and lived with them on terms of equality. He was inclined to the party of Savonarola, and brought up his son carefully and well—" santamente " ; and he did him the inestimable benefit of saving him, in the days of Borgias and Medicis, from seeking riches and advancement by becoming a priest; though by no means to the satisfaction at the time of the ambitious young gentleman, who did not understand being balked by scruples of the benefices of his uncle the bishop :—

Nel detto anno morì Messer Rinieri, mio zio, che era arcidiacono di Firenze e vescovo di Cortona, e avea di entrata di benefici pressa a ducati 1500. E stimandosi per molti, quando aveva male che era infermità lunga, mi dovessi rinunziare i sua benefici, e io desiderandolo. non per poltroneggiarmi colla entrata grande come fanno la più parte degli altri preti, ma perchè mi pareva, sendo io giovane e con qualche lettera, che fussi uno fondamento da farmi grande nella Chiesa, e da poterne sperare di essere un dì Cardinale; e benchè M. Rinieri non fussi molto disposto a rinunziare, pure l' avrebbe fatto con rigresso, e massime quando ne fusse stato stretto da Piero mio padre, a chi portava riverenza grande,—finalmente, non se ne fece nulla. Perchè Piero al tutto dispose di non volere alcuno figliuolo prete, benchè avessi cinque figliuoli maschi, parendogli che le cose della Chiesa fussino molto transcorse: e volle più tosto perdere la utilità grande che era presente e la speranza di fare uno figliuolo gran maestro, che maculare la conscienza sua di fare un figliuolo prete per cupidità di roba o di grandezza; e questa fu la vera cagione che lo mosse, e io ne fu contento il meglio che io potetti.

Guicciardini had the habit, in important crises of his life, when reviewing his position and circumstances, of putting his thoughts into the shape of an address to himself. There is a curious mixture of outspoken satisfaction and genuine self-reproach, joined with a pleasant touch of his affection for his father, in the following call on himself for correction and exertion, which he has preserved among his papers probably because it was written just when he was on the point of losing his father, or perhaps when, without knowing it, he had already lost him. It was written during his embassy in Spain :—

Francesco, la età in che tu sei ora mai, avendo già finito i trent' anni, la grandezza di molti e infiniti benefici che tu medesimo ricognosci avere ricevuti da Dio, lo essere di tanto intelletto che tu conosci la vanità di questa vita, quanto i cattivi debbono temere e i buoni sperare della futura : ti doverebbono ridurre in uno modo di vivere, che tu doveresti deliberarti di voler procedere come si conviene alle ragioni sopradette, e come si appartiene non a uno fanciullo e giovane ma a un vecchio. E poi che Dio ti a dato grazia che nelle cose del mondo la patria e i cittadini tua ti hanno deputato liberamente e ordinariamente a gradi e esercizii sopra la età e li anni tua, e la divina grazia vi t' ha insino a oggi conservato drento con più riputazione e gloria che tu non meriti ; debbi anche nelle cose divine e spirituali accommodarti a questo medesimo maneggio, e fare tali opere che Dio per sua benignità ti abbi a dare quella parte in paradiso che tu medesimo desideri nel mondo. E certo la vita e i costumi tua non sono stati insino a oggi degni di uno uomo nobile, figliuolo di buono padre, allevato da piccolo santamento, nè di quella prudenza che tu giudichi in te: ne vi puoi sanza grandissima vergogna almeno teco medesimo perseverare.

But even filial reverence and affection could not make Guicciardini forego his habitual determination to see a man as he was; and even in favour of his father he could not pass by without animadversion the fault for which he had least patience, want of spirit :—

Fu Piero uomo molto savio, e di grande iudicio e vedere quanto alcuno altro che fussi a Firenze nel tempo suo : e così fu di conscienza buona e netta al pari di ogni altro cittadino, amatore del bene della Città e de' poveri, nè mai fece uno minimo torto a persona. Per le quali cose e per le qualità della casa e passati sua, fu insino da giovane cominciato a essere stimato assai, e così si conservò sempre, in modo che al tempo della morte era in grandissima riputazione : e si teneva che di cervello e gravità, da G. B. Ridolfi in fuora, non fussi in Firenze uomo che lo agguagliassi. E se alla bontà e prudenza sua si fussi aggiunta un poco più di vivacità, sarebbe stato più riputato assai : ma lui, o perchè la natura gli dessi così, o perchè lo richiedessino i tempi che correvano, che furono in verità forti e strani, procedeva nelle cose sue con poco animo e con sospetto grande ; pigliando poche imprese, travagliandosi nelle cose dello Stato adagio e con grande maturità, ne volendo se non quando la necessità o la conscienza lo stringeva dichiarare nelle cose importanti bene lo animo e parere suo. Per il che, non si facendo capo di parte o di imprese nuove, non era così sempre in bocca di ognuno ; non di meno questo procedere li servì ad altro effetto, che in tante turbolenze che ebbe a' tempi sua la Città, lui sempre si conservò in stato e sanza pericolo : il che non accadde a alcuno altro suo pari, che tutti li altri uomini grandi corrono in qualche tempo pericolo della vita o della roba.

II

GUICCIARDINI[1] began and ended as an historian. His first youthful work—unpublished till the other day, when it was printed from his autograph in the archives of his family—was an unfinished *History of Florence* under the "tyranny" (in the old Greek sense) of the first Medici, then under the restored popular government, down to the first great blow struck by the League of Cambrai at the battle of Agnadello or Ghiaradadda—a history in part of his own times, and a remarkable effort for a youth of twenty-five. His last employment, on which death found him still intent, was the great *History of Italy* by which his name is chiefly known. But active public business, not literature, was what he set before himself as his aim, and what was, in fact, the main occupation of his life. He was not an observer looking on at a distance, to whom to be occasionally conversant with the details and responsibilities of action is a novel and curious change to his ordinary habits. He wrote a great deal, and was fully conscious of his qualifications as a writer; but the object and purpose of his life

[1] *Saturday Review*, 13th March 1869.

was not to write and record and pass judgment on what was going on, but to play a leading and important part in it. He and, like him, Machiavelli were writers because they were ambitious and practical politicians, and they wrote out of the abundance of their very real and varied experience. Guicciardini's first literary attempt, his fragment of Florentine history, was probably intended, in part at least, for a practical end. The young advocate, who was diligently training himself, in the exercise of his profession and of the various civil functions which attended it, for the public career on which he had set his mind, and who had shocked his cautious father by laying a foundation for it in a marriage alliance with one of the most powerful houses of Florence, used his time of comparative waiting and leisure, before the stress of real work came upon him, in reviewing the circumstances amidst which he had to begin to act; in tracing back recent events and changes, as far as they were connected with the emergencies of to-day, and practically affected them; in collecting distinctly before his own mind the best judgments he could make about the men, some lately dead, some still alive, who had shaped the present with which he would soon have to do; in clearing and fixing his thoughts as to the tendencies which he saw at work, the dangers and obstacles that were either inherent in things or the legacy of past mistakes, and what in them was inevitable and insuperable, what admitted of resistance or remedy; the conditions which a citizen of Florence, desirous of her welfare and greatness, must take account of, in the state of the world in which he found himself, and the principles on which he might most wisely and hopefully deal with them.

But, with whatever view written, the sketch is the most interesting account which we have of perhaps the most interesting crisis in the history of Florence; the crisis which determined the fate of free and rightful government, and the chances of political improvement in Italy for three centuries to come. The seeds and germs of it were in the city of Florence alone; there only men had the intellect to imagine it, and the head and spirit to aspire after it, in however imperfect a manner. In that Republic alone, perhaps, on the Continent, the idea survived and was seriously entertained, that government is for the governed, and should be, to secure this, by the governed. And the struggle at Florence in the fifteenth and sixteenth centuries was to ascertain whether this was practicable. The verdict of events was against it. The power of the world, in vast and overwhelming and accumulating forces, was in the hands of those whose only notion of government was that it is for the advancement, the pleasure, the glory of those who could get hold of it. To an Emperor of the Romans, to a Vicar of Christ, to a King of France or of Spain, and to those who served them, the political ideas which prevailed at Florence seemed simply the height of impertinent and ridiculous childishness; and in the terrible shocks of war among these mighty and ruthless Powers, these ideas were crushed and perished. But the chimerical ideas which were current with the multitude in Florence, and which interested its public men, are now in substance the ideas of civilised society. With all their gross faults, and their incredible and grotesque blunderings, and with all their fruitless and tragic efforts to accomplish the impossible, Florence and Venice—alas! hating and jealous of one another— were spots in a world of selfish fraud and brute force in which public spirit really lived, and in which reason and justice were allowed to go for something in ordering the civil relations of men; and it was so in Florence more than in Venice. This will always give an interest to their history out of proportion to the smallness of the stage on which it was played, and unaffected by the complete and disastrous eclipse which for a time seemed to pass judgment on the principles which they prematurely sought to realise.

Guicciardini's sketch follows the course of the last two of those alternations which were continually succeeding one another at Florence, between the *Governo stretto* and the *Governo largo,* the "close" and the "open" system of government. Under the first Medici things were far from having yet arrived at the gross despotism of the later ones or of the Dukes of Milan, or even at the arbitrary rule of the men who became upstart "Signori" at Lucca or Bologna. The liberty of Florence, within as much as without, was not an idea without meaning, even to the mind of Lorenzo. But the eternal problem which

the statesmen of Florence were revolving was, how the
city might be free, and yet the wisest and fittest men
govern it; and the eternal oscillation was between
freedom on the one hand, with the chances and
results of ignorance and confusion, and ability and
wisdom on the other, tempting to ambition, usurpa-
tion and violence, and provoking conspiracy or
revolution. With the *Governo largo* power was, it
seemed, sure to come into the hands of unfit and
incapable men, and fit men would decline it or be
excluded. With the *Governo stretto* there might
be the rule of the most competent; but it seemed
equally inevitable that they should turn their power to
their own advantage, and ruin the rights and freedom
of the rest. These are the two sides of the question
which Guicciardini illustrates, with keen penetration
and grave and relentless impartiality, in the $\tau \nu \rho \alpha \nu \nu i \varsigma$
of Cosimo and Lorenzo (they knew the old Greek
term as well as thing); in the restoration of popular
government by Piero Capponi, Francesco Valori, and
Savonarola, and in the modified democracy with a
Gonfaloniere for life under Piero Soderini. The
history is a proof of what the civil education of
Florence was. The work of a young man of twenty-
five (we have the date incidentally given us, when he
was writing, 1508), it is not only a vigorous narrative,
but it is full of that keen discrimination between
appearance and reality which it takes reflection and
experience to give; and of delicate and subtle appreciation of motives, and still more, of the whole of a

complicated and varied character. And, except in the direction of cautious distrust of all things human, it is difficult to discern any bias; on each side he is free of criticism, but he is not afraid to praise. Such a work seems to presuppose great and active discussion of public matters among men of strong and free sense and keen wit, and an early familiarity with such arguments and such company among the younger men; and it illustrates what he says of the difficulty of governing a city like Florence:—

Massime sendo questa una città liberissima nel parlare, piena di ingegni sottilissimi e inquietissimi, e uno imperio piccolo, da non potere cogli utili pascere tutti i cittadini, ma sendo necessario che contentatane una piccola parte, li altri ne fussino escluse.

The narrative is written simply, easily, and succinctly; there is movement in the story as it unfolds itself; and it is written also with a kind of sly archness which reveals a great deal that is not directly shown. We have a companion picture to put beside it, the more mature work of Machiavelli, which goes over much of the same ground; and it does not seem to us that the work of the younger writer, younger not merely in date but when he wrote, suffers by the comparison. Compare, for instance, the account in each of the conspiracy of the Pazzi, or of the administration and character of Lorenzo. Machiavelli is fuller, and perhaps tells us more; but Guicciardini, with just as much subtlety, keenness of insight, and vivid sense of reality, is more rapid and more readable; he is, as yet, less studied; and there is the charm of fresh and personal experience which belongs to a man who is writing in the midst of the things which he relates, who has lived in the midst of the recent actors in them, and reflects what he saw in the scenes he describes, and heard in the circles which discussed them. Many of his passing remarks and criticisms seem the very echoes of the talk of Florence; such a sentence as this, in his character of Savonarola, whom he judges with a curious impartiality:—

Dottissimo in molte facoltà, massime in filosofía, la quale possedeva sì bene e se ne valeva sì a ogni suo proposito, *come se avessi fattala lui.*

Or in his concluding remarks on the Pazzi conspiracy:—

E questo è il fine delle divisioni e discordie civili: lo sterminio di una parte; il capo dell' altra diventa signore della città; i fautori ed aderenti sua, di compagni quasi sudditi; il popolo e lo universale ne rimane schiavo: vanne lo Stato per eredità; e spesse volte di uno savio viene in uno pazzo, che poi dà l' ultimo tuffo alla città.

The history breaks off abruptly in the midst of Soderini's government, the failure of which—as Guicciardini, when he was writing, clearly foresaw—was inevitable, though it need not have been ignominious Four years afterwards, while Guicciardini was in Spain, endeavouring to satisfy Ferdinand for the alleged offences of the Republic in standing aloof from the Holy League against France, and reporting home the fair words which the King gave him, the King's Viceroy in Italy surprised the Republic, upset the popular Government, chased away Soderini, who fled without trying to strike a blow, and with a Spanish army replaced the Medici in Florence. Long afterwards, in another and very different time of distress, when Clement VII. was trying to bargain with the Constable of Bourbon, who was marching on Rome, Guicciardini seems to have been remembering the fate of the Republic, and the way in which it was lost, when he gave the warning that the time of negotiation was in those days often the time for dealing the death-blow—"ricordandosi che spesso si danno i colpi mortali tra la guerra e la tregua."

But the issue of the long experiment, the recent course of which was the subject of the historical sketch which we have been noticing, decided his political views and his course. Soderini's government was the last chance for popular government, and he evidently thought that there was a chance of it if Soderini, who was an honest man, had been an abler and more energetic one. But Soderini shrank equally from what was violent, and what was wisely bold and strong. Guicciardini recounts his father's advice to Soderini, to let the exiled Medici come back and live like citizens at Florence, instead of, like fugitive princes in foreign Courts, stirring up intrigues and exciting pity; but Soderini's timid jealousy shrank from it. In a diary of the time Guicciardini thus writes of him :—

Siamo nell' anno 1512, ed è Gonfaloniere a vita già il nono anno Piero Soderini, ed è la città nelle cose di drento in questi termini; che lui si trova con grande podestà; gli uomini di qualità e a' quali pare convenirsi riputazione, depressi; ed i magistrati e onori si distribuiscono molto largamente e spesso in uomini che non gli meritano, o per ignobilità di casa, o per valere poco ed essere cattivi. Di questo nasce che essendo gran parte degli uomini prudenti quasi alienati dalle cure pubbliche, ed avendo si può dire abbandonata la città; e il Gonfaloniere facendo deliberare le cose ne' numeri grandi, perchè gli uomini savi vi abbino meno parte, e che le si deliberino più a suo modo, rimane la città quasi in sul governo di lui solo. Di che seguita che le cose pubbliche e dello Stato non sono ben governate, e si vive in molte cose quasi a beneficio di natura: perchè lui non può reggere tanto peso essendo solo, o non avendo tale parte, come la esperienza ha mostro, che si potessi meritamente chiamarlo uomo savio e valente (vol. x. p. 87).

He made up his mind, when Soderini fell, that popular government was an impracticable and hopeless attempt; and under the circumstances of the time, and in the condition of Italy and the world, there can be little doubt that, in so judging, he was right. The time for free government had been; the time for freedom, justice, and public spirit might come again, and it has come. But his age was one of those hours of darkness when justice in matters of government speaks in vain, and when the dictates of invincible reason and certain truth are forced, by the unhappiness of the times, to wear the aspect of the most extravagant dreams. It is undeniable that a man of sober sense could have very little hope, in the times which were passing then, of finding the materials of a stable and orderly government in the quick-witted but jealous and sensitive and changeable people of Florence, exposed to perpetual and remorseless intrigues, and made restless by unceasing alarms and terrible dangers; still less that the most honest government of freedom and justice could avail to save its independence amid the clashing and lawless ambitions of Popes and Kings.

A greater man than Guicciardini, when he recognised that the time was not ripe for the triumph of justice and truth, might have preferred to wait in faith, and meanwhile to be counted a fool for his principles and hopes. A lesser man might have weakly struggled to resist the irresistible, and caused misery and confusion by the attempt. Guicciardini, eager for work and conscious of power, was a man to make the best of things. "Nè i pazzi, nè i savii," was one of his sayings, "non possono finalmente resistere *a quello che ha da essere.*" When he came home from Spain, he ranged himself at once on the side of the Medici, and devoted himself to their service. To have a government of purpose, counsel, and force, such as, in that state of the world, it was vain to hope for from the disorderly assemblies and the uncertain and shifting authorities of the "open" democracy, seemed to him the only chance for the independence of Florence; and the Medici seemed the only men capable of heading such a government. To save independence, he was willing, probably with but qualified reluctance, to sacrifice freedom; yet he did not forget that the popular intelligence, which he fully recognised, and the long use of liberty, had made Florence peculiarly difficult to break in to despotism; and he knew the Medici well, though he was very far yet from knowing them as in the course of time he was to know them. But he could see no alternative. The following extracts are from a collection of notes and observations which he left to his family (*Ricordi politici e civili*). They belong to his later life, but they represent the conclusions to which he very early came :—

Più difficultà ha ora la casa de' Medici con tutta la grandezza sua a conservare lo Stato in Firenze che non ebbono gli antichi suoi, privati cittadini, a acquistarlo. La ragione è, che allora la città non aveva gustato la libertà e il vivere largo; anzi, era sempre in mano di pochi, e però chi reggeva lo Stato non aveva lo universale per inimico; perchè a lui importava poco vedere lo Stato più in mano di questi che di quelli. Ma la memoria del vivere populare continuata del 1494 al 1512 si è appiccata tanto nel populo, che eccetto quelli pochi che in uno Stato stretto confidano di potere soprafare gli altri, il resto è inimico di chi è padrone dello Stato, parendogli sia stato tolto a sè medesimo.—*Ricordi politici* (1528), No. 376.

Non disegni alcuno a Firenze potessi fare capo di Stato se non è della linea di Cosimo, la quale anche a mantenervisi ha bisogna de' papati. Nessuno altro, e sia chi vuole, ha tante barbe o tanto seguito che vi possa pensare, se già non vi fussi portato da uno vivere populare, che ha bisogno di capi pubblici; come fu fatto a Piero Soderini; però chi aspira a questi gradi, e non sia della linea de' Medici, ami il vivere del populo.—*Ricordi politici*, No. 377.

Chi non ha in Firenze qualità da farsi capo di Stato, è pazzo a ingolfarsi tanto in uno Stato [particular constitution or form of government] che corra tutta la fortuna sua colla fortuna di quello; perchè è sanza comparagione maggiore la perdita che il guadagno. . . Esempio abondante è a chi se ne ricorda Bernardo Rucellai; e la medesima ragione ci debbe consigliare a temporeggiarci, e intratenerci in modo con chi è capo di Stato, che non abbia causa di averci per inimici e sospetti.

Io sarei pronto a cerrare le mutazioni degli Stati che non mi piacessino, se potessi sperare mutargli da me solo; ma quando mi ricordo che bisogna fare compagnia con altri, e il più delle volte con pazzi e con maligni, e quali non sanno tacere, nè sanno fare, non è cosa che io abhorrisca più a pensare che a questo.—*Ib*. No. 379, 380

Guicciardini, then, frankly accepted what he considered to be the necessities of a Florentine citizen who wanted to take part in public life. He served Leo X.; he served Clement VII.; he served Alessandro, and then, as far as he was allowed, the second Cosimo. And he served them with his eyes open, knowing perfectly what sort of men they were, because active life on any other conditions seemed to him impossible or useless. Every purer and nobler road was closed. His was not that "prudence which makes a man keep silence in an evil time." He saw the world round him with much the same eyes as Machiavelli; but he took what he found with the grave earnest of an accomplished and deeply occupied official, too busy and too positive to speculate on the right hand or the left, to complain, or even much to laugh at things, except in passing; with a touch of involuntary amusement and sarcasm, but with little trace of that grim, terrible humour, telling of intense scorn in the background at the wickedness and still more the weakness round him, which we feel to pervade every line of Machiavelli in his most direct, and even in his most tragic, passages.

Guicciardini's official correspondence, first from the Court of Ferdinand of Aragon, and then as the Pope's representative clothed with supreme civil and military authority in the Emilia and Romagna, is at least as interesting as any portion of this collection. His letters are of much value as documents illustrating the history of the time, and they show a good deal of the man himself. The Spanish Embassy led to nothing, and there was not in reality much to do. The crafty old King amused the young Ambassador with civil speeches, which Guicciardini perfectly understood, and treated him, as he is careful to report, with "discrezione e umanità grandissima," while his Viceroy was plotting and accomplishing the overthrow of the

Ambassador's country. But it gave Guicciardini a near view of a specimen of the kings of the time, and an opportunity of studying for himself one of these formidable potentates; and he was deeply impressed with the King's immense ability, his immense dissimulation, and his terrible power. He quotes the proverb, which he says the Moors have of "this Majesty"—*"che questo Re scrive le lettere a modo suo, e che Dio gliene soscrive tutte."* He appears to have been particularly struck with the military order and organisation which he saw in Spain. Ferdinand's perfect craft and mastery of all indirect ways was long remembered by him with hardly dissembled admiration. The crown of it was that, known to be a deceiver, yet Ferdinand got men to go on trusting him:—

Ancora che uno abbia nome di simulatore o di ingannatore, si vede che pure qualche volta gl' inganni suoi truovano fede. Pare strano a dirlo, ma è verissimo, e io mi ricordo, il Re Cattolico, più che tutti gli altri uomini, essere in questo concetto; e nondimeno ne' suoi maneggi non gli mancava mai chi gli credessi più che il debito: a questo bisogna che proceda o dalla semplicità o dalla cupidità degli uomini; questi per credere facilmente quello desiderano, quelli per non cognoscere.—*Ricordi politici*, No. 105.

The letters of so quick an observer are not likely to want for incidental touches of interest. Spain was not a pleasant place for a foreigner; and he especially notices the contrast of character between Spaniards and Englishmen, then in close alliance with Spain, which was soon to lead to such fierce national antipathy :—

E vedute queste diffidenze comminciate a nascere tra gl' Inghilesi e costoro, si può facilmente dubitare, che avendo ad essere in uno medesimo campo, possa nascere fra loro ogni giorno disparere; massime che le nature non sono conformi, e anche naturalmente queste due nazioni sono molto inimiche.

The correspondence also contains the letters to Guicciardini from his relatives and friends at home. Among them is one with an animated description of the battle of Ravenna, and another with an account, written on the spot, of the overthrow of Soderini's Government.

In the *Carteggio*, a correspondence relating to his government under Leo X. and Clement VII., he plays a much more important part. He shows the qualities of an able and energetic officer, placed in a very difficult and hazardous post, with dangers all round him, with very slippery masters to serve, and expected, as was common in those days, to do the most important work with the most inefficient and desperate means. He was to keep order and peace in the Pope's new conquests, with the corruption and lawlessness of the Court of Rome countenancing and stimulating the disorder of the native factions. He had to maintain the Pope's power by bands of brutal and plundering mercenaries, and to get the money to pay them as he could, in fitful and inadequate supplies.

He was, if we may judge by his correspondence, indefatigable, resolute, vigilant, and, what was very necessary, patient; not fond of severity, but perfectly ready for it. He tells with great satisfaction how, at his first entrance on his office, he had seized a troublesome military partisan of the neighbourhood, of good connections and formidable character, and had him summarily tried and beheaded, without giving him any chance of appealing; a proceeding which he considers to have produced a very good effect. If we are to believe him, his stern but just and impartial rule earned him popularity in these provinces, where plunder and oppression were usually the order of things. But perhaps the most interesting portion of the despatches is that in which he follows day by day the march of the Constable of Bourbon's fierce companies—a fresh invasion of the barbarians on their own account, rather than the advance of a regular army set in motion under the orders of a belligerent Government—to sack Rome, and put the Pope to ransom. It was a mad enterprise, except against an opponent made utterly helpless by his absolute reliance on the devices of insincerity. The band of adventurers marched through Italy in the midst of hostile camps, by almost impassable roads and amid deluges of rain. It was only to attack them; and there were the soldiers to attack them; but the soldiers would not fight without money, and for this the money was not forthcoming, while Clement was vainly offering huge sums to buy off the invaders. Guicciardini's urgent counsels are characteristic of the time. Florence, the Pope's first resource for money, was exhausted. The Pope, he urges, must raise money himself now. It is no use for him to be nice about the means. Let him sell as many Cardinals' hats as he can, and not listen, at such a crisis, to weak and vain scruples. Later, the time for resistance has passed; and then he is urgent about raising the money, if not to fight Bourbon, at least to buy him off:—

Questo capitano franzese (Marchese di Saluzzo) non può essere più debole, nè pensare manco alle cose: la gente d' arme sua male pagata, e i fanti suoi sanza uno quattrino, fanno tanti mali alli amici, che li inimici non so se ne fanno tanti; d' onde nasce la desperazione di populi, il serrarci le terre in sul viso, e tanti disordini; nè lui vuole, può, o sa provvedervi. Dio mi è testimonio che io muoio ogni dì mille volte, trovandomi in tanto caos, necessitato a pensare, a ricordare e importunare ogni minima cosa, e alla fine impotente a farla eseguire. . . . E adunque unico rimedio lo accordo, conosciuto bene da voi, ma mal aiutato; perchè non posso credere che a Firenze siano ora tanti contanti che bastino a fare ritirare costoro [the Imperialists] e vorrei che se non potessino supplire loro (i Fiorentini) ne fussino aiutati da voi; e voi non avendo altro modo, *mettessi mano agli estraordinarii*, i quali non so per che maggiore necessità o maggiore pietà s' abbino ad adoperare: e se voi pensate mettervi mano seguendo la guerra, quanto è meglio farlo ora per levarsela da dosso, e quanto sarà più santo e più pio. E se non vi ne risolvete al presente, vi interverrà come di molte altre cose che fuora di tempo avete voluto fare ... in queste ambiguità vostre e diffidenze di altri veggo che o sarete presi una mattina nel letto, o vi converrà fuggire. Però per l' amore di Dio risolvetevi che l' accordo abbia effetto traendo di qualunque luogo quelli danari che non si possino cavare di Firenze : perchè questo è minore male che qualunque altro.—Al Datario (Giov. Giberti), 11 Aprile 1527.

"Choose the least evil" is his continual appeal ; and selling Cardinals' hats is a less evil than the ruin of Rome and the Pope ; but, at any rate, *choose ;* to fight in earnest, to buy off in earnest, or to throw up the game and fly. The temporising Romans irritate him by telling him that he is too hasty ; that his last alternative is a "partito pazzo e disperato" :—

Non volli allora dire in mio linguaggio altro, se non che è necessario non differire più a risolversi ; e se i mali che si aspettino di questa ruina, sono i maggiori mali che possino essere, stimare manco *tutti gli altri rispetti che questo,* quando anche ce ne sia qualcuno che vaglia più ; dico che s' ha a tornare a gittarsi in terra, *e quanto più presto l' uomo sa quello che ha a essere, tanto è meglio.* 18 Aprile 1527.

The next day—in a little more than a fortnight afterwards Rome was sacked—he returns to the charge. He urges the spiritual mischief of a victory by heretical Lanzknechts as a set off against the scruples of those who hesitated to sell Cardinals' hats to raise money to resist them. It may be doubted whether he cared so much about the spiritual evils themselves which he described, as about the effect on the Pope's measures which his enumeration of them might produce :—

E perchè il punto principale è di provvedere alle spese, e che Firenze da per sè non basta, sendo esausta come ognuno sa, e danneggiata da' soldati inimici e amici, non so che resoluzioni saranno le vostre, e se continuerete in volere più tosto perire che aiutarvi : o se quello che non ha fatto la ragione e la necessità passata, lo farà almanco ora lo sdegno e la desperazione. Non vogliono li inimici, da Nostro Signore e da noi, se non tutto quello abbiamo : non hanno instrumenti e arme seco che solo offendino il temporale, ma ruinano le chiese, profanano li sacramenti, mettono eresìa nella fede di Cristo : alle quali cose chi può fare conato di provvedere e non lo fa, massime essendo in grado chi è obbligato a farlo, credo sia sottoposto alla medesima infamia, alle medesime pene, e alla medesima offesa di Dio che loro. Se in Nostro Signore è tanto animo che possa patire primo perdere la gloria del mondo ; perdere lo stato temporale che hanno acquistato i suoi predecessori ; vedere ruinare la sua patria, che nè per nobiltà nè per qualità di ingegni, nè per li ossequi che ha fatto a casa sua, non lo merita ; privare il sangue suo di quello grado e di quello splendore, che non gli hanno già dato i pontefici, ma le virtù e fortuna degli avoli suoi ;—se tutte queste cose gli paiono vili rispetto a uno proposito (direi parole più gravi, se la riverenza non mi impedissi) che s' ha messo nel l' animo di non volere con fare cardinali e con modi simili evitare tanta ruina, non gli debbi parere vile la autorità spirituale, la fede di Cristo, che perdendosi questa guerra se ne va in preda di Luterani. Non l' ha eletto Dio per suo Vicario a questo effetto, perchè lasci ruinare la chiesa e la fede sua, e empire il mondo di eretici; nè per difendere le cose sacre, la salute dell' anime, la fede nostra, può con buona coscienza scusarsi di fare provisione alcuna. Non è buon capo lasciare andare in preda le cose sante, non coscienza lasciare ruinare la fede di Cristo, non virtù lasciare i Cattolici in preda delli eretici. Ognuno che ha buon gusto conforta e prega Sua Santità a non tardare più a fare danari; a difendersi, poi che non può avere pace; e non voglia per l' amore di Dio differire tanto che siano tardi.

This is certainly not a high view of things. To save the Christian faith by deliberate and wholesale simony appears to him the obvious and reasonable course. But in Guicciardini's world and age it was not so unnatural. He might think that if the Papacy —which as an Italian he wished to support—were rightly maintained by the ordinary courses familiar to all the world in the daily policy of the Popes, a sacrilege more or less, in a moment of extreme danger, could not do much harm, and was not worth standing out about. If Cardinals' hats were constantly sold one by one, he probably could not understand why, in such desperate straits, they should not be sold in a lump. Guicciardini's unscrupulousness must be measured by the service in which he was engaged; and his being in that service at all must be judged of by reference to the conditions of his time.

To follow public life in Italy, when the Most Christian King was Francis I., the Catholic King Ferdinand of Aragon or his grandson, and the Holiness of our Lord the Vicar of Christ was represented in Popes who were also Medici or Farnesi, condemned a man to strange necessities. What is to be said of men like Guicciardini and Machiavelli—who, seeing no escape from these necessities, accepted their evil times as limits of irresistible fate, and made the best of the degraded Sparta to which they were born—is that they were men who, from real public spirit, could not bear to be idle; that they never deceived themselves as to the evils which yet they put up with, because they saw no way to remedy them; and that though the double character of servants and accomplices of fraud and violence, and its clear-sighted and unsparing denouncers, is not a pleasant one, yet they were the pioneers of improvement; they were among those reformers of a transition time, unable to extricate themselves from old trammels, whose acts are too much stamped with the evil habits of the past, but whose words, inconsistent as perhaps they may be, prepare for a better future.

Guicciardini, with the strongest confidence in the force of reason and the power of good counsel, had also the strongest sense of the limits of human foresight, of the immense part in human affairs of the unthought of and unexpected, and of the vanity of wasting strength on refractory obstacles which nothing but time could touch. He had no patience with the restlessness which frittered away a lifetime in varied experiments after what promised to be better, instead of throwing its whole force into one solid and concentrated effort in one direction, which after due balancing of good and bad seemed, if not the best, yet the least bad. His type and continual byword of incapacity was the accomplished but changeable and never satisfied Bernardo Rucellai, as Machiavelli's *bête noire* was Piero Soderini. But he looked in the face, and judged with cold merciless reason, the evils from which he saw no present escape. His plain-speaking has been the warning and lesson to the times after him. To us it seems cynical. But this cynicism has been the way in which in Italy men, short of the highest force of character, or hopelessly kept down by their circumstances, have given vent to their restrained indignation; and it was one side of a genuine and deep desire after that nobler lot of which they felt their country, with all its crimes and follies, to be worthy. Guicciardini, the officer, and an energetic and faithful one, of the Popes and the Medici family, has also, like Machiavelli, faithfully transmitted the tradition which has descended in our days to Giusti and Cavour. He has left the following judgments on that policy and system to which, on national grounds, he gave the main work of his life :—

Non si può dire [he says, commenting on and qualifying Machiavelli's famous chapter on the Roman Church in the *Discorsi* on the First Decade of Livy]—non si può dire tanto male della corte romana che non meriti se ne dica più; perchè è una infamia, uno esemplo di tutti e vituperii e obbrobrii del mondo.

Io non so [he says in his *Ricordi politici*] a chi dispiaccia più che a me la ambizione, la avarizia e la mollizie de' preti. Nondimeno, il grado che ho avuto con più pontefici, m' ha necessitato a amare per il particolare mio la grandezza loro; e se non fussi questo rispetto, avrei amato Martino Lutero quanto me medesimo, non per liberarmi dalle leggi indotte dalla religione cristiana nel modo che è interpretata e intesa communemente, ma per vedere ridurre questa caterva di scelerati a' termini debiti, cioè a restare o sanza vizii o sanza autorità.—*Ricordi politici*, No. 28.

He repeats it again in broader terms :—

Io ho sempre desiderato naturalmente la ruina dello Stato ecclesiastico; e la fortuna ha voluto che sono stati dua pontefici tali che sono stato sforzato desiderare e affaticarmi per la grandezza loro; se non fussi questo rispetto, amerei più Martino Lutero che me medesimo, perchè spererei che la sua setta potessi ruinare o almanco tarpare le ale a questa scelerata tirannide de' preti.—*Ibid.* No. 346.

Tre cose desidero vedere innanzi alla mia morte; ma dubito, ancora che io vivessi molto, non ne vedere alcuna:—uno vivere di republica bene ordinato nella città nostra:—Italia liberata di tutti i Barbari:—e liberato il mondo della tirannide di questi scelerati preti.—*Ibid.* No. 236.

XI

LECKY'S HISTORY OF MORALS[1]

Mr. Lecky's *History of European Morals* may be looked upon as a complement to Mr. Buckle's *History of Civilisation*. Mr. Buckle had regarded the growth of European civilisation mainly as an intellectual progress. In man's increasing knowledge, and increasing power to use the faculties which enable him to extend it, he found the sufficient account of all social improvement. Of course he recognised such a thing as moral improvement; but he could find no reasonable cause for it, except in intellectual improvement. Mr. Lecky believes in another distinct and original source of the advance or deterioration of society. Closely connected as moral improvement or imperfection is with intellectual, it yet is, he holds, not simply dependent on intellectual conditions, but has roots and laws of growth of its own. Morality is something more than an intellectual result, much as it may be helped or impeded by what the intellect does:

[1] *History of European Morals from Augustus to Charlemagne.* By W. E. H. Lecky, M.A. *Saturday Review*, 1st May 1869.

it has its own great and separate phenomena, and the moments of its success or failure are not necessarily coincident with those which mark the history of mere knowledge. European civilisation requires to be regarded on its moral side, for itself, not in an aspect purely subordinate to the study of its intellectual changes. To supply what is wanting or kept out of sight in Mr. Buckle's generalisations; to recall a great and broad side of historical truth at least as important as that on which he has dwelt, and one which is absolutely necessary as the counterbalance and correction of his powerful representations; to trace in their early stages and early changes the springs and beginnings of the great ideas of duty and right which make European civilisation what it is, and which mark it with its peculiar and characteristic notes as much as its conquests in the realms of knowledge; to compare the different steps and alternations of the long battle between what raises and what depresses and injures man's moral nature—this is the subject of Mr. Lecky's great attempt. For a great and remarkable attempt it is, whatever may be our judgment on its success.

Mr. Lecky begins by defining his point of view, and discussing the comparative merits, as theories of morality, of utilitarianism and of what he calls the Stoical or intuitive scheme of morals. He is quite right in doing the first; it was not necessary to do the second, and it may admit of a question whether he was wise in doing it. For Mr. Lecky's business is history, not a philosophy or system of morals; and while he is abundantly entitled to be credited with having thought out for himself his moral doctrines, the great controversies about them are hardly to be settled in an introductory chapter; nor does he seem the man to do it. Mr. Lecky's *forte* is his power of bringing a great number of scattered social phenomena to a focus, putting a distinct meaning on what he has brought together, and connecting these generalised appearances one with another; but in the stage beyond this, where we pass from stating broad facts to philosophising, and where everything depends on sensitiveness to differences, and on the force which at once seizes them with precision and truth, and is able to keep a whole body of them, with all their contrasts and relations, before the attention simultaneously, he does not seem so strong. He seems to us to fail in that kind of powerful and exact handling which goes to the quick, and under which the mind feels that it has made a new and real step in disengaging and precipitating the tangled elements of a difficult subject. He is generally ingenious, but he is often loose. Thus he remarks that "more intense" pleasure is "usually obtained from the grotesque and eccentric than from the perfection of beauty"; and then in the next sentence he lets us see what he means by "intense." It turns out that he takes it for "violent"; "the pleasure derived from beauty is not *violent*, and is in most cases peculiarly mixed with melancholy," as in the contemplation of a lovely landscape. A writer's command over words is imperfect who says that the pleasure of a great tragedy or a great piece of music is less "intense" than that of a good farce, when he only means that it is less "violent." The sentiment that "it is probable that the American inventor of the first anæsthetic has done more for *the real happiness of mankind* than all the moral philosophers from Socrates to Mill," would do passably as a smart impertinence in the mouth of a fast young lady with smoking proclivities; but it is an odd remark to come from an historian of morals. We suppose that Mr. Lecky generalises from his own experience when he gives us the following quaint illustration of the undoubted truth that our æsthetic ideas are affected by association; to us the connection of a blue blouse with "ferocity," even in a butcher's boy, much more in quiet-looking French peasants in diligences, is certainly new :—

I suppose there are few Englishmen into whose first confused impression of France there does not enter a half instinctive feeling of repugnance, caused by the *ferocious appearance* of a peasantry who are all dressed like butchers.

After reading Mr. Lecky's preface, those who are intuitive moralists will probably feel that he has made some forcible and pertinent remarks on their side, and those who are utilitarians will remain utilitarians still; but neither, we take it, will think that he has brought them to the bottom of the subject. It is difficult to be satisfied with Mr. Lecky's term "intuitive morality," when intuition fails completely in every respect as a test and source of virtue, except when explained, as he explains it, as the result of progressive cultivation. The cultivated eye and ear perceive intuitively the merits of Phidias, Raffaelle, or Beethoven; but it cannot be said, in any intelligible sense, that these judgments are derived from intuition. Cultivated and improved man sees at a glance the superiority and the claims of truth, honour, and purity; but to say this tells us nothing as to where he got these sentiments. Mr. Lecky is right in saying that utilitarianism fails to account for them; but we do not see that he solves the riddle. To say that all men have an idea of higher and lower within them, and of the rightful subordination of the lower to the higher, is to tell us little of the life and substance of morality.

His forcible and striking pictures of moral progress show beyond doubt that "unity of tendency" in which he finally places the unity of mankind in moral sentiments. So, too, would a history of art, of painting, or of music, each great step of which marks, not the triumph of mere arbitrary fancy or taste, but of reason, good sense, and truth, capable of abundant and unanswerable justification. Yet to carry back these to any original natural powers—natural and universal, in the sense in which the functions of the eye or ear are natural—is a harder and more complicated task, involving more numerous and more obscure steps, than Mr. Lecky seems to allow for. That human morality under education certainly and distinctly moves in this or that general direction, and not in others; that time and favouring circumstances are necessary elements in its development; that it changes and grows as truly in the race as it does in the progress from the moral ideas and condition of a child to those of a man, is one thing; and of this Mr. Lecky is the able and intelligent expounder. To trace out and disentangle in human nature all the infinitely complicated roots of this growth and development, is another. But if, as it seems to us, he has not been so successful here, he has only been baffled where others have been baffled before him.

Mr. Lecky's proper subject is not philosophy, but history, and here he is more in his element. He has drawn a most impressive picture of the evolution of Christian morality, especially in its early stages, out of the civilisation of the Pagan empire, of the various changes of moral type and standard, of the successive degrees of prominence or decay shown in different classes of virtues, of the proportion between different virtues in the ideal character of the time, and of their influence on one another, to be remarked in the course of this great moral recasting of society. Mr. Lecky has excluded from his plan a number of important points connected with his subject—among others, the question of the real nature of Christianity as a religion; and he professedly confines his inquiry within the limits of the first eight centuries, while the necessities of his subject force him continually to follow it out of these bounds to its later and more instructive developments.

A history of European morals which stops short at Charlemagne, though it really takes in, as of course it must, much of their history to the present day, betrays an imperfect plan; and Mr. Lecky's accumulation of materials, which is very great, is almost too great sometimes for him to know quite what to do with it. There is a want of concentration, of checking one broad statement by another, of keeping in the mind together two or three different views of a subject, and bringing out from them a joint and harmonised result. His learning is sometimes exuberant and ill-digested; and there are occasional marks of haste, as when he makes Euripides the author of the *Eumenides*, and talks of Clarke "following in the steps of the Stoics and of *Butler*"—of Butler the "gentleman in Gloucestershire," and student at a Dissenting Academy, who first became known to Clarke in the character of a humble suitor for the explanation of certain metaphysical difficulties. But after all allowances made for imperfect execution, and for the great diversities of judgment which must inevitably arise on Mr. Lecky's subject, his book occupies a field which no one in England has yet attempted to master; and if he fails to satisfy us, he gives us plenty to think about.

The great and characteristic change, in Mr. Lecky's view, from the ancient to modern morality, may be described as a reversal in order of pre-eminence among the virtues. Mr. Lecky distributes the virtues into groups—the heroic, the amiable (the latter including benevolence, purity, reverence), and the intellectual virtues connected with truth. In classical times, down to those of the Pagan empire, the ideal and type of human excellence made the heroic virtues paramount. The result of Christianity in the world has been to invert this scale. The primary virtues of the old world have become secondary; what were then secondary have been elevated into primary. Christianity first gave new fulness and strength to the amiable virtues, and then placed them on the height once occupied by the heroic ones. Purity foremost, benevolence next, threw into the shade, in the early ages of Christianity, the great virtues of heathen military and civil life—courage, patriotism, magnanimity; and, with more or less variation, they still keep the place they gained. Further, the course of civilisation, especially in science and trade, has brought into prominence a class of virtues which the heathen world honoured, though not in the first place, but which the Church is accused of systematically and deliberately ignoring—the virtues of the intellect, veracity, honesty, fearless love of truth. The victory of Christianity in Europe has raised the standard as regards one set of virtues, those connected with humanity and the relations between the sexes; it has lowered it as regards another, those of the high heroic type of public spirit and self-sacrifice; and it has required the corrective of an antagonist and partly hostile spirit, to force it to give their due place and rank to the great moral duties connected with the exercise of the mind on the facts of the world and existence. We have gained, Mr. Lecky thinks, immeasurably in our care for human life and happiness, in gentleness and sympathy, in the domestic ideal and the refinement and conquest of the lower instincts. We have lost in as great a degree in the loftier and more severe virtues, the noble devotion to the State, the stern unselfishness of the ancient citizen and soldier. We are only beginning to estimate at its due worth the moral passion for mere truth, and to be alive to obligations which religion, as it has been hitherto regarded, has done little to foster, and has often flagrantly violated.

Generalisations like these are brilliant things to read when stated and enforced as a writer like Mr. Lecky states them. They contain in them great elements of truth. Yet the qualifications which they require are so important as to leave us with the misgiving whether, after all, as contributions to real and fruitful knowledge, they are not mental efforts all but thrown away. Doubtless there is truth in Mr. Lecky's leading position, that the scale of the virtues has been sensibly altered between ancient and modern times. There have been changes in what he calls—using, it seems to us, a bad, because equivocal, term—the "rudimentary" virtues of different times; meaning the characteristic and dominant virtue of a period, like patriotism in antiquity, or obedience in monastic times. And he dwells much on the fact that Christianity and civilisation, while they have fostered the amiable and social virtues, have diminished the value and the capacity for those of which Stoicism upheld the type while the great ancients realised it—virtues which rested on the two essentials of an unselfish disinterestedness, able even to dispense with a moral ruler and a future world, and of the subjugation of the affections to the reason. Well, the Stoical ideal was very grand; and public virtue often showed itself very nobly even under the Empire. But when we are told that public virtue, with its high sternness and self-devotion, has given way, both in general estimation and in its capacities for great deeds, under the progress of modern civilisation, it seems to us that Mr. Lecky's instruments for collecting the rays of truth, though they may form a neat and clear image, cut off a great deal of light. They cut off from entering into his field of view some of the grandest and loftiest political spectacles which the world has ever seen. In the civil and military history of the Italian Republics, of France, of England, of Holland, of the United States, terrible deeds have been done, and fatal mistakes committed; but the last thing that can be said is that, in comparison with antiquity, there has been any want of "public souls," or of the highest ideal of public duty. Civilisation, and even religion, under certain conditions, have impaired the heroic type of virtue; it has been a common superficial fallacy to assume that they do so always; but, in an observer like Mr. Lecky, it is a grave mistake in the final result of his calculations, and one which weakens our confidence in his power of generalising from complicated and conflicting elements, that he should bring out as an ascertained law or tendency that under civilisation the virtues which demand effort and self-sacrifice are less thought of, and, when called for, are less ready to come.

Mr. Lecky does full justice to Christianity as a moral movement, though he is apparently unable to make up his mind what to think of its supernatural pretensions. What heathen morality attained to under the Empire was, he says, a very high standard of the heroic virtues in a very select class; but even in that class there was an insensibility to the social and benevolent virtues, and still more to those of purity, though this hardness was much softened down in characters like M. Aurelius and Julian; while in the multitude there was a degradation without control and without hope, going deeper and deeper down in every generation in brutality, licentiousness, vileness of feeling and deed. Wherever Christianity came from, it brought the remedy for this. With its strong leaven of charity, of purity, of fearless assertion of conviction, and with its immense sympathy for the despised and lost, it gave the impulse which began the regeneration of the world. All this is vividly and forcibly exhibited. The picture does not seem to us complete, and it wants those more subtle and delicate touches which test the insight of genius; but no one can deny its vigour. Mr. Lecky is fair in representing the results of the great moral revolution which has brought us to where we are; he seems to us harsh and inconsiderate in his judgment of the conditions under which it was made. He traces the great changes in the standard and practice of humanity. He devotes a remarkable chapter to the position of women in the ancient world and the new. He is, on the whole, full and just in his estimate of the breadth and fruitfulness of these and analogous changes. But he is impatient of the religious temper that went with them, and of the intellectual, and some of the moral, habits which it engendered—habits more or less the natural accompaniments of a religion which believes itself certain. The moral change, he quite allows, depended on religion; but the Church, he thinks, taught men to lie for religion, to persecute for religion, to run wild for religion, to think that they could know what they could not know, and to shut their eyes to what they might see, in the name of religion. The result of its training has been, besides much good, for which we ought to be thankful, much evil which is hard to be undone.

Here, again, Mr. Lecky seems to give us the truth, but not the whole truth. When commenting on the looseness of inquiry and looseness of assertion which no doubt, as he says, are to be seen in early Christian literature, as they mark the intellectual character generally of its time, a writer who is not a sceptic ought to have remembered—and remembering, to have qualified a good many of his statements—to whom the world is indebted for the idea that there is a Truth, and that it is worth working for, suffering tor, dying for; to whom it owes the word "martyr." Mr. Lecky does not bear in mind his own leading doctrine, that the moral growth of mankind has different ages, as widely removed from one another as the stages of bodily development. Things that are absolutely absurd to us were inevitable once; people knew no better, and it was impossible, in the nature of things and the conditions of their age in the world's history, that they should know better. The Church had a great cause to advance—the cause of morality, as even Mr. Lecky sees; the cause of man's relationship to God, as Christians believe. And it had to do this in the face of obvious disadvantages, from the state of society, the narrowness of all possible knowledge, the still backward education and imperfect experience of the human race. It did the work; not as we should do it now, perhaps, but in the ways which seemed the natural and only practicable ways of doing it then. It was a conquest; and Mr. Lecky too summarily blames the Church spirit which is seen in the Fathers for having the necessary virtues, hard and stern, as well as great, of conquerors—of those who risk or sacrifice all for an idea or a conviction which shall benefit mankind. Its exclusiveness, its absolute positiveness, its intolerance, its zeal, its scorn, nay, its occasional unscrupulousness, it has in common with all the great movements which have affected mankind — in common with the modern spirit of reform, with Mr. Bright, Mr. Buckle, and Professor Tyndall. We may perhaps yet learn that doubt can be as intolerant of seeming or claiming to know as faith and conviction ever were of doubt. All this belongs to it as realised in human nature, under given conditions of time and development; it belongs to whatever force of intense conviction has moved and swayed man, and exacted from him the great sacrifice of self-indulgence and the present. To say that the Church had all this on a great scale is only to say that its aims and work were on a great scale, and that its fervour and resolution were in proportion to the greatness of its pretensions and the seriousness of its purpose. Mr. Lecky appreciates the magnitude of the moral change then made; but he seems to us to underrate the enormous difficulties of creating modern morality and the society which accepts it; the obstacles, in themselves and in things round them—often utterly hidden and obscure at the time, and only plain to us—in the way of those who had the heart and daring to attempt it.

To take an instance in his treatment of the history of asceticism. We have seen, from its beginning to its end, the whole course of that history. We have had experience enough to entitle us to form a judgment on the working and ultimate results of the ascetic principle; and if there is a question of it in our own time, this experience may supply weighty reasons against it. Mr. Lecky, naturally enough, thoroughly condemns it, though he does in one place seem to regret the suppression of monasteries as correctives to excessive industrialism; and he has an easy task in painting a repulsive picture of this once powerful ally of Christianity. His details of the lives and deeds of Egyptian and Syrian devotees are undeniable; and though he must be charged with greatly understating one whole side—all that in spirit and aim gave meaning and elevation to what was so extravagant and disagreeable—yet, after all, with all the admissions in its favour, the system does fairly appear extravagant and disagreeable. In our stage of moral development, and under our circumstances, it would be intolerable; but the thing to be borne in mind is that it flourished in a stage of moral development and under circumstances which were not ours. You must take men, even Egyptian monks, not only for what they are, but for what they can be; and it is a perpetual mistake in historical judgments to insist on requiring from men what it was impossible, in the nature of things, that at the time they should be. The ascetic fervour of the early and middle centuries is wrongly judged unless, with all our dislike of it in itself, we look upon it—as indeed we can see it to have been—as a first step, not perhaps in intention yet in fact, tentative; an attempt, rude and wild, to apply to life the Gospel standard.

When we remember what were the enormous, blind, intractable forces on the other side, in the days when it arose, of fierce, reckless, unrestrained sensuality, it seems as if nothing but such an enthusiasm, as inconsiderate and unmeasured, could balance or swing back, on a scale necessary for the progress of the world, the tremendous, ever-renewed, and accumulating pressure in favour of self-indulgence. The severity of the early Church was a rebound and strong medicine against the ruinous dissoluteness of the decaying Empire, which no remedy but a heroic one seemed able to stay. It was undeniably, in its aim and effort, a great stroke in favour of virtue and perfection. Doubtless there was dreadful waste in it—waste of character, affection, happiness, life; but it must be looked upon as a great war, the only one which could have made any impression on the world of that day; and when we think of the waste of men in monasteries, we should remember the waste of men on the other side. The monks and ascetics have perished, as soldiers and workers have perished; but what have they left behind? What have they done to print images, softened now by distance, of moral greatness, strength, height, unselfishness on the mind of society? What would those ages have been, being what they were, and separated by impassable intervals from the possibility of what is so commonplace to us and ready to our hand—what would they have been without this direction given to their grossness and fierce temper, without those examples of fierce self-bridling, and of proportionate discipline? So asceticism taught mankind, though by extravagance and with degeneracy and failure at the end, the hard lesson of the incomparable superiority of the higher over the lower nature. We may doubt whether the greatness of free modern morality—of which part of the greatness is that it is a thing, not of a school or of a choice aristocracy of feeling and mind, but popular, common, and public—could ever have been formed and fixed without passing through the terrible agony of asceticism. All these histories of monks, which lend themselves so easily to our sarcasms, and seem to us almost as disgusting as immorality itself, may be viewed in another way—as the crude, clumsy, distorted, absurd sketches of beginners, who yet have the heart and boldness to try to copy a great and difficult model. They are like the stiff, ungainly figures drawn by the early masters, of the saints and hermits themselves, which, in the hands of the later ones, come to forms of the highest nobleness and beauty. But the early steps must have been passed to reach the later perfection. All this is not, indeed, overlooked by Mr. Lecky; but he does not give it the prominence it deserves, nor remember it sufficiently in his vehement and sometimes almost feminine denunciation of the ascetics.

The same imperfect grasp of the idea of a progress, the same defective appreciation of the suitableness and proportion for one time of what another time may have utterly outgrown, marks Mr. Lecky's generalisations—often very sweeping and trenchant ones—on the intellectual character of the early and middle ages. He denounces at every turn the cast-iron decisions of theology, the intolerance of priests, the stagnation of mind under the rule of the schools. The truth is that there is a good deal too much in his book of these sneers. They come so very glibly to our tongues in these days that a writer with so great a subject before him might have been expected to guard himself against them. Flings and incidental sarcasms against philosophers and reason are justly accounted impertinent in theological writers; they are not better in philosophers against theology and divines. All indiscriminate generalisation is foolish; if with an animus, unjust; if the mere repetition of a commonplace, vulgar; and it ought to be borne in mind that calling men "priests" by way of scorn or disparagement is just as grave an offence against truth, justice, and the real interests of morality as, with the same invidious purpose, calling them freethinkers and rationalists.

Mr. Lecky is abundantly justified in protesting against any such views, philosophical or religious, of those early times, as represent them as ages of perfection to which all succeeding ages ought to look back for their standard and model. But when he uses the very strong words which he ordinarily does of their blind submission to authority in religion, of their hard, unreasoning, and uninquiring faith, their indifference to physical knowledge, and their intellectual barrenness, besides that there is much loose over-statement of the fact, he disappoints those who look to him for a broad and fair comparative estimate of the differences of times. There is a time for everything. There is a time for construction, for building up positive beliefs for practical needs, when men take what on the whole has the recommendation and attraction of apparent truth as an inestimable treasure by which to live and work. At such times, whether they come in regard to religion, or politics, or even mechanical progress, men take foundations for granted; they are too keen about what may be realised to sift and ask questions about them; it was so just as much when a new polity like that of the United Provinces or the United States was called into existence, and a great war carried on, as when Christianity was set up as the religion of Europe. Of course, at such times of positive building up there is abundance of what seems, to cooler or unfriendly observers, unreasoning impatience of inquiry; there is plenty of intolerance; for what at a distance seems only difference of opinion seems, when near, mischievous opposition; what at a distance seems mere party variance, looks near like disloyalty and treason.

The early ages were times when of all things the most impossible to those who lived in them was that keen criticism and subtle inquiry which seem to us so natural and rational. They could judge of things by broad marks; but it is simply inconceivable that they should have examined as, with our means of knowledge and long-trained habits of thought, we can examine. It seems idle to expect it of them, and harsh to complain of them for failing in what would have been in them premature and futile. It is well for us that their belief was so much stronger than their spirit of inquiry. We do not yet know what may come of that spirit in our own more experienced hands; but in those days of narrow knowledge—knowledge confined by limits then absolutely and literally impassable—it would have been like gun-cotton and electricity in the hands of a child.

Mr. Lecky further strangely overstates the stagnation of mind in those times. Mind is employed either in tracking out the knowledge of things outside it, or in examining its own thoughts and history. Its activity ought to take both directions; in the Middle Ages it long shrank, not without intelligible reasons, from the first; but surely the mind cannot be said to be idle when it puts forth its strength on the second. Now, though there was a vast deficiency in that hunting out and ascertaining the facts of nature and history which is so great a work in our days, there was no deficiency in that which is more properly thought—profound and patient and exact consideration of what goes on in the mind, of its efforts to know, of its materials and processes. The Schoolmen have become a commonplace for sneers. But no one who ever studied any of the great ones among them could possibly say that mind in them was dormant. No one could ever say that men like Anselm or Aquinas did not treat the most difficult questions with a freedom and originality which are ordinarily supposed incompatible with their religion. In all that is of most essential consequence, not only in the exhibition of what we know, but in grasping it firmly, clearly, comprehensively, in taking in all the sides of a question, in mapping out all its ramifications, in the sheer hard work of purely intellectual action on ideas and words, they are still our unequalled masters. Most surely, if they led, in their keen and subtle speculations, into many false and useless roads, they paved the way as nothing else did—as certainly neither ancient speculation nor Mahommedan science did—for modern philosophy. They laid out the ground and prepared a language for Spinoza, Leibnitz, and Kant. Those ancient and unwearied pioneers of real thinking deserve more respect than they always meet, from all who know that real thinking is as necessary as the actual discovery of facts, for the true and solid advancement of knowledge.

XII

MORISON'S ST. BERNARD[1]

We have been tardy in noticing Mr. Morison's volume on St. Bernard. But a late notice in some measure makes up for delay by recalling a book to the recollection of readers after its first chance among the new publications of the season has passed. A book may not need this. But if it is a good book, the interest of it deserves and will bear fresh remark, though it is no longer new, and has been much read. And Mr Morison's *Life of St. Bernard* is a very good book.

Mr. Morison has one eminent qualification for the biographer of a man like St. Bernard, and one eminent disqualification. The qualification is a rare faculty of insight and sympathy, which, without committing him in the least to agreement with his hero's ideas, or drawing him into partiality in judging his conduct, yet enables him to comprehend, not merely justly or even generously, but really and completely, his hero's

[1] *Life and Times of St. Bernard.* By J. C. Morison, M.A. *Saturday Review*, 16th September 1871.

position in relation to his times and to the progress of human history. It is obvious that, except with regard to the simplest and most primary elements of all morality and greatness of thought, Mr. Morison does not think with St. Bernard. One who is more than a Protestant traces the character and career of the greatest of mediaeval saints; one who owns the full influence of modern secular civilisation draws the picture of the thoroughgoing and unflinching ascetic, to whom this world was but a short exercising ground—greatly profitable for trial and discipline, but for nothing else—to prepare him for the endless world of his hopes beyond. Yet no sympathising Catholic, no enthusiast for monasticism, has ever entered with greater interest into this combination of the dogmatist with the ecclesiastical statesman, so uncongenial to days like ours, or has traced with more reverent admiration and with more attractiveness the portrait of the Cistercian reformer, with his mixture of austerity and sweetness, of repulsive harshness and irresistible grace. To do this well, without affectation, without the strained and forced efforts arising out of an artificial and unreal position, soberly and as a matter of simple truth to nature and history, is a great proof of power; and this is the great qualification which Mr. Morison has.

His disqualification is one which he shares with some other distinguished writers who have wished to do justice to great mediaeval names. It is a negative disqualification, yet it is a serious one.

He views religion, the spiritual life of the Christian soul, only from the outside; fairly, admiringly, in a higher and worthier way than very many religious men, yet still only from the outside. That sight of the unseen, that burning and inextinguishable love of an object beyond the veil, the new life inspired by this never-failing faith and this ever-growing love—these were the real roots and springs of all that Bernard thought or wished or did. Mr. Morison understands and appreciates the historical greatness and power in which they issued, but he shows no signs of feeling about the things themselves as Bernard felt about them. A representation may be very masterly, yet must be imperfect, which, in describing a saint, discloses a want of power to respond to his devotion, his inward deepest love and aspirations; it may be his likeness, but it does not open to us the living image and expression of his soul, nor adequately even of his mind. It is like writing of a fine artist or a fine musician without feeling music or being moved by art; it may be quite possible to appreciate the man if he has any greatness in him, but imperfect sympathies with that which he loved and lived in cause a great gap. The spiritual and essentially religious side of St. Bernard may not be an easy one to treat as well and as honestly as Mr. Morison has treated his career as a great man in an eventful time; but it must be noted that he has failed to give one, as he has given the other.

St. Bernard has always seemed to us one of those

great religious personages who produce effects very strange and unexpected on some of those who observe them. One of the very foremost and most thoroughgoing representatives of religious completeness, religious effort, religious severity, and uncompromising zeal, he has, on the one hand, attracted the interest and admiration of those who have the very least in common with his religion; and, on the other hand, there is a large class of religious persons, deep and fervent in their religion, and that the religion of the Church, who know that they ought to like and admire St. Bernard, but who cannot get themselves to do so; who, in spite of themselves, feel themselves not drawn to him, but with uneasy and dissatisfied feelings, repelled by the general result of what they see and read of him. This double effect, inverting what might have been anticipated — disturbing and alienating sympathies which might have been thought certain to arise, and kindling into veneration, and sometimes even into enthusiasm, minds far sundered on the questions which are the very hinges of all thought and life—is a phenomenon which, though not common, is far from unique. One part of it is more deserving of notice than the other. The respect and warm reverence of Liberal writers of our day for some of the great ecclesiastical champions and saints is not difficult to understand; it rests on that honest and impartial appreciation of public spirit, originality and ardour, love of justice, unselfish care for others, and fearlessness of personal consequences, which is at the foundation of Liberal principles, and without which their boasts and claims are vain. But the distaste felt by religious men, not so much for the views and principles as for the personality of a great religious leader, is a thing of more subtle and also of more significant character. Of course we are not speaking of those deep theological differences which have a natural power in averting sympathy and engendering dislike. St. Bernard is a great saint, whom many who thoroughly accept his view of the Church, of Christian truth and doctrine, even of ascetic self-discipline and self-conquest, and who are fully sensible of his genius and eloquence, yet regard with an instinctive and unconquerable want of cordiality. They respect and honour him, but they do not like him; they do not quite trust him; and the question why they so feel opens a curious subject of inquiry.

There are two features, very broad and vague ones, yet still very real and certain ones, in St. Bernard's character which seem to help us to understand why a certain class of religious minds, and that a very respectable class, are indisposed to a very cordial interest in him. St. Bernard was a writer and preacher, one whose words are full of a flavour of the highest devotional unction, and of the most refined spiritual emotions. St. Bernard, also, was the busiest and the most powerful man of his time, with the Catholic world of his day as the field of his statesmanship, wielding his influence over all powers and authorities round him, the master and guide of the crowds and of their princes, of Kings and Emperors and Popes. Every one knows, of course, that he did not seek this great position; it came to him; it forced itself on him. He said himself—it has been said for him, with perfect truth—that he could not help himself; it was by no wish of his that he was mixed up in every business that went forward, that he was the oracle of Europe, that he directed its energies and took part in its great disputes. But still, the sense of incongruity, the persistent, uncomfortable, dim, yet obstinate feeling of jar remains between the unction of his writings and the distractions and the vigilant all-embracing energy of his practical life. The poetry, the expansiveness, the unguarded bursts and flights of his soul in the highest sphere of devotional self-abandonment, these mark his manner of teaching and exhorting; and they speak of another manner of man from him who, by what he did and became, must have been a sober, shrewd, and cool watcher of human hearts, human wills, human weaknesses. There is too much exhibition of the mysterious depths of the spiritual life for so resolute and self-possessed a statesman; or there is too much of the willingness for work, the inflexibility, the unscrupulousness as to means, the familiarity with evil, of one who plunges into human affairs and feels his competency to direct them, for one whose language implies the tastes and aspirations of the lover of seclusion and solitude.

That St. Bernard should have joined the two is, with many, one of his titles to praise and admiration.

It is eminently a case where the ordinary suspicions which arise against churchmen who are forward and successful in the world's debate are excluded by all the manifest probabilities of human nature. But a man like St. Bernard does not play such a part as he did in the world without choosing to do so, and without thinking that it was a good thing to play it. To say that he was forced into it is only a manner of speaking; he did not seek it, but when it came, he made no effectual resistance, and threw himself by degrees into it with the whole force of his nature. No one could have worked and ruled as he did without feeling the greatness and the pleasure of ruling. And people who are jealous of the soberness and reality of even the highest forms of devotional and spiritual expression come away from the comparison of his writings and his life with the suspicion that, though there was nothing to blame in his activity, yet with so busy a life he sometimes spoke and wrote too fast, without commanding the rush of emotion or measuring the consistencies of language. After all the coarse doubts about purity of aim and motive have been, as they ought to be, utterly swept away and put out of sight, there still remains that obscure, ill-defined, inscrutable region where the mistakes and temptations of self-deceit have their play out of the sight of men, and insensibly take off the sharp edges of truth and reality, making a man, we hardly can tell why, less great and perfect than we should wish to believe him.

As the prophet and enlightener of his age, Bernard would have been greater and more complete if he had not been the preacher of the Crusade and the vanquisher of Abelard, or even the stern satirist and reformer of the corruptions and abuses of his distinguished pupil's Court at Rome. He was meant for the privacy and quiet of a life of thought, and all that such a life creates. He added to it the dazzling glory of a life of brilliant practical achievement. The pages of history have gained more from it for their varied and sad display than has the perfectness of character in him, who was to bear the torch of spiritual light to his age, the last of the Fathers. He is a warning to all Christian explorers and expounders of truth—a warning all the more emphatic for the singular disinterestedness of his purpose, and the success of much that he attempted —not to be tempted, by the influence which their work in retirement has given them, into those entangling and difficult paths of public activity from which, when once a man has entered on them, it is hard to draw back, and in which it is so easy for the thinker, the divine, the teacher, to pass into the religious partisan, the religious manager and meddler and contriver, forgetting, at once in the purity and elevation of his purpose, and in the intoxication of success, the inherent snares and dangers of power in any human hands.

XIII

IGNATIUS LOYOLA[1]

A REALLY good and discriminating life of one of the most remarkable men of modern Christendom, for such Loyola certainly was, would deserve our warmest thanks and welcome. There is no religious achievement comparable, in brilliancy and in the glory of this world, to that of having founded the Company of Jesus. And it would have been a great triumph for a writer to have enabled the nineteenth century really to enter into the character of one who embodied the spirit of the sixteenth, and to have written of him without sneers and flippancy, and without slavish fascination and worship, yet with enthusiasm and sympathy, which are by no means incompatible with freedom of judgment. Mr. Stewart Rose is a diligent writer, and a devout admirer of his hero; but the eye of the great captain seems so fixed upon him, and his own nature is so imbued with the spirit, not of the

[1] *Ignatius Loyola and the Early Jesuits.* By Stewart Rose. *Saturday Review*, 25th February 1871.

master, but of the feebler and more obsequious of his adoring disciples, that instead of a biography we have only an unnatural and exaggerated panegyric; and his volume, though not wanting in curious and interesting narratives, must fall under that inexorable fate which always attends the violation of the laws of truth and likelihood, which are quite compatible with pictures of almost superhuman sanctity, but which are terrible touchstones of the factitious and conventional perfections of those whom the will and fancy of man, or the traditions and blind reverence of sects and systems, have made into saints.

Mr. Rose begins at the beginning, and tells us, in passable fashion, of Ignatius's family and birthplace. Then he goes on to the period of his youth, which was spent at the Court and in war. What has he to tell us of this early time, usually supposed to have had considerable influence on his after life? "He was generous, even to enemies," says Alban Butler, "but addicted to gallantry, and full of the maxims of worldly honour, vanity, and pleasures." Mr. Rose, apparently, is not satisfied with this. He tells us that Ignatius wrote love poems, but "they were often of a religious character"; "he also wrote a long poem in honour of St. Peter." "With his heart and imagination thus occupied," Mr. Rose proceeds, "he was not tempted to indulge in the common excesses of young men thrown on Courts and camps; he avoided even gambling, the dominant vice of Spain." As far as we can make out, this, except the statement about gambling, in which all accounts agree, is simply Mr. Rose's surmise. Again—

He was scrupulous in speaking always the strictest truth, holding that as indispensable to true nobility; his words were ever guarded and modest, such as a lady might have heard; he was master of his wrath, and never drew his sword on slight occasion.

And so on, with all the characteristics of a true knight and gentleman of the model type. Mr. Rose is indeed a little carried away by the recollection of his hero's "marvellous eyes," full of fascination, and is tempted to admit that "when young he was conscious of his good looks, delighted in gay and splendid attire, and in paying his court to ladies"; which makes one think whether, considering the manners of the time and his way of life, Ignatius was so very much above them as Mr. Rose paints him. But at the end of two or three pages of this kind of writing, the object of which is to produce the impression that even in his unconverted days the saint was very different from the society round him, and even then was a pattern, comes the innocent remark that "of this early portion of his life very little has been left on record, and of that little scarcely anything was derived from the saint's own lips." Why then draw a pretty and sentimental picture of what there is no means of verifying; and why give it a rose colour, about which all the probabilities are that it is utterly unlike the truth? Ignatius is at any rate too great a man to be drawn as a washed-out copy of one of the heroes of Florian's *Gonsalve de Cordoue*. Why not be satisfied with his own simple and straightforward avowal? "He said of himself that up to his twenty-sixth year he was entirely given up to the vanities of the world." There is no need of putting worse into the confession than his words tell us; but neither is there any need of elaborately toning them down.

The fault of the book is indicated by this false start. It is the irretrievable fault of being, not biography, but hagiography; it describes, not a real man, but a character of guaranteed and certain saintship, every one of whose acts must be made to accord with and exemplify the perfection which is postulated of the saint. In first-hand accounts, the accounts of eye-witnesses and friends, such writing is often very interesting and instructive, and almost always pardonable; it shows us a side of a man's nature as persons believed that they actually saw it, and we naturally and easily make allowances for their tenderness and their partialities. But it is different when people sit down, not to record recollections and impressions, but to write a book from documents. The hagiographical style is a vicious one in itself, and it defeats its own purpose. A man who adopts it is pretty sure to be careless about his authorities and evidence, and to blunt his perception of the most ordinary probabilities of character, conduct, and results. And on all but those whose admiration is as exaggerated as his own he produces the effect that it is impossible to discriminate, from his account, between what is really and credibly great in his hero, and what is mere embroidery and fancy-work of his own. Mr. Rose has much to tell us about the great Ignatius, and he can, on occasion, tell it with spirit and interest. But his attitude towards his saint is one of such unreserved and even abject worship that all differences are lost, between what is great and small, between what is high and low, all shades of character are confounded and effaced; and, in the anxiety to give magnitude to the least admirable extravagances and more questionable displays of natural temper in the great man, the proportion disappears between them and what is really original and wonderful in him.

The parallel between Ignatius and Luther, the two polarities of the religious tendencies of the age, is a familiar one, and is not forgotten by Mr. Rose. Loyola became in due time the founder of a great organisation of which the popular, and in a great degree the true, idea is that its object was to place a final barrier against fundamental changes in the Church, by leading and encouraging the freest adaptation to the circumstances of the day in things which were not fundamental. That was the result of his activity; but the great schemes of great men are only partially in their own power, and just as Methodism has become something very different from what Wesley originally meant, so Ignatius did not begin with intending to found the Jesuits. He began with something at once humbler and greater. He began, as Luther began, with a violent and indignant reaction against the blindness and dulness of a firmly settled Catholicism, which had lost eyes and heart for the primary simple realities of its own overwhelming creed. To take religion literally at its word, and not in the shape of authoritative and official compromises, was the great resolution from which sprang the careers both of Luther and of Ignatius. But they took religion on its different sides—the German, on the side of knowledge, intellectual truth, the necessities of the heart and sympathies; the Spaniard, on the side of doing, of practice, obedience, service. To realise in imagination and in conscience the actual truth of the example and words of Christ, and to subdue his own will to a thorough and unqualified compliance with them, was the first great thought of Ignatius; and often as the attempt has been made, it is always in each age an original one, and leads to unthought-of results. He asked no questions; he took what he found; he was troubled with no intellectual doubts; he started with the accepted ideas of the Church about the distance between God and man, and what had been done to bring God and man together; and thence he proceeded with inexorable and unshrinking consecutiveness. And to make others feel like him about the elementary realities of religion, with their natural consequences on life, was all that he at first proposed to himself. In the humbleness of his forecasts, all that he further designed, in the first yearnings of his zeal, was, not to reform Christendom, much less to stem heresy or threatening innovations, but to lose himself, like St. Francis before him, in the hopeless task of bearing witness for the Gospel to the infidels of Palestine. It was like Wesley, with whom the likeness of the great Jesuit founder starts up at each step, going to preach to the Indians; and, like Wesley, Ignatius was sent home again by brethren whom his zeal frightened and offended. Like Wesley, too, the very simplicity and plain thoroughness of his method of realising religion, combined with his spiritual pretensions and his decisive and peremptory calls, long puzzled and disturbed the religious authorities about him. They could not understand any one, not having some heretical notions and aims, living so absolutely according to the Sermon on the Mount as he tried to do; they could not understand that mixture of loftiness and humility, of meekness and force; they could not understand those little knots and companies of young men, partly students and altogether beggars, associated solely for the purpose of confirming one another in stricter and harder lives, and more complete separation from the world; they could not understand his lay preaching, not because lay preaching was thought a strange thing, but because it was so powerful in its plainness of speech. The Inquisition dogged Ignatius from Alcalá and Salamanca to Paris and Venice, and added many a dreary hour of cold and painful prison to his voluntary privations, though he was always in the end released, sometimes unconditionally and with full acquittal, more than once with restrictions. Long after Ignatius had entered on that method of soul-discipline which he embodied in the four weeks of the "Spiritual Exercises," long after the first assembly of the eight companions at Montmartre on the Feast of the Assumption, 1534, the one distinct object in his mind was simply to deepen and strengthen the reality of religious life; and his instruments were self-subjugation, with as little of traditional forms and as much of keen, substantial truth as possible; and next, a study of the influences which affect, take hold of, and guide other minds, and by which souls are converted, and, when converted, trained and secured.

Both the enemies and the eulogists of Ignatius have often assumed that behind all this was the scheme of the great Society which was in time to come. Mr. Rose, seeing, as he generally does, through the eyes of those who ascribed to Ignatius from the first gifts of divine inspiration and prescience, sometimes speaks as if he shared this notion. But the merit of his narrative is that, after all, it leaves what we believe to be the true impression of the early career of Ignatius; as that of a man bent simply on giving reality to the recognised religion round him, and doing it with the extravagance, rudeness, and intemperateness, but also with the enthusiasm, dauntless bravery, and resolute perseverance, which marked the character of his countrymen at that time. The thoroughness, the plain and absolute self-devotion, the skill, narrow in its range yet within its limits most consummate, which brought success to the work of these unshowy and unpretending, but well-tempered and well-tried soldiers of religion, made their Company a power in that age when everything was balancing doubtfully and perilously in opposite directions. Its power, recognised in time, was thrown into the direction of complete and inexorable conservatism and stern and unsparing resistance, when this direction was finally resolved on at Rome; and the Company—sanctioned and incorporated, not without great difficulty and hesitation, under the Farnese Pope, Paul III.—speedily grew, under him and his successors, and under his fierce namesake, Paul IV., Caraffa, once a suspicious observer of the Spaniard, for whom Caraffa's cherished Theatines were not good enough, into the Company of Jesus.

And the Company of Jesus was from the beginning a very different thing from the association which Ignatius first imagined, and from that which he gathered round him at Montmartre; almost as different as the later Jesuits became from the disciples who lived under the eye and guidance of the founder himself. It was full of strange power, and it could do great things; but its power was not of the kind to resist the lowering influences of the policy of the Roman Court, of which in an evil hour it made itself the special champion, and which it undoubtedly saved in the time of danger, but at the cost of passing from a single-hearted enthusiasm for the reform and regeneration of religion to an engine for maintaining at any cost the spiritual supremacy of an unreformed theocracy, with all its insolent pretensions, all its accumulated abuses, and all its falsehoods.

Mr. Rose's book shows very clearly, though he seems entirely unconscious of what he is showing, the transition in the mind and aims of Ignatius from the simple unreserved service of religion to the service, as unreserved, of the Papal cause in the Church. Every word of the admirers of the Company about the deep and general ignorance and corruption which made the enterprise of Ignatius so necessary, about the character of his teaching, about the opposition which he had to surmount, is so much added to the indictment against the government which had brought the Church and religion to such a pass; yet to uphold and extend this government, reformed or unreformed, and to do so with blind and absolute obedience, became the fourth and characteristic vow of the Jesuit rule. The passage from the simpler and nobler ambition of the early attempts to the more magnificent and more definite, but most perverse and fatal, conception of applying the craft and cunning bred in an unprincipled and most corrupt state of society to the purposes of the highest charity, in order to defend the threatened interests of the Church, was a gradual one, but a rapid and a marked one. The original direction of Ignatius's religious reforms was turned aside, first by contact with the theology of the University of Paris, with its rude independence, and with the alarming specimens in it of the novel teaching; next, by his closer view, during his sojourn in Venice and North Italy, of the impending dangers to the traditional Church system from the German religious revolt, and from the dangerous political attitude of Germany and France; and finally, by his residence in Rome, and his immediate connection with that seat of spiritual empire, where the highest religious aspirations and the vilest and foulest intrigues both found their congenial home. The misfortune for Southern Christianity was that its great Reformer, powerful in all those gifts which make a man strong to subjugate his fellows, irresistible in will, overpowering in influence, keen and piercing in speech, matchless in that skill which probes men's folly and uses their weakness, was an ignorant, vehement, self-confident, dauntless Spaniard, whose mind nothing could have opened beyond the narrow range within which he saw with undoubted clearness, and who made up for his incapacity for knowledge by the most unqualified trust in the revelations which he thought were given him, and by the most absolute obedience to the religious authority which he chose to believe to be, in spite of all the tokens of evil upon it, the sole representative of God on earth.

The enthusiast, fighting at any sacrifice against "shadows of religion," and the General of the Order, directing every movement of a vast organisation, and every impulse and purpose of each of its members, with the sagacity and often with the pitiless harshness of a soldier, are distinct characters. The second may be the greater, but, let men say what they will, not the greater in a religious point of view. But it is very manifest that early in his career the seeds of mischief showed themselves which afterwards grew to such a height. That love of power over the souls of others for its own sake, which in some minds, and those of high temper, seems to replace all other objects of ambition and desire, is very visible from the first. It grew with his growth, his sufferings, his devotedness, his success, till it became the marked and formidable characteristic of his Society. The defenders of the Society are as shallow as its ordinary assailants—and that is saying a great deal—when they point triumphantly to the fact, as to a proof of the perfect purity and disinterestedness of the institute, that the Jesuit rules forbade the acceptance of Church honours and power; as if to sway those who sway the world was not worth, to men like Ignatius and those whom he formed, all the preferments and all the titles on earth. Another feature is the stress which he lays on catching the great and the clever among those whom he tried to win over to religion. "He was already allied," writes Mr. Rose, "in close friendship with a remarkable scholar, Simon Rodriguez, whose family was noble; he himself had much talent; his exterior was comely and graceful; he was one of those who verified the sagacious remark of Loyola, that they who were best fitted to succeed in the world were also the best and most useful servants of Christ." "Let them avoid all relations with women," was one of his early cautions to his companions at Rome, "unless those of the highest rank."

He was pleased to find the qualifications which he required in young men of noble birth; "the endowments," he repeated, "which fit a man for eminence in the world are highly valuable in a devout life, and he welcomed such persons as were best fitted to transact the business of the Society and help on God's work with sovereigns and men in power." There may not be much harm in such sayings, but what they led to at last, in the history of the Jesuits, is a proof of how strong was the impulse given by Ignatius to the policy which they indicate.

When Ignatius was at Paris, among the many efforts made by him in the cause of religion and righteousness, Mr. Rose tells the following:—

It came to his knowledge that an unhappy man, probably a Spaniard, was engaged in an illicit amour with a married woman, and in constant danger of losing both life and soul together. Warnings and remonstrances having proved ineffectual, the Saint adopted another expedient. Ascertaining that, on his way to visit the object of his guilty passion, he had to cross a bridge over the lake of Gentilly, Ignatius repaired to the spot in the dusk of the evening, and, taking off his clothes, stationed himself in the water up to the neck, awaiting the moment when the infatuated man should pass over. It was winter, and the water icy cold; and the Saint passed the time praying God with tears to have mercy on this madman, who had no mercy on his own soul. Absorbed in the thought of his criminal purpose, the adulterer neared the bridge, when he was startled by a voice from the water which was vehement in its earnestness. "Go," it said, "and enjoy your odious pleasures at the peril of your life and of your immortal soul. I, meanwhile, will do penance for your sin. Here you will find me when you return; and here every evening, till God, whom I shall never cease imploring, shall bring your crimes, or my life, to an end." At these words, and still more at the sight, he beheld the man stand abashed and confounded . . . he abandoned his guilty purpose, and changed his whole course of life.

This is extravagance; but it is the heroic extravagance of the purest Christian charity, the boundless enthusiasm of the love of holiness and the love of our neighbour. Ignatius at the bridge of Gentilly is the earlier Ignatius. The later is seen, in equal extravagance, and still in heroic self-devotion, but in his new phase, the servant not merely of righteousness, but of a great earthly system supposed to be absolutely divine, in the following story, in which his grand and memorable saying does not alter the mischief and folly of its application :—

He was now past sixty years old, infirm, and broken in health, yet he often said that at a sign from the Pope he would take his staff, and go on foot into Spain, or embark in the first vessel he found at Ostia, without oars, sails, or provisions, not only willingly, but with joy. A nobleman who heard this said, in surprise, "But where would be the prudence of doing this?" "*Prudence, my lord,*" said Ignatius, "*is the virtue of those who command, not of those who obey.*"

And the man who could so obey insisted with

relentless peremptoriness on being so obeyed. Mr. Rose tells much of his sweetness and forbearance. But the stories which have obviously struck Mr. Rose most, and which give a character to his later narrative, are stories of Ignatius's stern discipline. They are sometimes instances of unintelligible harshness, as when he would turn away a member on the spot, rousing him from his bed in the dead of night, for failing in the spirit of the Society; or as when he " dismissed an infirmarian who had led an exemplary life, and though all the Fathers entreated for him, only for an unbecoming jest; and the poor man was dismissed without his habit or money, to travel 1200 miles home." At other times they are relieved with a touch of grim fun, as when he obliged a shy novice, who in some trifling errand had shown more modesty than obedience, to stand in the refectory, ringing a bell, and repeating aloud the words, " *Volo et nolo non habitant in hac domo.*" In the later Ignatius we see one whose single and devoted zeal for religion, as such, had been turned into the narrow channel of religion as it accorded with the interests of the Roman Court; and whose inborn hardness and spirit of command, reviving in his old age, made him a great captain of a widely-dispersed army, but a perilous founder of an institution which was to sway and mould the souls of human beings.

XIV

BOSSUET'S EARLIER SERMONS[1]

CONSIDERING that Bossuet was, if not, as they think him in France, the greatest of modern Christian preachers, at least one of the first, the literary history of his sermons is curious. In one of those careful and elaborate investigations which the French call *études*, and which, if sometimes spoilt by sentiment and fine writing, often display a method and conscientious labour above all praise, and furnish results of great value, M. Gandar has traced this history, and has shown how it is that of these famous sermons anything whatever has come down to us; for it was not Bossuet's own doing that the great mass of them got into print. This is one part of the book, and perhaps the most curious. But, besides, it undertakes to trace the processes by which a great artist like Bossuet worked, as far as they can be recovered; and further, to follow step by step the expansion and

[1] *Bossuet Orateur: Études critiques sur les Sermons de la Jeunesse de Bossuet* (1643-1662). Par E. Gandar. *Saturday Review*, 23rd May 1867.

perfecting of his powers, the changes in his manner of preaching, and the gradual progress by which defects were thrown off, and the final direction and concentration of his intellectual forces determined. M. Gandar's literary judgments partake sometimes of the exaggeration natural to any exclusive study, especially if the student be a Frenchman, and the subject Bossuet. To say that Bossuet was "the most accomplished orator who has appeared in the world since Demosthenes" shows that M. Gandar has something to learn both about Demosthenes and the history of the world. But he has brought great zeal and intelligence to his work, and has spared himself no pains; and Bossuet is sufficiently great to make an inquiry of much interest, which exhibits in authentic detail how he prepared himself for his task as a preacher, and how his great gifts unfolded and shaped themselves.

Bossuet was so emphatically a preacher, that not one of his innumerable sermons was destined by him to be printed and read. In his works there are contained nearly two hundred sermons, either whole or in fragments. Of this number not more than seven were published by himself, and these reluctantly. The funeral sermon on Henrietta Maria was printed at the urgent request of her daughter, the Duchess of Orleans; and when he had preached ten months later over the daughter's tomb, it seemed natural to make the same request, and to accede to it. The precedent had been set, and four other funeral sermons—those on the Queen, the Princess Palatine, Le Tellier, and the Prince of Condé—were printed to gratify family wishes. The funeral sermon on Nicolas Cornet, his old master and the framer of the Five Propositions out of Jansenius, and the sermon at the "Profession" of Mdlle. de la Vallière, were printed in Bossuet's lifetime, but without his consent, and much to his displeasure. He did not, he said, recognise in them his own work. The great sermon on the *Unity of the Church*, preached before the Assembly of the Clergy in 1681, was a sort of public manifesto to Rome and to the whole world, and there was a special reason for printing it. But, besides these, none of Bossuet's sermons were printed by himself, or by others in his lifetime. Further, when Bossuet's friends began to gather up their recollections of him after his death, it was their way to say that he never wrote anything but the divisions, and perhaps the opening, of his sermons on some rough scrap of paper. This was said in his funeral sermon preached by the Abbé de la Rue. It was said by his first biographer Burigny. More remarkably still, it was repeated by the Abbé Ledieu, who had been his secretary, and lived in his intimacy for twenty years:—

Ce n'est, pour la plupart, qu'une ou deux feuilles volantes, où est un texte en tête, un raisonnement, avec ce mot en marge : *Pour l'exorde ;* une division en deux ou trois membres toujours marqués distinctement à la suite du texte et du dessein de l'exorde ; et pour le corps du discours, l'on n'y trouve que quelques passages des saints Pères, beaucoup des Grecs. . . . Hors les grands panégyriques et peu d'autres actions d'éclat, *aucun de ses sermons n'a la forme d'un discours achevé, et plusieurs sont en latin.*

No one could be a better witness than Bossuet's secretary, and there is not the least reason to doubt his account. But it is a curious instance of the way in which stories get about with only half the truth, and in a shape which impairs the interest of that half. Nothing could be more natural than to conclude from this testimony that Bossuet never wrote his sermons ; and it was true enough for the latter part of his life, the twenty years during which Ledieu had been about him. But it was not true that he never wrote them. On the contrary, he began by never preaching without first writing. It was only true that whereas he had begun with writing them, most often from beginning to end, and some of them many times over, he had come at last, partly by long practice, partly by having vast stores of prepared materials to fall back upon on every occasion, not to need such preparation any longer :—

Son secrétaire le voyait d'ailleurs à tout instant préparer ses instructions ; il se faisait alors apporter la Bible ou saint-Augustin ; après avoir relu avec une attention profonde et de suite quelques chapitres de l'Écriture, il lui arrivait de jeter sur le papier quelques notes ; c'étaient en effet, des textes, ou l'indication sommaire d'un plan, la division du discours ; puis il s'absorbait dans sa pensée, méditait, priait, jusqu'au moment de monter en chaire. Il parlait alors sans étude, familièrement, de l'abondance du cœur.

Mais Bossuet n'avait pas toujours procédé ainsi. On a su plus tard, par l'étude même des manuscrits autographes, mieux que par les assertions de ses familiers, mieux que par son propre témoignage, quelle méthode il avait suivie d'abord, et durant de longues années, dans son travail, et quel était le contenu de ces portefeuilles que Ledieu a vus, mais qu'il paraît n'avoir jamais ouverts. Naïf admirateur de son maître, il aurait été ravi d'y trouver tant de discours achevés, et du premier coup d'œil, il aurait reconnu que Bossuet, en préparant ses sermons, n'écrivait en latin que les textes tirés de l'Écriture ou des Pères.

But the story, besides being only half true, was likely to be mischievous ; for if Bossuet had never written his sermons, what editor of his works would think of looking for such manuscripts? M. Gandar reflects with consternation on the risk to which this gossip exposed some of the treasures of French literature. Bossuet's nephew and heir opened and used his uncle's portfolios, which Ledieu his secretary never looked into, and found them full of manuscript sermons ; but he confined himself to making a practical use of them, copying them himself and lending them to the clergy of his diocese. In this way some sermons were lost ; but, in the passing from hand to hand, they dissipated the belief that Bossuet had never written sermons. Yet, when it was first proposed to collect his sermons, no one had any idea of what there was remaining. The Royal Library in 1768 bought fifteen or twenty sermons in Bossuet's own handwriting, but nothing was known of the real state of the case. The person who rescued the sermons and restored them to French literature was one of those indefatigable and obstinate Benedictines, long-winded, prosy, and not always critical, but whom no trouble or labour could daunt, who have done so much for history and letters. Dom Déforis is the perpetual object of attack to all recent editors and critics of Bossuet; but, as M. Gandar says, it is to him that they owe it that they have the mass of Bossuet's sermons at all. He got on the trace of what no one else knew of or cared about; and though much that he recovered was in a fragmentary state, which he did not always treat in the wisest fashion, yet in what he saved were included some of Bossuet's finest and most characteristic sermons :—

J'aurai fixé la juste mesure de ce que nous devons à Déforis, quand j'aurai dit que, depuis la mort de Bossuet, plus de soixante années s'étaient écoulées sans qu'on eût imprimé un seul de ses discours ; que les cinq volumes publiés en 1772, 1778, et 1788, en contiennent près de deux cents dont une centaine sont des chefs-d'œuvre et que, depuis quatre-vingts ans, toutes les recherches de la critique n'ont pas grossi ce recueil d'un seul discours complet.

Poor Déforis, attacked in the eighteenth century by the polite and tasteful Maury for not caring enough for Bossuet's reputation, and for doggedly refusing to suppress or soften his rough and obsolete phrases, and in the nineteenth for bungling additions and want of critical insight—after toiling manfully and not unsuccessfully, for more than twenty years, through a work which at the time brought him little thanks or credit—was charged, when the Revolution broke out, with Jansenism, and with being the author of the Civil Constitution of the Clergy; then, when he indignantly denied the charge, he was imprisoned for the zeal with which he repelled it, and at last sent to the guillotine.

Much the same thing happened to Bossuet's sermons, when they were first edited, as happened to Pascal's *Pensées*. A mass of papers came into the editors' hands, some complete, some in every degree of imperfection; and the editors took what was at that time thought the most judicious course to make them intelligible and useful. They arranged and pieced together; out of two or three fragments they constructed the best they could in the shape of a whole; they dropped what were repetitions, and intercalated bits of their own to connect and clear up the imperfect remains. This process was carried much further by the Portroyalists in the case of Pascal than by Déforis in the case of Bossuet. The Portroyalists, publishing a book for edification, and having a horror of everything violent and excessive in language, omitted a good deal, and softened and toned down more, of Pascal's most characteristic fragments. Déforis did not alter language, and incurred reproach from the narrow purists of his time for introducing such a man as Bossuet in the uncourtly roughness of his early style. Maury complained of his "collecting even Bossuet's dirty linen." But Déforis did not see the importance of exact dates, and he was too ready to play the interpreter of Bossuet. He did this by explanatory additions; but, besides, when he found two or three recensions of the same sermon or paragraph, according as Bossuet had rewritten it, sometimes more than once, and at considerable intervals, instead of giving each bit as he found it, he worked up the whole as well as he could into one composition. He had, as M. Gandar says, to consult the taste of his time, which wanted something which it could read off at once, and did not trouble itself much about critical accuracy in modern classics. They thought it a sensible proceeding when Déforis, finding two sermons on Christmas Day, the later of which repeated portions of the earlier, instead of printing both, to show how Bossuet revised and improved on himself, took what was new in the second sermon, and, in order to avoid repetition, incorporated it in the first, wherever it could be done without "spoiling" the text. Accordingly, the work of all the recent editors of Bossuet has been to pull to pieces all that Déforis had patched together, and to get back all the remains of the sermons into their original state; to determine their chronology, and to exhibit fragments as fragments in their true order; to give us, as they say, "Bossuet, tout Bossuet, et rien que Bossuet"; and great is the complaining of some of them against the blunderings of Déforis. M. Gandar, who appears to be engaged in a work of this kind, is much more reasonable and just. He points out clearly what are now found to be the inconveniences of Déforis's way of working; but he also points out that no one thought them inconveniences in Paris a hundred years ago, and that Déforis was really in advance of his time in his notions of the right way of editing. In the course of his work M. Gandar justifies the stress which he lays on accuracy of editing, by some interesting instances of the way in which Bossuet worked up afresh his previous compositions, preserving the main idea and much of the old language; but cutting down without mercy, striking out what was pretty or ambitious, and bringing what was a diffuse and florid piece of amplification into the compass of a few nervous, compact sentences, where every word is one of common use and every word tells.

The original manuscripts in the Imperial Library, and at Meaux, have been diligently studied, and as it seems to much purpose, by several critics—the Abbé Vaillant, M. Lachat, and especially by M. Floquet. M. Gandar, who has spent five years upon them, finds in them satisfactory indications of Bossuet's way of working. Nothing is met with among them belonging to the time of his Episcopate at Meaux except a few rough notes; and thus Ledieu's statement is confirmed as to his not writing his sermons at this period. Before this time he seems often to have used old material, "revising former compositions, and marking with pencil here and there what was to be left or kept." But allowing for his having then to a certain extent "lived on his store," M. Gandar thinks that up to 1669, when he was made Bishop of Condom, he was in the habit "of writing before he preached." Sometimes this was a hurried sketch, varying from mere notes and outline to a composition unequally finished, with portions only indicated and others more completely developed. M. Gandar in the papers before him detects the marks of the work :—

Quelquefois Bossuet n'a jeté, en effet, sur le papier qu'un sommaire ou des fragments ; quelquefois aussi, bien que le développement paraisse complet et que les phrases soient achevées, il est sensible que nous n'avons sous les yeux que le travail rapide de la dernière heure. La plume court et l'orateur, même en écrivant, improvise. Nous tenons de lui que, dans sa jeunesse, on lui reprochait de se laisser toujours être presser par le temps ; il commençait donc son sermon la veille, un peu tard, résolu à prendre, s'il le fallait, sur son sommeil. Il allait alors toujours devant lui, sans s'arrêter, même pour jeter un regard en arrière. Mais voici que le moment approche où il faudra quitter le cabinet ; à peine aura-t-il assez de loisir pour écrire en toutes lettres les dernières lignes de la conclusion ou l'avant-propos du sermon, qu'il écrivait ordinairement après tout le reste, sur le premier papier venu, et dans le trouble d'un orateur qui déjà se sent en présence de son auditoire.

But at other times he wrote at full leisure; and the character of the page or the deliberateness of the writing shows that he was not working against time :—

Souvent, au contraire, Bossuet écrit dans le recueillement ; il a d'avance embrassé d'un ferme coup d'œil le commencement, le milieu et la fin de son discours. Tantôt les râtures se multiplient et avertissent que l'orateur serre de près les moindres détails de son argumentation et de son style. Tantôt la netteté de l'écriture montre à quel point il s'est rendu maître, par la réflexion, de chacune des idées qu'il exprime, de chacun des termes qu'il emploie. Nous avons ainsi plus d'un discours, dans le Carême des Minimes, par exemple, et surtout dans le Carême du Louvre, auquel on peut dire que Bossuet a mis la dernière main.

We can trace in these manuscripts, M. Gandar thinks, the increasing severity of taste and judgment in the writer. The earlier ones seem to flow rapidly, without any thought of correction ; but as Bossuet grows older, he leaves space in his paper for possible changes, and he is more ready to make them :—

Si les manuscrits ne nous rendent pas l'accent de la parole de Bossuet, ils nous font entrer, plus qu'il n'était possible à ceux qui l'ont entendu de leurs oreilles, dans l'intimité de son commerce, au moment même où il s'enfermait pour méditer son discours. Dès qu'on s'est mis à les parcourir au hasard, ce qui frappe d'abord le plus vivement, c'est la fécondité naturelle d'un génie auquel rien ne coûte ; de bonne heure, il a conscience de ce qu'il peut, et donne carrière à sa plume, sans reserver sur le papier ni une margi, ni un bas de page, ni même entre les lignes assez d'espace pour recevoir autre chose que l'indication d'une variante ou des corrections de quelques mots ; du premier effort, la trame du discours est ourdie et serrée. Ou si parfois Bossuet efface la phrase commencée, c'est pour la reprendre un peu plus loin ; mais, dans l'intervalle, il aura enrichi son développement d'un tour heureux qui achève de mettre l'idée en lumière ou de quelque idée nouvelle qui est venue s'offrir elle-même, déjà revêtue d'une forme, et qui a pris sur le champ sans aucune violence la place qui lui convenait dans la suite de l'amplification oratoire ; il semble qu'on voie jaillir de la source vive et monter le flot puissant de l'inspiration.

Cependant les progrès de l'âge et la réflexion mettent Bossuet en garde contre les illusions de la jeunesse, au moment même où elles semblaient justifiées par le bruit flatteur des applaudissements. Les sermons prêchés au Louvre en 1662 ont cette marge réservée aux corrections, qui manquait encore sur les manuscrits du Carême de 1660 ; à Saint-Germain, en 1666, Bossuet a pris cette coutume qu'il gardera jusqu'à la fin, de plier en deux le feuillet ; c'est qu'il prévoit la nécessité de condamner son premier travail et de le refaire entièrement. Reprend-il désormais les sermons qu'il a déjà prêchés ? Il barre, il efface, ajoute et corrige sur l'ancien texte ; il déchire le feuillet pour remanier plus librement un passage ; insensiblement il se décide à sacrifier l'ouvrage entier, dont nous ne savons même plus l'existence que parcequ'il en a laissé subsister, comme par hasard, quelques lambeaux.

But the written sermons were not, says M. Gandar, written to be repeated by heart. This, Bossuet said himself, he could not do; he would have lost all his force and freedom and energy if he had simply exacted of himself a great effort of memory. He wrote beforehand to make himself sure of his subject and his thoughts, and thoroughly familiar with the ground which he was to go over; then he trusted himself to his powers, and to the circumstances and inspiration of the moment; and probably the sermon written often conveys but an imperfect idea of the sermon preached. But the thing to be noticed is that a preacher of such resources and gifts took so much pains with his pen in preparing himself beforehand, just as if he could not trust himself to find words on the moment, and was going to repeat or simply read his sermon. With an imagination and readiness equal to Fénelon's, says his critic, Bossuet left little to chance; he resembles Pascal in his resolute will, his exacting and scrupulous reason, his severe taste; and he is an instance of a man who had natural gifts enough to gain admiration by their mere exercise, but who for forty years never ceased working, to satisfy his own standard and make himself more perfect.

After giving the literary history of the sermons, M. Gandar proceeds to the main design of his book, which is to trace the gradual unfolding of Bossuet's oratorical genius, and to point out, as far as possible, his modes of study and the influences which affected him. This is done at length, and with ample citations from the sermons; it seems to us, considering the results gained, with some prolixity. For, after all, though it is interesting to go with an intelligent critic like M. Gandar over the sermons of Bossuet, the light which he has to throw on the sources of them is but limited. M. Gandar professes to show us how Bossuet laid deep a foundation of theology in the study of St. Thomas, at the College of Navarre, and then threw himself, first into the Bible, and then into the Fathers, especially Tertullian and Augustine. St. Paul, commented on by St. Augustine, supplies both his doctrine and inspiration. But the bare fact in this case is nothing new, and we do not see that M. Gandar is able to furnish any fresh illustrations of it. So, as to the inquiry how far Bossuet learned from any of his contemporaries, M. Gandar says all that is to be said, but it does not come to much, and most of it is ingenious conjecture. He thinks, and perhaps with justice, that he can trace the effect of Pascal on Bossuet's style. Bossuet professed to have been a sparing reader of French: he knew Corneille and Balzac, and had read some translations from the classics; but to books written in French previous to the *Petites Lettres* he had been indifferent. The year during which Pascal's letters came out (1656 and the beginning of 1657) was just the time of Bossuet's first prolonged stay in Paris, after quitting his college and gaining considerable provincial reputation as a preacher at Metz. Bossuet must have read them as they appeared; their subject had the deepest interest for him; and we know that he spoke of their "force, vehemence, and grace" with admiration, though M. Gandar rejects Voltaire's apocryphal story that Bossuet once said that, except his own works, he would rather, of all others, have written the *Provinciales*. But M. Gandar points out with some force that Bossuet was in some danger from his own tendency to magnificence and pompous amplitude, a tendency which the taste and feeling of the time fostered; and that to this tendency the undeniable combination of simplicity and power in the *Provinciales* probably acted as a fortunate check. A change accordingly is, he thinks, discoverable in Bossuet's style after the date of the *Letters*. Bossuet still followed the bent of his genius to majesty and richness; he did not attempt to exchange it for an unnatural endeavour after a more severe and unadorned manner; yet he wrote with more chastened taste, and with a keener sensitiveness to the merit of not saying too much. It seems more doubtful whether, as M. Gandar thinks, the substance of Pascal's letters produced as important an impression on Bossuet as the astonishing originality and perfection of the style. It was not necessary to be a Portroyalist to have strong opinions against the *morale relâchée;* and Bossuet did not need Pascal to quicken his zeal, in theory, at any rate, against it; but Bossuet's pride was to keep the difficult balance between ancient theology and modern necessities, and to be tolerant of inevitable facts, at least in his own Church, at the expense of logical consistency; and this moderation it was the glory or the folly of the *Provinciales* to refuse.

M. Gandar also goes at length into a comparison between a number of passages, certainly full of striking resemblances, from the sermons and the *Pensées*. It has been a question of late between the admirers of the two great writers—such as M. Havet on one side and M. Floquet on the other—whether Bossuet imitated Pascal, or whether many of the *Pensées* are not echoes of the sermons. The coincidence, in a number of passages which M. Gandar brings together, is no doubt very remarkable. Plagiarism has been established before now on less proof. But M. Gandar's conclusion seems the sensible one—that both writers drew from a common fund of thought and language to be found in the religious, philosophical, and ascetic works with which both were familiar, and which passed from these works into the current ideas and discourse of the religious society of the time, which was active-minded and interested in such subjects to a degree far beyond anything among ourselves. And though it is possible that Pascal may have heard Bossuet, and more than probable that Bossuet read the *Pensées* as soon as they were published, yet there is no reason to think that the similar language and touches which each used about the same great and familiar commonplaces of man's nature and condition are more than can be accounted for by the sameness of the atmosphere of feeling, studies, and tradition in which both lived, and by their immeasurable superiority to their contemporaries in the gift of thinking powerfully and clearly, and saying what they thought. The likeness is found, too, before they could have been acquainted, as well as afterwards; and M. Gandar observes, in giving instances of their parallel treatment of the same thought, that " the difference of their genius is perhaps never more clear than when it has happened that each has said nearly the same thing in nearly the same words." We do not always make sufficient allowance for the degree in which great writers are the mouthpieces of the common talk round them, expressing in its easiest and most natural form what all are saying. Their coincidence often means that each has seen for himself what is in many minds, and has caught the secret of putting it into its right shape.

Bossuet was a preacher from his youth, and M. Gandar accepts the story told by Tallemant des Réaux, and confirmed by Ledieu, of his being sent for when a boy of fifteen to the Hôtel de Rambouillet, and having a subject given him, on which he extemporised a sermon before the select audience, which lasted till past midnight, and gave occasion to Voiture's *mot*, " Qu'il n'avait jamais entendu prêcher si tôt ni si tard." But they were accustomed to preach, or to *prêchoter*, early in those days. De Rancé, says M. Gandar, was preaching, not to private companies, but in the churches at Paris, at fifteen years old. Bossuet, however, was something more than a wonderful boy; and it is not surprising that he felt his powers, and from the first formed the purpose, which it is plain that he did, and kept with unyielding tenacity, to become a great preacher. He distinguished himself by his addresses in the chapel of the College of Navarre while still a student; but it was during the half-dozen years of his residence at Metz— years of retirement and combined hard study and practice—that he laid the foundations of his power. He always spoke of them as his years of severe yet delightful preparation. In his Metz sermons his characteristics appear—his fire and swing and vehement flow, his power of infusing a sense of serious reality into the commonplaces of the pulpit, his unrivalled gift of sarcasm, and his readiness to use it. But he falls into bad taste, and often does not know when to stop and disengage himself from a thought which has got hold of him. Yet the interval between Bossuet at Metz and Bossuet when first beginning to preach at Paris is not so great as between Bossuet's first *carême* at Paris in 1660 and his third in 1662. The last stride in perfection is the most rapid and the most marked. It is curious to observe, while in tone and general manner he is the same—as indeed he is from the beginning, too declamatory for our English taste, yet undeniably full of deep and real observation of the broad facts of life—how great is the improvement in command over his powers and his subject, in robust and nervous vigour, in largeness of view and aim, in strong and lucid statement, after living in contact with the society of Paris. But for the detail of all this we must refer to M. Gandar's book. It is a volume of intelligent, equitable, and refined criticism ; and the writer has prepared himself for instructing us on his theme by the trouble and the thoroughness of the study by which he has made himself master of it.

XV

JANSENIST EXPOSITIONS OF SCRIPTURE[1]

A RELIC of the later Jansenist literature—and that an elaborate exposition of the figurative language of Scripture—is rather a singular work to be republished in modern Paris by the bookseller of the Institute and the Senate. Neither Jansenism, apart from the genius and the sufferings of its early leaders, nor that close and minute study of the Bible which is familiar to English religion, is supposed to be very popular or very much respected in France; and the circle there, we should think, must be a narrow one, which is likely to enter with any interest into the ideas of a writer who founds a scheme of religious history, past and present, on a comparison and arrangement of the symbolical language of prophecies and parables. But the work before us is not the only one by the same writer, and bearing on the same general subject, which has been lately reprinted in Paris. It may be that

[1] *Histoire de la Religion représentée dans l'Écriture Sainte sous divers Symboles.* Par M. l'Abbé d'Etémare. *Saturday Review*, 14th March 1863.

these republications indicate new currents of religious feeling and thought—that a reaction against the fashionable and rampant Ultramontanism is setting some independent and serious minds in the direction of views which are a byword with Ultramontanism, and of studies for which it has no sympathy, and is inclining them to study the Bible as devout and zealous Protestants study it, or even to look with reviving favour on the almost silent and forgotten teaching of the "Appellants" from the Bull "Unigenitus." Unlikely as it seems, and as in fact it is, that the leading ideas of Jansenism should again gain ground in France, there are circumstances in the situation of the country, and permanent elements in the French character, which make it not inconceivable that something of the kind should come to pass. If Jansenism had a lame and inglorious end, no Frenchman can ever forget its magnificent beginnings; and in this age of surprises more extraordinary things might happen than to see some Frenchmen, austere, extreme, uncompromising, and learned, going back to seek for weapons against religious shallowness and social corruption at the hands of Pascal and his companions, or even their successors.

The Abbé d'Etémare, some of whose works on the Interpretation of Scripture have recently been republished, is a person whose name many a modern reader would own without confusion that he never heard of. Yet he was a very considerable person in his day, in that later development of the Jansenist party which has now fallen into the dimmest background of history, but which during the first part of the last century kept things alive in more senses than one, and gave trouble enough, not merely to Bishops and controversialists and Theological faculties, but to Kings and Popes themselves. His long life connected the days of Louis XIV. with those of Joseph II. and Frederick the Great. He was alive while the great Arnauld was still living, and he was a hot and vigorous fellow-combatant for the same cause with Arnauld's successor, Quesnel. He was one of the earliest and most indefatigable of the famous band who appealed to a future Council against the Bull "Unigenitus" of Clement XI., which was meant to dispose finally of Jansenist doctrines, and which has always been taken in the Roman Church to be their inexorable condemnation. He lived to see Ganganelli Pope, and almost lived to see the suppression of the Jesuits, and the acts of Scipio de Ricci, and the Synod of Pistoia. In the whole later history of Jansenism he was a prominent figure. He had all the Jansenist activity, the Jansenist conscientious obstinacy, the Jansenist unwearied perseverance, the Jansenist flow of facile, even writing, the Jansenist mixture of disinterested humility with impracticable pertinacity of opinion. Seeking nothing for himself, he would go with the most unfeigned spirit of general submission and subordination to the verge of stout rebellion on the one point in dispute. He committed himself deeply to the miserable displays of fanatical extravagance to which the successors of

Port Royal at last descended. He accepted the exhibitions of the *convulsionnaires* at the tomb of the Deacon Pâris, as the outpouring of Divine and miraculous power, witnessing to the truth taught by his party. He vainly attempted to control the mad outbursts of frenzy, and to distinguish between the true and the false miracles, between imposture and grace; and he was involved in all the bitter war of recrimination which followed.

Jansenism never recovered the crushing discredit of those great scandals; and M. d'Etémare's reputation, not altogether uncompromised even with his own party, sank with the cause which, leaving argument and a pure ideal of Christian life, had risked an appeal to supernatural sanction, and fallen into the hands of the coarsest and basest of its supporters. But M. d'Etémare had all the characteristic stiffness and staunchness of a Jansenist. In spite of the loss of character and influence following on the exhibitions of the *convulsionnaires*, he held on his way, stout in his convictions, sanguine and undismayed. He was not one of those who flinched from going with his party, or who despaired of it because it seemed to be rushing into absurdity; and he received honour accordingly. He was a depositary of all the Jansenist traditions; and M. Ste. Beuve refers continually to his papers, as preserving recollections about his predecessors and friends which would otherwise have been lost. It is from him that he quotes a story about Pascal which is typical of what has often happened where wit and learning have encountered one another. Pascal had once a long conference, for two hours, with the Père Thomassin of the Oratory, one of the most learned ecclesiastics of that learned age:—

Et au sortir de là, le P. Thomassin disait: "Voilà un jeune homme qui a bien de l'esprit, mais qui est bien ignorant." Et Pascal, une fois le dos tourné, se prit à dire: "Voilà un bonhomme qui est terriblement savant, mais qui n'a guère d'esprit."

The specimens of the Abbé's writings lately reprinted are not directly connected with the controversies of Jansenism; but they are highly illustrative of the Jansenist teaching. The first thing to be noticed of them is that they are, to a degree unusual in most orthodox Roman Catholic writings, Biblical. They concern themselves entirely with the structure of the Bible. They make its texts the exclusive basis of argument and illustration, and they handle its language with a freedom and familiar knowledge which is not commonly found except among persons accustomed, as Protestants are accustomed from their childhood, to the reading and use of Scripture. It was one of the earliest tendencies and efforts of the friends of Port Royal to popularise the Bible, and to make it in their own Church the household book of devotion and religious teaching which the schismatic and heretical Protestants had succeeded in making it. In their controversies, in their austere self-education and self-discipline, in their straining after the highest ideal of

Christian perfection, their taste for the simple and the solid led them back to the most sacred and authentic monument of religious truth, and made them feel the contrast of its rude but venerable words, fresh from the lips of Prophets and Apostles, with the subtleties and theories, the accommodations and refinements, the pretty elegancies and the dangerous softenings down of the popular modes of religion, and even with the wholesome and necessary learning with which they were themselves so amply furnished, drawn from the Fathers of the Church and the schools of theology. New translations of the Scriptures, and plain practical commentaries and reflections upon them, were the labours on which they set most value, and among these were some of the books which brought them most into trouble. De Saci's translations, especially the New Testament of Mons, and above all the *Réflexions Morales* of Quesnel on St. Matthew, the source of the 101 propositions of the Bull "Unigenitus," were famous books in the long controversy between the Jansenists and their opponents. Nor were the greater spirits of the French Church without sympathy with them in their desire to make people study and feel the Bible. Bossuet was so great a quoter and translator of Scripture texts in all his writings that a French New Testament, if not a French Bible, has recently been published, made up almost completely by piecing together the Scripture extracts dispersed through his works. Bossuet, doubtless, unhampered by controversies and the necessities of his position, would have urged the reading of the French Bible on his flock as strongly as the Portroyalists ; but, as it was, he left it to them to recommend the Bible as a book, not only of theology for scholars and divines, but of comfort and guidance for the unlearned reader. The Portroyalists were the first, we believe, whether among Roman Catholics or Protestants, who distinctly conceived and executed consistently and intelligently the plan, familiar enough to us, of a "plain commentary," without any show of learning, and intended simply for practical instruction and simple explanations. From them this familiarity with the Bible passed into the Jansenist school generally, and it is a conspicuous feature in the representative and specimen of that school whom we are noticing.

But M. d'Etémare's book is also an example of a very peculiar method of Scripture interpretation and application. He is one of the most systematic, thoroughgoing, and ingenious exponents of the idea that Scripture was, from first to last, so constructed as to be one great intentional parable, containing in itself countless other parables, figures, and enigmatic symbols, about the dealings of God with men and with His Church. The idea itself, in its general aspect, is a very old one, and one claiming high sanction. "Which things are an allegory," expresses not only the Apostle's judgment of the use to be made of the older Scriptures, but the natural and inevitable effect on the mind, to the end of time, and in thinkers of the most opposite schools, of perceiving the reflection, especially if it be in ancient and sacred words and histories, of what most powerfully interests and affects ourselves. Loosely and unsystematically, but purposely, the principle had been applied by the earliest interpreters of the Bible; and it had naturally attracted the attention of the thinkers of Port Royal. Pascal had been deeply struck and captivated by what seemed to him the manifest purpose of figures and symbols, and the surprising correspondence of the later truths and facts which accounted for them and gave them meaning. Yet he had given a warning that, if there were figures which were clear and demonstrative, there were others "qui semblent un peu tirées par les cheveux, et qui ne prouvent qu'à ceux qui sont persuadés d'ailleurs." It was many years after Pascal, yet probably not uninfluenced by his remarkable fragments, that Jansenist divines began, in their systematic and methodical manner, to lay down rules and general principles for the interpretation of Scripture as a great figurative scheme. M. Duguet, of whom Ste. Beuve gives a characteristic sketch in his book on Port Royal, and from whom even Bossuet seems to have caught fresh ideas, was the first master of this use of the Bible. M. d'Etémare was his pupil. His book carries the idea to great lengths. It is a favourable contrast, in point of good taste, sober expression, and orderly arrangement, with most Protestant treatises on the same subject, from which in spirit and sentiment it is not very distant.

And it is a curious example of that union of extreme and exaggerated conclusions with severe modesty of statement, and clear yet temperate argument in details, which is so often seen in the school on which Arnauld and Nicole had set their mark.

His notion is, that any expression in Scripture drawn from nature, or the works of art, or the ways of man, is a definitely intended symbol of something spiritual; and that each set of symbols drawn from one class of objects form in themselves a whole. The symbols from light—the sun, moon and stars, lamps and candlesticks, brightness and darkness, form one set; those from stones and buildings, from houses and temples, form another; those from corn and harvest, from the relations of marriage, from the wine and the vineyard, yet other sets. And each set, followed out in its completeness, represents the same great series of truths respecting the dealings of God, the conduct of men, and the destiny of the Church and the world. But in Scripture these sets of symbols are mixed up and interwoven one with another; for the understanding of them is not meant to be obvious at first sight, but to be discerned in the due and fitting time, and also as the reward of patient and diligent labour. "L'Écriture," he says, "n'est autre chose que le tissu de toutes ces énigmes entrelacées les unes dans les autres." So the business of the interpreter is to disengage and disentangle these different sets and series of parables, as they run into one another, and, following each class of images, as they break off in one place and reappear in another, to reinstate them in their true order and connection.

C'est ainsi qu'il suffit que dans un seul endroit la même nation soit représentée sous la figure d'un vase et en même temps sous celle d'une épouse fidèle ou infidèle, pour nous apprendre que ces deux symboles nous représentent les mêmes objets, et pour aller chercher dans la parabole prise des vases le supplément de celle qui est prise des épouses ; pour nous faire comprendre que tous les endroits de l'Écriture qui parlent de l'une ou de l'autre figure sont dépendants les unes des autres, et pour nous porter à rassembler les traits épars en divers livres, à les remettre dans leur ordre, afin de rétablir l'une et l'autre parabole dans sa suite naturelle.

Il faut faire en cela à peu près ce que font ceux que l'on appelle des compositeurs en termes d'imprimerie. Avant de composer la forme qui doit servir à imprimer une feuille, ils ont chacune des lettres de l'alphabet, ou plutôt une multitude de chaque lettre rassemblée dans la case qui lui convient séparément de toutes les autres. C'est ainsi que l'on trouve tous les *a*, tous les *b*, tous les *c*, et ainsi des autres. En composant cette forme ils dérangent cet ordre, mêlant, les unes avec les autres, toutes ces lettres qui étaient séparées. C'est un pareil mélange qui est fait en composant chaque livre de l'Écriture, qui se trouve entremêlé d'une multitude de différents symboles. Or, il est question de prendre de nouveau chacun de ces symboles et de le remettre dans sa place naturelle, en imitant ce que font ces compositeurs, quand ils rompent leur forme ; car alors ils reprennent toutes, les unes après les autres, ces lettres qu'ils avaient mêlées et confondues entre elles, pour remettre chaque lettre dans la case qui lui est propre avec toutes les autres du même nom et de la même forme.

The parallel is ingeniously expressed. But it does not seem to occur to the writer that in fact he does much more than "restore the types, of which the printing was composed, each to its case." When he has done this, he sets to work to rearrange them, and out of them to make words of his own, according to the "copy" before him. He not only sorts the symbols and figures, but he presents them in a very distinct combination—in an order determined by the interpreter himself. The various series of symbols, separated and drawn out in a connected array, certainly do, under his disposing hand, represent the ideas and the course of events which he tells us that they represent. But they are made to do so, in obedience to a principle of arrangement already in the writer's mind.

The key of the arrangement is in the view taken by the Jansenist party of the Roman Catholic Church and their own relations to it. They held the Church, of which the Pope was head, to be the one and only Catholic Church; but they also held that, though the Church could never fail, it might be filled, even in its highest places, with corruption and apostasy, and that truth and hope in it might come to be represented by a feeble remnant, who, as long as, in spite of persecution and oppression, they clung to the Church, were safe from being confounded with the schismatics who denied and disowned the Church. This is the view which governs this ingenious, yet often really thoughtful and striking, application of Scripture parallels and imagery. While the "ignorant Catholics," we are told, dwell exclusively on the promises made to the Church, and, appealing to them, refuse to see the plain facts of evil and error within it, and while the "pretended Reformers" dwell equally exclusively on the prophecies of apostasy and punishment, the Jansenist view reconciles both sets of facts.

And it must be confessed that the idea of great and highly-favoured institutions falling away and becoming degenerate, and of a minority witnessing for truth and goodness against error and hypocrisy in high places, is one so consonant with what is shown and dwelt upon in Scripture, and with the nature of things itself, that it is not difficult to see how it would lend itself to the use which a fervent Jansenist would make of it. The parallel between the "Synagogue"—the proud and learned, and yet corrupt representative of the chosen people, which had Caiaphas and Herod for its chiefs—and the Papal Church of the days of Louis XIV. and the Regency, admitted of being effectively drawn out. What had to be assumed was, that the Jansenists were the counterpart of the rising Christian Church, *in* the Synagogue, and yet not of it—joining in its worship and acknowledging its authority, though regarded by it as an heretical sect, but destined to outgrow it, and see its judgment and ruin. It was an assumption which the Jansenists found no difficulty in making.

M. Ste. Beuve transcribes the report of a conversation between Bossuet and Duguet, on the evils and scandals of which their days were full, and which Duguet wound up with the exclamation—"Monsieur, il nous faut un nouveau peuple." The words were not vague ones. They express the great governing thought of the Jansenist party. They thought that things had come to such a pass in the Christian world that the hour of vengeance and deliverance was close at hand; that the rejection of the greater portion of professing Christians was as certain as the rejection of the Jewish Church of old; that the faith and hope of the Church was to be continued and preserved in the despised and excommunicated remnant which maintained the doctrines of grace, and had appealed against the injustice and error of the Pope; and that the "new people," which was to take the place of a fallen and reprobate society, and to renew yet more auspiciously the glories of the early Church, was to be formed by the conversion of the Jews, who were to be joined to the faithful remnant. The conversion of the Jews, imminent and certain, is the *point de mire* of the Jansenist explanation of prophecies and types. As far as appears, less was done to try to bring it about than is attempted by our sanguine societies. Still it was the practical turn of affairs, the coming sign on which the Jansenists' hope seems to have rested. At a time when their prospects appear most visibly on the decline, they are convinced that their troubles are but the certain proof that a new era of triumph was about to open. " En un mot," as Ste. Beuve says, "ils croient que Port-Royal est *un commencement;* tandis que c'était trop manifestement une fin."

XVI

FÉNELON'S MYSTICISM[1]

MYSTICISM, like metaphysics, is a word with a core of substantial meaning, but with an envelope of nebulous praise or dispraise which has little or none. Something of the same kind bids fair to befall the antagonist word "positive" when it is a little older. "Mystical" stands conveniently for something at once grand and hazy, whether we mean, in thus qualifying what we speak of, to express reverential admiration or a contemptuous sneer. It is a word pretty sure to occur in describing Buddhism and other Oriental schools; or Plato, or the Alexandrians, whether Jewish, New Platonist, or Christian; or the method of allegorical interpretation, or the devotional writers of the middle and modern ages, from the writers of the school of St. Victor and Tauler to St. Theresa. Unsympathising critics would fix the name of mystical on Hooker's description of man's aspiration after good "beyond the reach of sense; yea somewhat above capacity of

[1] *Le Mysticisme en France au temps de Fénelon.* Par M. Matter. *Saturday Review*, 14th December 1867.

reason which the mind with hidden exultation rather surmiseth than conceiveth"; or on M. Guizot's account, lately quoted in our columns, of the obstinate faith of the beaten "party of good sense and moral feeling" in the power of truth, honesty, and justice; or on arguments for the truths of natural religion, based on men's moral sentiments and ideals, which, if not constant and universal, are indestructible as facts, and are allied to what is greatest and noblest in their nature. The epithet mystical, applied in such cases, is understood to be a sort of broom which sweeps away cobwebs and saves time; but so vague and so imposing is it, that what was intended by one party as a sarcasm would sometimes be heartily accepted by the other as a compliment. It is a word of which, in spite of its convenience, a careful writer will be shy, for it is one of those words which, as commonly used, eminently contain a concentrated *petitio principii*. And it has, moreover, a meaning of its own. M. Matter employs it in its proper and definite sense, as a special system of doctrine treating of the relations of the soul to God, and a method, distinct from, and even opposed to, the intellectual processes of ordinary theology, for attaining direct knowledge of Him and union with Him.

From the time when men's thoughts began to be turned in upon themselves, there has been mysticism in some shape; and mystical theology is an acknowledged and large department of the Christian science of divine things. For, supposing religion to be true, and to be conversant with the highest possible objects of thought, love, and hope—objects too great for man's intellect to master, but open to and inviting all his affections—it is natural that this amazing unseen world of goodness and beauty should call forth corresponding sympathies and efforts in proportion to the capacities to which it is presented, and should become a centre of the most attractive interest. If religion is real at all, its objects have a right to exercise the most powerful influence on the affections; and this influence, like everything else, may be studied and variously directed. There is nothing far-fetched or unnatural in this; it is in strict analogy with what we are accustomed to in poetry, or art, or in the exercise of the affections among ourselves. A great poet sees the world of feeling, thought, and action, a great painter sees the world of nature, with different eyes from ordinary men; and a great critic is able, by a direct insight denied to others, to see what the poet or painter saw, and to interpret and establish its truth by reasons, manifest and convincing when stated, but which had escaped duller minds, and perhaps required trained minds to feel their force. The family and social affections are common to mankind at large, and their objects in a general sense are the same; but we all know how infinitely different, in depth, in richness, in refinement, in purity, in strength, in the delicacy of their shades, in the play and vigour and variety of their exercise, are these affections in different characters, and how great is the interval between their extremes of rude and of high development. If the affections are to find objects at all in religion, their exercise, which will certainly be often slack and dull, must also be expected to be in other cases energetic, intense, absorbing; and this exercise must always come near to what both friends and enemies call mysticism. Its degrees are necessarily infinite. But any one who disbelieved in the possibility of the fitness of the affections being really directed to the unseen world would find mysticism in the Psalms and St. Paul, in Dante and Wordsworth, in Hooker and Bishop Butler; and from his point of view, fairly. In all religious writing in which the affections come in, there must be, if it is real, an element more or less of what must bear the name of mysticism. It is simply the same thing as saying that there cannot be poetry without feeling, or art without insight, or affection and friendship without warmth of heart.

But as there are false poetry and false art and extravagant and false affections, so there is a false and mistaken direction, as well as a true and right one, of the religious affections; and it seems hardly saying too much to affirm that the mischief done to religion and to human society by the misdirection of the religious affections is, as far as we can see, out of all proportion greater than that done by intellectual error, and by the divisions created by what has been deemed intellectual error. Perhaps it is only to be paralleled in the mischief done by misdirected social affections. Intellectual error at least does not directly sap men's strength; and often, in the earnest conflict to which it leads, it provokes the force which is to overthrow it or keep it in check. But the disasters following on the misdirection of the religious affections have been of a more fatal nature. They include not merely all the train of evils attending on what is forced, unreal, and hollow, but the irreparable exhaustion, and weakness, and failure of tone, which succeeds the fever of minds wound up to overstrained states of exaltation; the credulity, the mad self-conceit, and the perverse crookedness which never can be cured; and in opponents and lookers-on, influenced by the reaction of disgust, the scepticism, the hardness, and the mocking and cruel temper, which the sight of folly, and possibly selfishness, clothing themselves with the most august claims and taking the holiest names in vain, must inevitably call forth and confirm.

Fénelon has had a bad name in connection with one of these forms of misdirection of the religious affections. He was accused and condemned in his own day for complicity, at the least, with false and mischievous mysticism. M. Matter's object is to point out distinctly the true state of the case before a tribunal in which, if it has its own prejudices, the passions are gone to sleep which were so active and so imperious in Fénelon's own day; and to show how far he is fairly chargeable with what Bossuet so fiercely imputed to him, and how far his own defence, though it did not avail him at Rome, is available. He is favourable to Fénelon; but he is an honest and temperate advocate. An English reader is tempted to mark what seem to him two faults. There is, it appears to foreigners, an occasional slovenliness or obscurity in M. Matter's language which we do not look for in modern French; and, except to those who have special knowledge of the time, he is not unlikely to seem prolix and over-minute, as he is sometimes wanting in arrangement, and fails to see where the subject demands, not allusion and suggestion, but direct statement and proof by reference to facts and dates. But his book strikes us as one which, though it need not have been so lengthy, and has defects of plan and faults of taste, well repays the trouble of reading it. A more skilful writer would have spared his reader some of the trouble. But the story which he tells is full of deep interest, in many of its passages extremely curious, in its general course and upshot not the least sad and touching of the tragic episodes which marked the religious history of Louis XIV.'s reign. It comes out in M. Matter's pages almost with the unity and effect of a novel. He is perfectly guiltless of having any such purpose in his mind. But he has intelligence and delicacy in catching the true combinations of qualities in the chief persons concerned, and their relations to one another; and the facts themselves, illustrated by the language of contemporary letters, do the rest.

The work is really a life of Fénelon as it was affected by the question of mysticism; the life of a churchman, with everything fortunate and promising for him in those palmy days of churchmanship, combining, in a degree universally acknowledged to be absolutely peculiar to himself, genius, the elevation and grace of a perfect nobleman, and further, the purity and enthusiasm of a winning and unsuspected piety—such a life and career cut across, and, in spite of superficial honours, really spoiled and overthrown, by the kind of fate which, almost against his will, entangled him with Madame Guyon and Quietism Bossuet himself, first his master and friend, then his implacable antagonist who ended by crushing him, is the best witness of what was thought of Fénelon's genius. "Qui lui conteste l'esprit?" he exclaimed in the hottest moments of the quarrel, "il en a plus que moi, il en a jusqu'à faire peur." No one doubted at the time, except perhaps Bossuet's friends, that though Bossuet was the greater theologian, Fénelon came much nearer to what was then considered the saint. People admired and dreaded the thunder of Bossuet, but Fénelon's words were music such as the devotion of the time thought it had never heard equalled. Fénelon was far indeed from being the greatest, but he was the most accomplished and most attractive example of the Roman Catholic religion of his age. He combined the strictest faith in dogmas, the most profound submission to authority, the most genuine devotional temper, and an absorbing and governing zeal, with the benevolence, the high spirit, the tolerant generosity, the polish and courtesy and largeness of mind, of which society was beginning to recognise the value and the grace. He, in fact, realised in the highest and purest form, and without intending it, that ideal of religious character which the Jesuits had constantly before their eyes, and strove so laboriously and with such imperfect success to create by their ingenious and artificial methods of discipline. It is to be observed that, in the great quarrel between him and Bossuet, the Jesuits, even the King's confessor, Père la Chaise, and whatever sympathies they commanded at Rome, were—timidly, no doubt, yet very distinctly—for Fénelon. Yet, while Bossuet's career was to the end a successful and brilliant one—and one, too, which has left its permanent mark on the great nation of which, while living, he was the oracle —Fénelon's career, though in some things he was Bossuet's equal and in some his superior, was a failure. Though his type of religion seemed on all its sides to recommend itself to his age, by its refinement and real goodness and charm, and by its philosophical tendencies and disposition to soften down what was harsh and rugged — and though his first achievements and first elevation were full of splendour— still Fénelon's career was a failure as a whole, though we do not forget his saintly episcopate. M. Matter calls him the master of modern mystics. We do not well know who they are; but it is a poor lot, compared with the glory of being the leader of the French Church, and the writer of the *Sermons* and the *Variations*—to be known chiefly as the author of *Télémaque;* or even for having done what Bossuet failed to do—made one of Louis XIV.'s family an honest man.

M. Matter has well caught one feature of Fénelon's character which is not always noticed. People speak of his gentleness and sweetness, and beautiful spirit of yielding and submission; sterner critics give these things the harsher names of suppleness and oiliness; and we must confess, for ourselves, that Fénelon is sometimes too resigned, too ingenious in finding out reasons why he should not complain, to suit our notions of what is natural. In the thick of his quarrel with Bossuet, when Bossuet is, as he often is, grossly and inexcusably rude and violent, nothing can be more beautiful than Fénelon's calm patience and devout cheerfulness. Only it is too beautiful; and it is quite refreshing when he breaks out sometimes into fierceness, and turns with no want of power on his great accuser. But the truth is that with all his sweetness, with all his professions of deference—which there is no reason to think insincere, though we may think them excessive — of deference to authority, whether to the authority of superior age and wisdom, as in the case of Bossuet, or of ecclesiastical position, as in regard to the Pope, Fénelon, as M. Matter repeats, was one of the most resolute and independent of men:—

On prend volontiers, en le jugeant, la rare souplesse de sa parole, qui répondait si bien à celle de sa pensée, pour de la souplesse de caractère; c'est à tort, et c'est une grande faute qu'on commet dans l'appréciation de sa personne. Toute sa vie durant Fénelon tient au contraire singulièrement à ses idées, à ses doctrines, à ses affections. Ses intérêts lui sont chers comme sa personne ; il a conscience de son droit et de sa dignité, comme de ses talents. Il s'y maintient avec fermeté ; toutefois, il le fait avec une telle mesure, avec une si parfaite subordination de ce qui est secondaire à ce qui est supérieur et de ce qui est supérieur à ce qui est suprême, qu'il ne heurte jamais le goût ni la modestie. . . . Sa parole est souple ; mais sa pensée est constante, son génie est un du commencement à la fin. Si nous manquons de détails sur son premier supériorat, nous pouvons être certains que ce qu'il fut depuis et partout, à Versailles, à Issy, à Cambrai, et à Rome, il le fut à Paris à vingt-sept ans : toujours et partout le plus docile des hommes pour qui sait éclairer son génie et pour qui a sur lui autorité ; dans tout le reste, le plus indépendant et le plus lui-même de tous les mortels. Ne lui a-t-on pas reproché l'engouement poussé jusqu'à l'entêtement, la constance exaltée jusqu'à l'obstination ?

Madame Guyon—who occasioned the failure of a great career, who caused to the Court and Church of France trouble and scandals almost equal to those of Jansenism, for whose sake friends like Bossuet and Fénelon were turned into implacable antagonists, and who excited so much compassion by the brutality with which Bossuet and the King treated her—seems, after all, to have been a very ordinary sort of person. Such women are about everywhere, in germ. Her piety, which there is no reason whatever to doubt, was of a strongly marked type, which had been developed in

Spain, since the revival of Catholicism, out of the maxims and outlines of the earlier theology, and had been adapted to the French temper by St. François de Sales and Madame de Chantal. She was enthusiastic, audacious, self-confident, and probably eloquent, at any rate attractive and persuasive; and, in spite of some unfavourable rumours, when she came to Paris, she captivated Madame de Maintenon, and the select circle—select both as to birth and piety— which met at the house of the Duc de Beauvilliers, Colbert's son-in-law. Nothing would satisfy Madame de Maintenon but that she must have Madame Guyon at St. Cyr, to carry forward her teachers and scholars there in the ways of spiritual perfection. If Madame Guyon's head was turned, it is not very surprising. It was none of the strongest, with an eager, forward, adventurous character; and she had before her St. Theresa and Madame de Chantal as examples of women directing and governing in religion. Her mysticism passed from the mysticism of thought and contemplation into that of sensible experience of the most extravagant sort. Her books spoke of states of prayer which seemed to exclude all active religion, and of doctrines which seemed to invert every human idea and motive. The theologians and those whom they influenced began to complain. The King took alarm; he even snubbed Madame de Maintenon when she read to him from her friend's books. He could see nothing in them but dreams, and he declared that Madame Guyon was the maddest woman in France.

The wise Madame de Maintenon, with the prudence of a schoolmistress anxious about the character of her school, threw her overboard at St. Cyr, and then altogether. Madame Guyon attempted to re-establish her character by putting herself and her writings into Bossuet's hands. It was her ruin. The courtesy with which he received her at first turned, as he learned more of her, to the most intense disgust and the most unrelenting persecution. It is difficult to find the parallel, for oddness, to Bossuet's implacable wrath against her. If she had been the most terrible of heresiarchs, instead of a very silly and self-conceited but most submissive devotee, he could not have pursued her more fiercely. Long and earnest conferences of bishops and theologians sat about her books. She was attacked in articles—the "Thirty-four of Issy"—*mandements*, condemnations; she was confined in monasteries, hunted by the police, shut up in State prisons. Her son, a distinguished officer, perfectly innocent of Quietism, was dismissed because he was her son. If it had not been so brutally cruel, nothing but her own dreams could have equalled in ridiculous extravagance this combined rage of Church and State against her. Yet she was not tenacious of her ambitious hopes, if she had any, and lived and died, after the storm had passed, in edifying submission and obedience.

And Fénelon, who suffered as her supposed champion, had not, after all, according to M. Matter, any special interest in her. They both were students and admirers of the same books, the writings of the masters of the new spiritual devotion of the time, Spanish and French. Madame Guyon appears to have tried to win Fénelon; but Fénelon himself strongly warned Madame de Maintenon against the high pressure of her books and influence at St. Cyr. There is little trace of correspondence between them, and Fénelon, though he maintained that she meant well, was very free in admitting that she spoke crudely and ill. But he thought her hardly used, and refused to lend himself to Bossuet's insatiable desire to crush her. This, M. Matter thinks, was the cause of his being involved in her disgrace. Bossuet's jealousy was roused, and turned from her on a more important victim—a friend who had questioned both his temper and judgment, and, in this particular question, his knowledge. M. Matter brings out the case with much appearance of truth. But it seems to us that he leaves without explanation something which does need to be explained—what were, in fact, Fénelon's relations towards Madame Guyon. Fénelon, with all his spirit and courage in speaking for her, writes like a man who is shy of an old acquaintance; and it seems unlikely, in those days of spiritual letter-writing, that where an active and intimate correspondence at some period or other appears to be taken for granted on all sides, it should not have existed, because the traces of it have disappeared.

In the dispute between Bossuet and Fénelon, M. Matter sees with exultation a magnificent jousting match between the first writers and first divines of the day. To us it does not seem so brilliant. The real spirit of it is to be found in Bossuet's letters, especially to his nephew at Rome, than which anything more bitter, untiring, and unscrupulous in the display of feeling against an opponent it would not be easy to find. Bossuet seems unable to sleep or rest for M. de Cambrai and his detestable *Maximes des Saints*. All the world condemns them, yet it is all over with the Church unless they are censured at Rome. The two men parted the right and the wrong of the quarrel between them. If Bossuet was overbearing, rude, and violent, Fénelon was not always quite ingenuous and straightforward, and had his distinct reserves when he was professing the most unbounded and most simple deference to Bossuet's judgment. Bossuet was right as to the general good sense of the question, and in pointing out the absurdity and the practical mischief of the high-flown and monstrous refinements of spiritual feeling of which Madame Guyon's writings were a sample; but Fénelon was right, too, as to the general authority which the tradition and language of acknowledged saints gave them, and in insisting that common-sense is not always the fittest judge of the subject, and that one man's ideas of devotion and religious perfection, as of poetry or affection, are often incommensurable with those of his neighbour. But the inexpressible oddness of the whole matter is that Bossuet himself, as M. Matter shows, had, in his letters of spiritual counsel to the ladies whom he directed, his own mystical language, which, though it may be different from Madame Guyon's and Fénelon's, is every bit as exaggerated, as startling, and, to our ears, as mischievous.

The truth is that it was a poor quarrel, and a sign of degeneracy. It was not like the great controversies of Port Royal, or even those which Bossuet had carried on against Protestantism, a dispute involving questions affecting all the world, and demanding robust and masculine intellect. It was a question interesting only to high society and the Court, with its dependent convents; a question touching devout fine ladies, and the directors whom they tired out and dragged down with their scruples and fancies. In the provinces they did not care a straw about Madame Guyon and Quietism. It was the malady or the need of a fastidious and over-refined society. Bossuet was right in his instinctive dislike, though he had largely helped to bring about the result which filled him with indignation. But controversy had sunk many steps when it came down from debates about grace or morality to debating the necessity of condemning the proposition that a man in a state of perfection ought to hate his own salvation, or that the highest form of love is loving God for nothing [in himself].

XVII

LAMENNAIS[1]

I

THE literary representative and the relatives of Lamennais quarrelled about the publication of his letters, and so these letters are given to the world in separate parcels. One portion, comprising those which Lamennais had in his possession at his death, and published by M. Forgues, his literary executor, has been already noticed in our columns.[2] But Lamennais's family interfered, and prevented him from publishing any others. M. Forgues's collection was accordingly very imperfect in some important respects, and the note *Lettre supprimée*, recurring constantly, kept before the reader's mind the gaps to which a legal decision had condemned him. The family, in the person of Lamennais's nephew, M. A.

---

[1] *Œuvres inédites de F. Lamennais.* Publiés par A. Blaize. *Saturday Review,* 16th March 1867.

[2] This collection of Lamennais's Correspondence, which, though published in 1863, contains letters of a later date, is reviewed in the succeeding article.

Blaize, now bring out their portion of the correspondence. With the private quarrel, which seems to have been a very pretty one — M. Forgues accusing M. Blaize, the nephew, of spiteful jealousy because his uncle had passed him over in his will, and M. Blaize accusing M. Forgues, to whom Lamennais had deliberately entrusted all his literary property, of incompetency for his task and ignorance of Lamennais's life and mind—we have nothing to do. But it is inconvenient to the public that the two gentlemen should not have been able to come to some understanding. There is nothing in M. Blaize's volumes equal in value, for the middle part of Lamennais's life, to the correspondence which Lamennais himself had collected, and which M. Forgues has published, with M. de Coriolis, M. de Vitrolles, and above all with the family of De Senfft—letters unfolding at great length and with much care his ideas, at a critical time, to persons whose intelligence he respected. But the second collection has an interest of another kind. It illustrates that part of Lamennais's life on which M. Forgues's work threw no light—the early part of it, before the *Essai sur l'Indifférence* gave him his sudden and fatal renown. The letters generally of M. Blaize's collection, many of them to the elder brother Jean, are far less elaborate than those of M. Forgues's volumes. They are more off-hand, familiar, and unguarded. But M. Blaize is right in saying that they reveal the man more fully even than those which Lamennais himself destined for publication.

Félicité Lamennais was one of the sons of a hard-headed, public-spirited St. Malo merchant, half trader, half privateer owner, with quite as much taste for ventures of the latter sort as for those of more peaceful commerce. Among other things which these letters show is the keen interest which Lamennais, in the hottest times, when he was fighting Gallicanism and laying down metaphysical foundations for Infallibility, always took in a speculation as such, and the zest with which he entered into the details of an account, the probabilities and operations of an adventure, or the niceties of a question of profit and loss. There was always a vein of the keen St. Malo man of business in the subtle theologian and abstract system-maker; and there was a kind of analogy in the invariable ill success of his bold and confident calculations, and the unexampled breakdown of his peremptory and absolute theories. Lamennais passed his boyhood under the Revolution and the Reign of Terror. Probably, as M. Blaize says, a naturally nervous temperament was strongly acted on by the conditions of the time. The boy, in his case, was the father of the man; small, frail, and sickly, with a head too big for his feeble body, he is described as irritable, wayward, solitary, and subject to accesses of rage which ended in fainting fits. He used to tell a story himself, that when only eight years old he was with his nurse on the ramparts of St. Malo, watching a storm at sea; and, as he expressed it, "il crut voir l'infini et sentir Dieu." Then, astonished at his own thoughts, and looking at the other spectators, he said to himself, " They are looking at what I am looking at, but they do not see what I see." His comment in later years was characteristic :—

Il ne racontait jamais cette anecdote sans ajouter : " Toutes les fois que mes souvenirs me reportent vers ces temps éloignés, une telle pensée d'orgueil dans un enfant de huit ans me fait encore frémir."

He was right, and his theological enemies were right, in talking about his extravagant pride. But his pride was just as evident when he was their triumphant champion; only they did not find it out then.

Neither M. Blaize's introduction nor the letters show very clearly what it was that threw Lamennais into his peculiar line of religious thought. St. Malo had its full share of suffering under the Terror. The clergy, especially, says M. Blaize, both suffered and took their revenge. On the one hand, Lamennais's father, though he had been ennobled under Louis XVI., had the uninterrupted confidence of the revolutionary Government, and filled important municipal offices; on the other hand, his house was one of those where, at the risk of their lives, the proscribed clergy celebrated mass :—

A St. Malo, on accueillit mal la déesse Raison, difficile à reconnaître, il est vrai, sous les traits de la fille d'un cordonnier sans-culotte nommé Oré. Le danger exaltait la foi ; on risquait sa tête pour adorer son Dieu. Parfois, le soir, un prêtre non assermenté, l'abbé Vielle, se glissait à l'aide d'un déguisement dans la demeure de la famille La Mennais. On se réunissait à minuit dans une mansarde. La chère Villemain, si dévouée à ses maîtres, veillait au-dehors. Deux bougies brûlaient sur une table, transformée en autel. M. Vielle, assisté de Jean de La Mennais, alors âgé de treize ans, disait la messe ; avec quelle ferveur on priait ! Le prêtre bénissait les vieillards et les enfants et se retirait avant le jour. Ces scènes de nuit avaient frappé si fortement l'imagination de Féli, que, cinquante ans après, il n'en parlait qu'avec émotion.

Probably the religious opinions and sympathies of the family were sharply contrasted ; and the elder brother Jean, afterwards the founder of a great educational order, and long the counsellor and second self of " Féli," had already devoted himself enthusiastically to the priesthood. But the younger brother at least was not brought up under ecclesiastical influence, or that influence does not appear. His chief instructor was a clever and childless uncle, M. des Saudrais, who went with them by the name of Tonton : far from a freethinker and eighteenth-century philosopher, but also far from straightlaced strictness or zeal—something of a humorist and a critic, a poetical translator of Horace and the Book of Job, and a great reader of Montaigne, Pascal, and La Bruyère. He turned young Lamennais loose into a miscellaneous library, for the boy to read what he liked ; he wrote letters to him of literary comment and counsels, putting sensible commonplaces into neatly turned epigrams, and recommending above all things the condensation and strength of the old French classics. He had his playful sarcasms on the positiveness and the uncertainty of metaphysics, and he rallies his nephew on his hard reasoning: "Ta logique, mon cher Féli, est bien serrée, bien raide, et bien rude; ne pourrais-tu pas en atténuer les conséquences?" But there is nothing in all this to account for the peculiar religious turn of Lamennais's mind. It accounts for his being a reader of Malebranche and Pascal, but not for his hostility to the doctrines current among the French clergy, unless the feebleness, cowardice, and shallow ignorance with which they were maintained account for it. "Tonton" was the declared enemy of everything violent and overstrained, both in thought and in taste; and it was not from him that his nephew learned to hate compromise and halting theories. He passed his early youth in his father's counting-house, and found a merchant's life and home very dull. "Il a écrit," says M. Blaize, "cette boutade. L'ennui naquit en famille—une soirée d'hiver." He had thoughts, which came to nothing, of going out to the Isle of France to make his fortune; he fought a duel; he read Rousseau, and went through a phase of doubt, astonishing the priest who undertook to prepare him for his first communion. His youth, says M. Blaize in a common and intelligible French phrase, "ne fut pas sans orages"; but it ended in strong religious convictions, and in 1807, at twenty-two, "he made his first communion, and his brother Jean was ordained priest." During the next few years he seems to have been either in retirement with his brother at

La Chênaie, a little property near Dinan which he was to make famous, reading Pascal, Malebranche, and the Fathers, plunging deep into philosophy, ecclesiastical history, and controversy, making some acquaintance with Shakespeare and Dryden, and interchanging literary ideas with "Tonton"; or else teaching mathematics in an ecclesiastical seminary which his brother and his friends had set up at St. Malo. When the correspondence opens (1808) we find him in full conflict with the University, in the cause of ecclesiastical rights and liberty of instruction, against the interference of a jealous and irreligious State system.

From this time forward he had taken his line; and everything goes forward in a rapid and natural development, to the *Essai sur l'Indifférence*, and the daring Ultramontanism of the *Avenir*. We soon get into the thick of his enthusiastic theories and prospects, and his enthusiastic and merciless hatreds; his fierce bursts of wrath against insidious and corrupt Governments—Imperial, and still more, Legitimate; his bitter sneers against the self-seeking, the ineptitude, the dull insensibility of the clergy brought up under the old system. In this there is nothing new; the interest of the letters is that they exhibit these feelings gradually taking shape and increasing in strength. M. Forgues's volumes had already shown how remarkably two things were combined in Lamennais—the passion and the power of abstract rigorous thinking, and an intense force and sensitiveness of feeling, quickly moved and insatiable in its demands, and issuing in the most unmeasured attachment and the most unmeasured detestation. Few men loved so tenderly and devotedly while his affection lasted, or hated so deeply, as this hard reasoner and theoriser. His nephew says that in his sympathies and antipathies he was alike apt to change :—

Dans la vie privée il apportait la vivacité des sentiments et l'esprit absolu que l'on remarque dans ses écrits. Ses amitiés se modifiaient comme ses idées ; elles avaient en quelque sorte une couleur locale ; aussi, sauf de rares exceptions, elles ont été plutôt des relations passagères que des attachements durables. . . . On savait son extrême facilité et on en abusait souvent. Il accordait de suite sa confiance et répondait à toutes les lettres qui lui étaient adressées. . . . Combien de fois il a été indignement trompé. . . . Après une de ces déceptions si fréquentes, il nous disait en souriant, "En vérité, je crois que si l'on m'assurait que la lune est tombée sur le boulevard Montmartre, je prendrais ma canne et mon chapeau pour l'aller voir."

But this is hardly a fair account; for though with the common run of people he was easily offended by opposition or even neutrality, and when offended was ready to exaggerate the offence into something gross and unpardonable, he had attachments which bore the severe strain put upon them, and endured in spite of the most disturbing changes. What these earlier letters specially disclose is, generally, the dark, gloomy, hopeless view of life which from the first had possession of Lamennais's mind; and particularly the remarkable circumstances which accompanied his resolution to enter into orders. As to the first point, young men sometimes indulge in sentimental melancholy; and the tendency to this was no doubt greater in the beginning of the century than it is now. But the gloom and despair of Lamennais was not sentimental; it weighed on him in spite of extreme activity and occupation of mind, and an absorbing interest in all that was passing in the world; and it was proof against a high-wrought and sincere devotion. In spite of bursts of fervid and mystical rapture, at bottom there is, as soon as he begins to disclose himself, not merely suffering, but an overwhelming depression which clothes everything round him, and his own fate, in hopeless darkness. He speaks of his "inexplicable torments," and of living continually in a state "of which anguish is the staple."

On corrige l'esprit [he writes to his brother], mais on ne refait point le cœur. La Providence a mis dans le mien une source de douleur qui s'est répandue sur ma vie dès sa naissance et ne s'épuisera qu'avec elle (December 1810).

He is thoroughly sick of life before he is thirty. "'There is not a soul in the world in whose remembrance he wishes to live":—

Toute liaison et même toute communication avec les hommes m'est à charge; je voudrais pouvoir rompre avec moi-même, et c'est aussi ce qui arrivera, mais malheureusement pas tout de suite. . . . Je ne me connais plus [he continues]. Depuis quelques mois je tombe dans un état d'affaissement incompréhensible. Rien ne me remue, rien ne m'intéresse, tout me dégoûte, . . . des désirs, je n'en ai plus. J'ai usé la vie ; c'est de tous les états le plus pénible, et de toutes les maladies la plus douloureuse comme la plus irrémédiable (La Chênaie, 1810).

And he continues in the same strain, letter after letter :—

Adieu, et à Dieu seul [he writes to his brother, with whom he shared all his confidence]. Je te verrais avec plaisir, et toutefois je ne sens aucun désir de te voir, ni toi, ni aucune créature. Dieu seul, Dieu seul !

But this "growing tendency," as he calls it, "to a dreary and gloomy melancholy," which made the future terrible to him, which covered the horizon with dark clouds wherever he looked, and made him believe that there was "no season for him but the season of storms," did not in the least affect the keenness of his judgments, or dull his grim relish of sarcasm and controversy. His melancholy depression did not prevent him, as all accounts agree, from being most genial and fascinating with those he loved ; but the one excitement which of all others had power to rouse him was when his wrath or his scorn was moved at the men and things round him; and the times swarmed with exasperating people and events. It was a necessary of life with him to have some one whom he thought a fool to lash, or some onslaught on his writings, the fiercer the better, to give interest to existence. He writes after an interval of quiet :—

J'attends la censure impatiemment, elle me réveillera. Depuis que je n'ai plus Tabaraud pour m'amuser, je ne fais que languir. J'avais besoin d'un peu de mouvement ; Dieu garde de mal celui qui veut bien venir à mon secours en cette occasion, et contribuer à mes menus plaisirs. (November 10, 1814.)

With such morbid hopelessness about himself, it is not wonderful that his views of everything round him should be, as they are, unmeasured in their savage and merciless bitterness. "Cet épouvantable enfer qu'on appelle la France" expresses his habitual feeling towards the society about him. Nothing less than a good curse can relieve his hatred against the University :—

Maudites soient la fille et la mère, l'ancienne et la nouvelle Université ! Maudits soient les fabricateurs de cette infernale engeance ! Maudits soient ceux qui l'ont fait naître, et qui contribueront à l'élever ! Maudits les chefs, maudits les subalternes, maudite toute cette infâme canaille. (March 6, 1815.)

He can see no hope or chance of salvation for mankind. " Le genre humain tout entier marche à grands pas vers sa destruction ; il est dans le travail de l'agonie, et comme un malheureux blessé à mort, il se débat et se roule dans son propre sang " ; and his religious faith only gave him the terrible pleasure of being able to look on without sympathy :—

Ce n'est pas sans une sorte de joie que je sens trembler sous mes pieds ce monde corrompu et corrupteur. En le voyant chanceler comme un homme ivre, je me dis, il tombera bientôt, et je hâte de tous mes vœux l'instant de sa chute, qui sera celui de la consommation de l'Église et du triomphe de son chef. (August 1, 1815.)

And what Lamennais was at the beginning, he was to the end. Christian or unbeliever, he could see nothing about him but what was dark and evil; the only change was as to those on whom, with equal positiveness, he successively threw the responsibility of the evil.

The other point on which these letters give new light is Lamennais's ordination. Even after he had conceived the idea, in conjunction with his brother, of changing profoundly the opinions of the French clergy, he had by no means made up his own mind to become a priest. He received the minor orders in 1809, but he shows no sign of going further in the ecclesiastical course. Indeed he seems to have given it up, for later on he writes, "ce n'est sûrement pas mon goût que j'ai écouté en me décidant *à reprendre* l'état ecclésiastique"; and in fact we find him in 1814 at Paris, undecided, and balancing between various plans. He had projected a great ecclesiastical history which was to take the labour of his life, and a work on "the spirit of Christianity"; he was very busy and eager about projects for a newspaper; he had not given up all thoughts of a mercantile life;

and he was inclined to go into a monastery. In the midst of these schemes Bonaparte returned from Elba; and Lamennais, who, with his brother, had published a book against the Emperor's Church policy, thought himself safest in England. There he met a French *émigré* priest, the Abbé Carron, whom he describes as a saint on earth, and by whose influence and counsels he was led to devote himself to the priesthood. He writes about his resolution, and the motives which decided him, in a tone which shows that he had been worked up to a most intense pitch of exalted self-sacrifice. He had placed himself absolutely in M. Carron's hands to settle what was to become of him; and the first idea on both sides seems to have been that he should " serve the Church in the regular clergy, that is, in the Company of Jesus." After the first excitement, his misgivings and reluctance returned :—

> En me décidant, ou plutôt en me laissant décider pour le parti qu'on m'a conseillé de prendre, je ne suis assurément ni ma volonté, ni mon inclination. Je crois au contraire que rien au monde n'y saurait être plus opposé. . . . Demande à Dieu pour moi la grâce de supporter la vie. Elle me devient tous les jours plus à charge. (October 19, 1815.)

And he thought, with inexpressible "sinking of heart," of his books, and the fields at La Chênaie, from which he believed he was parting for ever. But he had put himself into M. Carron's hands; he came back to France, where his brother Jean seconded the impulse given by M. Carron, and in 1816 he was ordained. "Cette démarche," he writes, after receiving the subdiaconate, "m'a prodigieusement coûté." But he went forward. One friend writes, to console him, that he was going as a victim to the sacrifice, and that it had pleased God to allow him to taste neither the happiness nor the glory of his new office. "Il lui a singulièrement coûté," writes his brother, "pour prendre sa dernière résolution. M. Carron d'un côté, moi de l'autre, nous l'avons entraîné, mais sa pauvre âme est encore ébranlée de ce coup." To those who felt misgivings about the painful struggle, M. Carron wrote, "Reposez-vous sur mon cœur, et bien spécialement sur ma conscience, du sort de ce bien-aimé Féli; il ne m'échappera point. L'Église aura ce qui lui appartient." A month after his ordination we have the following cry of bitterness and despair addressed to his brother—the Atys of Catullus in too literal prose:—

> Miser, ah miser, querendum est etiam atque etiam, anime.
> Ego Maenas, ego mei pars. . . .
> Ego vitam agam sub altis Phrygiae columinibus.
> Jam jam dolet, quod egi, jam jamque poenitet.

Quoique M. Carron m'ait plusieurs fois recommandé de me taire sur mes sentiments, je crois pouvoir et devoir m'expliquer avec toi, une fois pour toutes. Je suis et ne puis qu'être désormais extraordinairement malheureux. Qu'on raisonne là-dessus tant qu'on voudra, qu'on s'alambique l'esprit pour me prouver qu'il n'en est rien, ou qu'il ne tient qu'à moi qu'il en soit autrement, il n'est pas fort difficile de croire qu'on ne réussira pas sans peine à me persuader un fait personnel contre l'évidence de ce que je sens. Toutes les consolations que je puis recevoir, se bornent donc au conseil banal de faire de nécessité vertu.... Quant aux avis qu'on y pourrait ajouter, l'expérience que j'en ai a tellement rétréci ma confiance, qu'à moins d'être contraint d'en demander, je suis bien résolu à ne jamais procurer à personne l'embarras de m'en donner ; et j'en dis autant des exhortations.... Je n'aspire qu'à l'oubli, dans tous les sens, et plût à Dieu que je pusse m'oublier moi-même ! La seule manière de me servir véritablement est de ne s'occuper de moi en aucune façon. Je ne tracasse personne ; qu'on me laisse en repos de mon côté ; ce n'est pas trop exiger, je pense. Il suit de tout cela, qu'il n'y a point de correspondance qui ne me soit à charge. Écrire m'ennuie mortellement, et de tout ce qu'on peut me marquer, rien ne m'intéresse. Le mieux est donc, de part et d'autre, de s'en tenir au strict nécessaire en fait de lettres. J'ai trente-quatre ans écoulés ; j'ai vu la vie sous tous ses aspects, et ne saurais dorénavant être la dupe des illusions dont on essaierait de me bercer encore. Je n'entends faire de reproches à qui que ce soit ; il y a des destins inévitables ; mais si j'avais été moins confiant ou moins faible, ma position serait bien différente. Enfin elle est ce qu'elle est, et tout ce qui me reste à faire est de m'arranger de mon mieux, et, s'il se peut, de m'endormir au pied du poteau où l'on a rivé ma chaîne ; heureux si je puis obtenir qu'on ne vienne point, sous mille prétextes fatigants, troubler mon sommeil. (June 25, 1816.)

His brother remonstrates, as may be supposed; Lamennais answers that perhaps his words are too strong, but he adheres to the substance, and begs that the subject may never be mentioned—"Tout ce qui me le rappelle, de près ou de loin, me cause une émotion que je ne suis pas le maître de modérer." He takes to writing, and plunges into controversy, but his interest fails him:—

On me presse pour la quatrième fois d'écrire sur le concordat. Peut-être m'y déciderai-je, quoiqu'avec répugnance. . . . Je sens d'avance qu'enchaîné pour le choix des questions à traiter et pour la manière de les traiter, j'écrirai avec dégoût, mal par conséquent, et il est triste de s'ennuyer pour ennuyer les autres. C'est pourtant l'occupation des trois-quarts des hommes. Je regarde que tous mes malheurs, de conséquence en conséquence, viennent de ce que mes parents, bien contre mon gré, m'ont forcé d'apprendre à écrire, et il n'y a pas de jour où je ne redise, avec un sentiment profond, ce mot d'un ancien, *Utinam nescirem literas!* (January 4, 1817.)

By and by we find him deep in a new work, which his friend Tesseyre has made him undertake. "Never did I write anything with less taste for it." "I should have left the thing alone thirty times over, if Tesseyre had not pressed me to go on." And this is the famous *Essai sur l'Indifférence*. He does not want encouragement and praise; he is alive to the magnitude of his own design to find a philosophical and demonstrative basis for Infallibility; "s'il était bon," he writes of it, "il tiendrait lieu de toute une bibliothèque." But this is not enough to console him for the irrevocable step :—

Je n'avance guère (he writes), mon ouvrage, il m'ennuie. Écrire m'est un supplice. Je déteste Paris, je déteste tout. Cette vie est pour moi un enfer. J'ai manqué l'occasion de vivre selon mon caractère et mon goût ; c'est sans retour. (May 13, 1817.)

Some months later :—

Je ne saurais prendre sur moi de travailler à mon deuxième volume. Tout m'est à charge. La vie est trop pesante pour moi. J'ai beau me dire à cet égard ce qu'on souhaite, ce qui peut-être est raisonnable au fond, ce sentiment l'emporte, il m'écrase. Quelle terrible pensée que celle d'avoir réduit un être humain en cet état ! (December 27, 1817.)

Yet he wrote on. Lamennais was keenly sensible to one pleasure, that of forcing men by logic to admit what they did not like. He triumphs thus in anticipation over a friend :—

Il m'a pris fantaisie de me plaindre un peu à M. de Bonald de l'universalité des louanges qu'il prodigue à la vie de Bossuet. Je ne saurais digérer 1682 ; c'est là-dessus que portent mes observations. Il ne répondra pas, mais il entendra. Ses principes le forcent à dire *amen* intérieurement, et pour peu qu'il veuille regarder devant lui, il verra ce redoutable spectre d'infaillibilité, tout vivant, tout-puissant, étendant ses inévitables bras pour l'embrasser. (February 25, 1815.)

The pain which his book costs him is poorly repaid by the praise it receives or the good it is to do. "Books do not change men." True, there is one all-rewarding compensation to which he looks forward with a kind of cruel and savage joy, as if he clenched his teeth as he was writing:—

Je sens toutefois la nécessité de finir le second volume; mais le courage me manque à chaque instant. Plus je vais pourtant, plus je me tiens sûr de contraindre ces gens si fiers de leur incrédulité à dire leur *Credo* jusqu'à la dernière syllabe, ou à avouer par leur silence, car je leur défendrai d'ouvrir la bouche, qu'ils ne peuvent pas dire : *Je suis*. (January 9, 1818.)

Time had a strange fate in store for this haughty and defiant arguer, which has thrown a terrible irony into the impassioned fervour and merciless logic which was to crush all resistance; and this irony is heightened now that his letters disclose the state of mind in which he thus wrote with a conqueror's scorn. The world of thought, as well as the world of action, has its impressive lessons for those who in their intemperate self-confidence forget the measure of man's condition. Such was this history.

ὕβρις φυτεύει τύραννον·
ὕβρις, εἰ πολλῶν ὑπερπλησθῇ μάταν,
ἃ μὴ 'πίκαιρα μηδὲ συμφέροντα,
ἀκρότατον εἰσαναβᾶσ'
ἀπότομον ὤρουσεν εἰς ἀνάγκαν.

II[1]

Lamennais is one of the rare examples of men winning equal fame successively in two hostile camps; but it is also true that his career as a whole must be numbered with the most signal failures of his time. At a period when the cause of religion on the continent of Europe was low, and its defenders discredited, incapable, and perplexed, his undaunted and aggressive enthusiasm, and his rare intellectual vigour, surprised the world. He had found the argument which was to conclude for ever the questions of a doubting age in favour of Christianity, as Christianity is represented by the Roman Catholic Church; and his example, his eloquence, and his logical theories kindled such a flame in the young clergy of France, and gave such an impulse to their faith and zeal, as renewed and moulded a whole generation. A few years later, the original and self-reliant thinker who had invented a new basis of argument for Roman dogmatism, and had urged with peremptory rigour its extreme and exclusive claims, had become one of the foremost prophets of the revolutionary school, which, if we must not call it irreligious, understands religion in a different way from, not merely the Roman Catholic Church, but any of the Churches of Christendom.

[1] *Correspondance de Lamennais.* Publiée par E. D. Forgues. *Saturday Review*, 24th January 1863.

He is, perhaps, the most conspicuous instance of a form of change which is almost characteristic of our own times—in which zeal and conviction come first, in which the conversion is from settled belief and strong self-devotion to hostility and disgust, and a man's latter days are devoted to destroying the faith which once he preached. Such changes may be as inevitable and necessary as those of which former history is full, from indifference, or blind unintelligent bigotry, to the enlightenment of a new and satisfying faith; but the natural order of things is inverted when positiveness, and enthusiastic earnestness, based not on prejudice or authority, but on profound and laborious mental efforts, come first, and then disappointment, uncertainty, and the confession of having wasted life on a dream. A man who, on the greatest and most comprehensive of subjects, comes forward, in his mature years, with a deeply meditated theory of truth, by which he has been able to see, and to establish with clearness and certainty, the real relations of principles on which not only his timid and bewildered contemporaries, but the leading spirits of two centuries, have gone astray—who fearlessly and deliberately challenges the agreement of the whole Catholic, the whole Protestant, the whole philosophical world—who expends on the exposition of this theory all the resources of a penetrating and logical intellect, and all the hopes and earnestness of a most passionate nature—and who, after all this, for whatever reason, comes to believe that the grand theory for which alone he once lived has been but the sophistical propping up of the deepest wickedness and falsehood —cannot be said to have successfully done his work in life. The contrast is too sharp. His life is broken into two discordant parts, each of which is the condemnation of the other. His words were too stout, his conclusions too absolute, for such an utter and irreconcilable rejection of them to follow. For the latter portion of his career to have been joined by a less abrupt transition to the former, his first claims should have been more modest, his logic less unqualified and scornful. To have become so haughty and intolerant an apostle of the Revolution, Lamennais should not have been so haughty and intolerant a theologian.

Of the two parties which he served, he probably did most for that which he ultimately left. The *Essai sur l'Indifférence* filled a void, and suggested a new line of thought, in French theology, at a moment when French theologians could find little better to do than to go on repeating, more and more feebly, the thoughts of their ancient leaders. It was, indeed, suited especially for its own time—the slack-water time between two great tides, a time of lazy doubt and vague sentiment, of inactivity and barrenness of thought. It also suited better a race which values theories more than facts, than it would at any time have suited one which values facts more than theories. But it did what the romance of Chateaubriand and the paradoxes of De Maistre had not attempted to do—it gave a bold and definite answer to the ultimate questions and difficulties which were current about religion. Not unlike Bishop Butler's *Analogy* in its scope and purpose and breadth of argument, though so singularly different both in its spirit and its mode of reasoning, it has, not avowedly but really, filled the same sort of place in the French Church for the last forty years which the *Analogy* is supposed to have filled in the English Church. Lamennais provided his brethren with an imposing and complete popular theory of their position; and, in spite of the partial condemnation of it at Rome, they have not ceased to work it assiduously. The tone of the *Essai sur l'Indifférence*, its thoughts and reasonings, its generalisations and contrasts, its vigour of logic and recklessness about proof, its unfaltering assumptions and insolent sophistry, its best features and its worst, are to be widely traced in the theological literature of the modern French Church. No book of the time probably left its mark so deeply on a great class; no book ever did more to show them their way when they had lost it, to revive their spirits for an arduous struggle, and to strengthen their hearts with the confidence of triumph. That the French clergy have stood their ground and commanded respect in the revolutionary storms, that they have ceased to be necessarily identified with the unpopular side, that they have learned to have confidence in the theoretical and argumentative advantages of their position, and to press them with boldness and force, they owe to Lamennais. It may indeed be doubted whether the spirit and the principles which he imparted to them will be altogether for their benefit in the long run; but it must be confessed that it was something to have raised up a great and important body from the abject helplessness, and pettiness of action, and timid feebleness, in which he found the French clergy cowering and blundering under the Restoration, to be ambitious and independent, capable of intelligent interest in principles, and not afraid of the shock of argument in their defence.

But they have shown no signs of rising higher than their teacher; and, though he was immeasurably above those who have followed his path in the courage and originality with which he first dared to strike into it, he was not really a great thinker. He had the appliances and powers by which a great thinker might have expounded and impressed his thoughts; but he had not the mind which seeks, or which is able, to come into real living contact with the actual existing facts. The *Essai sur l'Indifférence* is a work of high aim. It attempts to go to the bottom of things—to view the great questions of which it treats from a high eminence. It is a great advance, doubtless, in philosophic largeness, on the apologies which it was meant to supersede. But who that reads it calmly can feel that he is brought into connection with a state of things which really exists in this world of ours? It is throughout the work of a mind which plays on the superficial aspects of the various forms of belief and opinion which it examines and contrasts. The writer never appears as grasping them in their true and living complexity; he never gives us the impression that he has honestly gone down to their roots and foundations; it is doubtful whether he ever felt the real pinch of the difficulties of which he disposes with such superb and annihilating logic. It is not, indeed, the work of a mere dialectician, brilliant and ingenious as his dialectics are. It is the work of a man who has felt deeply and strongly—the work of a man who hates and pities with all his heart. But it is not the work of a man who has seen, and compared, and judged, as a really great thinker sees, and compares, and judges. We may rise from the perusal of the book with the feeling of having been beaten in a game of chess—with the feeling that his skilful management, his resources of plan and system, his able and often unscrupulous style of argument, seem to have stopped all ways of escape from our perplexities, except those which lead to Ultramontanism or to Atheism; but we feel also that the postulate of the book is that we are living in a different world from the one which we know, and that our thoughts and actions are regulated on different principles from those which really govern mankind.

The line of thought in Lamennais's earlier writings is so forced and unnatural—there is such a violent bringing together of things incongruous and unsympathetic, and the victorious power with which this is done is felt so completely to be a triumph of mere argumentative skill, and not of reality and truth—that it is less surprising than it seems at first sight that convictions apparently so final and so rooted should have undergone such a ruinous overthrow. Lamennais thought that he should be able to open a new series of conquests for Rome, by compelling the Papacy of the nineteenth century into a close alliance with democracy and freedom of thought—by making the Pope the centre and guide of popular reaction against established misgovernment and tyranny, and by grounding afresh the existing dogmatic system of Romanism on the attempted proof that human reason necessarily stultified itself by accepting any divergence from the decisions of Trent. That he should have deliberately undertaken such a task seems to show two things—the intolerable pressure upon him of the state of things which he wished to revolutionise, and his deep ignorance of the real forces with which he had to deal. He probably only half knew himself. Then, when the delusion was dispelled, when old traditions and instincts proved stronger than his demonstrations, and the strained and unreal combinations which he had given his life to bring about proved vain and impossible, the old pressure which had driven him to contrive them returned upon him with increased strength. The theory, extravagant and fallacious, but novel and imposing, which had stood between him and the hollowness and rottenness of all things in the social state of Europe, had broken down; and the hollowness and rottenness of society produced their natural effect on an ardent and impatient mind, which had expected that the essential conditions of human nature would yield to its logic, and wondered that its unanswerable arguments did not make crooked things straight.

We naturally turn to his correspondence to find some indication of the intellectual process by which he passed from the most fervent and exacting belief to unbelief and deep hostility. Lamennais was a fertile letter writer, and it need not be said, wrote very well. He wished his correspondence to be published, as the explanation of his life; and though from private, and, perhaps, not unnatural difficulties, and the apparently singular decision of a French Court, his wishes have not been entirely fulfilled, yet his literary executor, M. Forgues, has been able to publish a great number of letters, and those to some of the most intimate and trusted of his friends. Considering what Lamennais was, the list of his chief correspondents in M. Forgues's volumes is a curious one. We have two religious ladies, who had shared the exile of the Bourbons, and who at the Restoration set up a house of charity in one of the dingy courts of the Rue S. Jacques, from whence they and the little knot of zealous priests, with whom they corresponded as the ladies of Port Royal corresponded with the Jansenist leaders, derived their nickname of *Feuillantines* and *Feuillantins;* an Austrian diplomatist, M. de Senfft, and his wife and daughter; an eccentric French marquis, given to political satires in verse, M. de Coriolis; and two very staunch but enlightened Royalists, M. de Vitrolles and the great advocate, Berryer. For some reason or other, the letters to M. de Vitrolles, who to the last continued on the most affectionate terms with Lamennais, and whose house was Lamennais's most frequent haunt, are not given in M. Forgues's volumes. All these correspondents belonged to the high Royalist and Legitimist party, and belonged to it on religious even more than on political grounds ; but the affection and sympathy and perfect openness which had been between them and Lamennais in the day when he had been of the same mind with them, appear to have continued, without the smallest abatement on either side, after he had entered on his new path. The correspondence in a great measure explains this. Whatever he was to the world without, to the little circle round him Lamennais was the most loving, the tenderest, the most interested, the most devoted and confiding of friends. Haughty, sensitive, and irritable, easily offended and not easily appeased in his dealings with men in general, with his friends he gives and takes without effort and without offence, letting the worthy old *Feuillantine* lady rate him for his rashness, making the tenderest inquiries about the humble dependents of the establishment, Jeanne, Jeannette, and Peggy, and remembering even the monkey, Mako ; giving particular directions for new watches for his nieces, and overflowing with every pleasant invention of playfulness and warmth of heart. In these letters, which are full of the great interests which occupied his thoughts and are the subject of his writings, and in which he unbosoms himself with that perfect freedom which comes from the assurance of perfect sympathy, we might have expected to find light thrown on the road which his mind travelled in its great change of belief. The letters, it is true, become scantier towards the end of his life; but a considerable number of them belong to the time when the change was going on.

It is rather remarkable that scarcely any traces are to be found of what may be spoken of as the intellectual side of the struggle, which resulted in the complete surrender of his ancient convictions. Of the changes of feeling, of hope, of confidence, there is abundant exhibition; but of the difficulties which address themselves to the intellect, of the doubts and questionings of the dissatisfied reason, we repeat, scarcely any. Remember what Lamennais had once held about the doctrine and Church of Rome—and then how utterly and finally he gave it all up—and it certainly seems strange that so little should be said in the letters of the mental cross-examination under which we ought to suppose that the lofty theories and crushing argument of the *Essai sur l'Indifférence* had broken down.

But if the correspondence shows little of the intellectual work and struggle of the change, it shows abundantly the man himself, and the mind and character in which the two great antagonist convictions grew up. In the first place, his mind was one in which intellectual struggles, and the debate of opposing reasons, had not much place. Notwithstanding his fame as a great reasoner, it was not reasoning that laid the foundation and determined the form of his characteristic views. He sought, in his own rare powers of argument and arrangement, a compact and ambitious theory for his views; but it was not through his theory that he had come to his views. They were dependent on something much simpler, and more immediate. Certain broad appearances in the state of society, in the state of thought, in the relations of men to men, struck with great force on his sensitive and ardent mind; they were received and fixed in it, as they came, in the gross,—unanalysed, unbalanced, unquestioned. To meet these appearances he constructed, with all the skill of a consummate advocate, the theory of a divine spiritual power in society, supreme over intelligence and faith. In spite of the theory, the appearances continued the same as before; *they* were what had the real power from first to last over his mind, and the elaborate theory of religion which he had devised dropped off of itself, and was abandoned without trouble and without regret, as soon as he could no longer make it suit his views of society. And these views, it is to be next remarked, were narrow views. The richness which reality gives to ideas is not to be found in Lamennais. In his letters, as in his works—in the keen argumentation of the *Essai*, as in the wild rhapsodies of the *Paroles d'un Croyant*—he never seems able to escape out of the circle of a few great thoughts; and even about these there is the barrenness and meagreness which belong to generalisations which shrink from the test of exceptions, to abstractions which do not care to expand into connection with the realities of life. But the feature of his mind which is most impressively brought out by his correspondence is the deep alienation and bitterness with which he regarded the men and society of his time. A deep melancholy and disgust at life seem early to have settled on his mind, and darkened everything to him. It is impossible to give an idea of the scorn and hatred which pervade his correspondence, and from which only his personal friends, and the collective abstractions of his successive creeds—the "Church" and the "people"— escape. "J'éprouve tous les jours une chose que j'aurais crue impossible, c'est un accroissement de mépris pour les hommes de ce temps." This was in 1825, because the Chamber of Peers would not pass a sufficiently strong law against sacrilege; but the sentence expresses the burden of his letters to the last. He goes on, daily increasing in his strength of contempt for his "siècle de boue, qui nous mène droit à un siècle de sang"; . . . "cette pauvre société idiote, qui s'en va à la Morgue en passant par la Salpêtrière." "J'ai tant souffert des hommes, depuis un an surtout," he writes in 1827, "que le monde m'est devenu comme une perpétuelle apparition de l'enfer." And his exhortation to one of his friends, in an early letter, is steadily followed by himself throughout:—

"Moquons-nous de notre siècle, Monsieur, et rions-en, toutes les fois qu'il voudra bien nous le permettre, en n'excitant pas l'horreur." No doubt the wickedness and folly of mankind are great truths; but, like other great truths, they require variety in their statement, and they require to be relieved. We have nothing to say against the piquancy and force of the persevering sarcasm, with which all governments, all public men, all nations, all laws and measures and forms of policy, are impartially scathed. The letters form a very curious running comment on the course of events after and before the revolution of 1830. But the effect at last is wearisome. No Calvinist ever dwelt with more determined pertinacity on the doctrine of total depravity than Lamennais does on the utter and hopeless corruption of European society. We have no particular love for the men who were the chief objects of his scorn—for M. de Villèle, or for M. Thiers—we can see a good deal to criticise in Louis-Philippe and Guizot. We no doubt find it difficult now to recall the gloom and exasperation of those days of triumphant despotism, which called forth such a burst of feeling as one that we find in a letter of the period :—"Si je ne vois pas le commencement d'un châtiment sans pareil pour ces monstres qu'on appelle empereurs et rois, *je mourrai désespéré.*" And we are willing to admit that prophets have their use in society. They are needed to tell it sharp truths in an impressive way, and Lamennais may be looked upon as one of these prophets. But even a prophet's despair is oppressive and forbidding, and in Lamennais all is utter despair—utter despair of any remaining good in society—despair until some frightful ruin shall have first changed the world. And what was this despair? It was the despair of a man who never mixed with society; who contemplated it from his retreat in the oak forests of Brittany; who knew nothing of the difficulties of active and responsible men; who never shows a sign of taking account of any good side in the varied aspect of society, or of recognising any compensation for evils. A prophet of ruin, he certainly saw several of his dark predictions realised; but he was too blind to foresee all that has also come to pass, of neutralising and counteracting good.

Such a man was not likely to endure what the Jansenists and Fénelon endured. When the Agamemnon of the time rejected the conditions and service of Achilles, Achilles only thought that Agamemnon had thereby sufficiently proved that he himself, too, was one with a corrupt and doomed society. To be sure, nothing could be more pitiably mean and contemptible than the way in which the Roman Court broke with its dangerous champion. Intrigue and jealousy dogged him there from the very first; and a letter of Cardinal Bernetti in 1824 is quoted by a zealous Roman Catholic writer, M. Crétineau Joly, in which the Pope, speaking of Lamennais, then at Rome, is made to shudder at his "face de damné," marked with "the visible signs of celestial malediction," which the Pope could not get out of his memory. As Leo XII. was at this very time welcoming Lamennais with the greatest warmth, as Lamennais's portrait and a picture of the Virgin are said to have been the only ornaments of the Pope's room, and as he gave out that he meant to make Lamennais a cardinal, it is to be hoped that Cardinal Bernetti told a lie or that his letter is a forgery. But the Encyclicals which condemned Lamennais's doctrine were undoubtedly extorted by base policy from base fears; and the wretched impotence with which they identified his doctrine with the axioms of civilisation, and denounced all liberty of speaking, or thinking, or acting, as being, in their vile jargon, something "deterrima, execranda, detestabilis, impudentissima," was almost a triumph for Lamennais.

Yet we cannot help feeling that the blow from the decrepit hand to which he had attempted to give such exorbitant power, served him right. The retribution was a righteous one for the extravagance with which he had strained all truth and reason to exclude every other authority in the world but that of Rome, that he should be taken at his word. At the time when he was insulting every one, as a fool or a scoundrel, who hesitated to place, not doctrine only, but every spiritual interest under the feet of the Pope, he might have known what the Roman Court really was, just as well as he knew Frayssinous and the French Bishops. There were signs enough in the world to check the recklessness of his confidence in Rome. The Nemesis that overtook him was as appropriate as it was natural.

XVIII

AN EIRENICON[1]

It is useful sometimes to try once more the working out of problems which have been given up as insoluble. The attempt may not lead to greater success than before; but collateral and indirect advantages may result from the investigation. It may incidentally open lines of thought which are worth pursuing, as alchemy led on, without intending it, to chemistry, or as the merely curious and apparently idle scrutiny of what was thrown aside for exhausted and useless refuse has sometimes issued in unexpected discoveries in science or its applications. A question which has really interested deep and serious minds must probably have something from which we may learn by examining it. And if the only gain be the apparently humble one of

[1] *The Church of England a Portion of Christ's One Holy Catholic Church, and a means of restoring Visible Unity; an Eirenicon, in a Letter to the Author of the "Christian Year."* By E. B. Pusey, D.D. Parkers, Oxford. *The Times*, Tuesday, 12th December 1865.

ascertaining that the question cannot be answered, or that the problem is not yet in a fit condition to be solved, it is never lost time to have made ourselves more sure of the limits of our knowledge or our power. It would cut off much useless labour, much restless pining, much vain striving against what cannot be helped and cannot be changed, if we only knew more clearly what we cannot know, or what we cannot do. And even when we feel that we have no right to forbid absolutely those who cherish a grand and noble hope which seems to us visionary from fulfiling what they deem the duty of following it even if it be unapproachable, yet we may do them service by putting before them the plain realities amid which they must act. Nothing can be more miserable than aiming at a great object in total and trifling insensibility to its arduousness, and to the obstacles that have to be overcome. Columbus would have been unworthy of his venture if he had not scanned and felt its doubtfulness and its hazards.

Such a hope, as it seems to us, very grand and very visionary, is that of a reunited Christendom. It is the most natural, the most inevitable of desires. That serious and devout men who believe in the documents of their religion and have imbibed its spirit should be led again and again to ask themselves whether division is never to have an end, is quite intelligible. And if they are fair and large-minded observers, with knowledge unobscured by the passions or necessities of controversy, they cannot help being

perfectly aware how vain are the attempts made by
all sides to deny the good things and the sound
reason that are to be found among their adversaries,
and to defend what is indefensible among themselves; they cannot but see that neither party shares
without mixture the right or the wrong; they see,
too, how the most formidable differences are apt to
sink into comparative insignificance when looked at
at a distance or in relation to the grander and more
essential features of the common creed. An impatient sense of the large part which stupidity and
pigheadedness, as well as both the more respectable
and the more unworthy influences, have had in
forging the barriers which keep churches and communions apart, mingles with an ever-recurring and
sorrowful conviction of the real agreement on the
greatest subjects of belief, which underlies divisions
never allowed to be forgotten, and which they who
feel it are not permitted to recognise. That Christians who can look out beyond their own particular
body should wish to see Christendom reunited seems
the natural consequence of the command of Christ
and of the immemorial understanding of the Church,
that His disciples should be one. And what is thus
to be desired is a reasonable subject of thought and
inquiry. It is not wonderful that great minds should
have been allured by the hope, and not been dis-
mayed by the apparent difficulties, of accommodating
the inveterate quarrels which make Christians of one
land or one communion seem like heathen men and

publicans to those of another. From one point of view the attempt seems so easy ;—only a few reasonable concessions; only a few misunderstandings explained; only a just allowance for the intrinsic difficulties of the questions involved; only a few honest acknowledgments of differences of conviction, with the equally honest determination not to make more of them than they deserve; only a little fair and manly giving credit on each side to the other, for having a real basis for its cause, for meaning what is reasonable and right rather than what is absurd and false.

The wonder at first sight seems less that such men as Leibnitz and Bossuet, Wake and Dupin, should have engaged seriously, as we are often told that they did, in a consideration of the possibilities of some such scheme, than that so few besides them among the higher order of minds which have interested themselves in theology, should have been tempted, by the noble ambition of being peacemakers of Christendom, to devote their attention to the subject. The wonder is rather that Christian society should have so long and so tamely acquiesced in an anomalous and scandalous state of things, in clear contradiction to the principles of its first organisation and the solemn language of its perpetually repeated creeds and prayers; and that with such keen and unabated interest in theology, scarcely any one should have thought it worth while to inquire whether a remedy could be found for the monstrous result of our controversies, that a devout English

Protestant in France cannot join in the ordinary Christian worship round him without a shrinking and guilty fear of being unwarily involved in fatal communion with some unholy rite, and that a devout Roman Catholic from abroad must look upon our churches here as the polluted and contaminating high-places of heretics under a curse, in whose company it is not safe to pray. That the teaching of the New Testament should have come to this, not in the dark days of Christian civilisation, but in the brightest, is so extravagant that it may well have prompted the wish, and with the wish the hope, that it might be possible to devise some means of ending such a state of things. Yet this hope, which looks so natural and reasonable, is one against which all experience has hitherto peremptorily declared; and the objections of reason against the possibility of its fulfilment are too obvious and too weighty to leave any doubt as to the soundness of the decision of experience.

Undeterred, however, by past failures, and by menacing difficulties that must present themselves to every one's mind in the circumstances of our times, Dr. Pusey has once more undertaken to examine the conditions on which rival communions might enter on the way of peace. The occasion which has led him to do so, and the form into which his inquiry has fallen, are both worth notice. He began the consideration of the subject, urged to it by Dr. Manning's adroit insinuations against the consistency of his former friend, which Dr. Manning based particularly on the recent course of events in the English Church, and in which he had and used the advantage always belonging to those who carry their principles to the extreme over those who, whether for good reasons or bad ones, stop short, and are either less logical or more large-minded. It is the answer to Dr. Manning's challenge—why, holding the principles which Dr. Pusey has professed, and seeing how things have gone lately in the teeth of all old theories, he should continue to trust the English Church, and refuse the claims of the Roman. Dr. Manning, ingenious, plausible, and impressive, as he always is, asks, with a lofty magnificent unconsciousness that any one can feel difficulties about Rome, "Why don't you yield?" A good many answers might be given. Dr. Pusey characteristically asks in reply, "Why are we fighting?" Controversy turns him to the inquiry whether there is not some larger and more reasonable way of dealing with the acknowledged and grave differences of the Churches than the way of treating them as irreconcilable, as breaches which no honest man would attempt to close, and which even a good man might wish to see widened. His reflections take the shape of an appeal to the letter of the Roman documents against the popular interpretations of them; an appeal to the comparatively temperate and liberal tone which it seemed once possible for even Roman theologians to take, from the unflinching and scornful hostility which is fashionable among so many of them now—

an appeal from the new Roman Catholics to the old. With the old, he seems to think that there might have been chances of accommodation; and he earnestly protests against these chances being narrowed or made hopeless by the extravagance or violence of their successors. This, it seems to us, is the view with which Dr. Pusey begins to write. It is curious to observe that unconsciously there is a change before he comes to the close of his work, and that the view with which he begins is hardly that with which he finishes. But of this more hereafter.

The idea and desire of a reunited Christendom could not spring up except in a large and generous mind, and they are calculated to draw forth to the utmost all that is most generous in it. Dr. Pusey, for the most part, in the tone and spirit in which he writes, responds fittingly to the grandeur of the theme on which he is engaged. He writes with a forbearance and an abstinence from vehemence and over-statement which are not common in controversy, especially on the questions which he handles; and if any one thinks that because he has strong and definite theological convictions he is narrow and exclusive in his sympathies, this book would show the mistake. Considering the life of warfare which he has led, it is striking to see the hearty warmth with which he speaks of people so opposed to everything with which he is identified as the Evangelical party in the Church, and the great body of Dissenters out of it. But dwelling on a great and fascinating idea, which may after all be but a dream, has its dangers and snares, and these, too, seem to be illustrated in Dr. Pusey's way of dealing with his difficult and slippery enterprise. Where a man's main basis is charitable hope and presumed goodwill, he is apt to take the things which he sees for more than they are worth, and to shut his eyes to those which stand in the way of what he knows to be desirable and right. There is the risk of weak concessions, of strained explanations, of unreal refinements on the obstinate evidence of common sense, of slurring over of substantial distinctions and critical differences, of gravely discussing mere suppositions, perhaps utterly without a foundation, as if they were solid facts. The test of a practical issue being far off, there is the temptation to go on arranging things as we think best, without fairly asking ourselves — What am I really aiming at? What is it that I expect or ask for? What am I coming to? When Dr. Pusey talks seriously of the Roman Church "giving explanations," or of the Thirty-nine Articles and the Decrees of Trent passing away and being merged in the decisions of an Eighth General Council, we are tempted to ask—Is he talking of the world as we know it? And yet it is hardly worth while to spend our pains about any other.

The reunion of Christendom is a vague word, and would have very different meanings, according to the differences of theological systems. With Dr. Pusey it appears to mean, not a fusion into one, but a pacification of the various organised communions of Christendom, which now more or less distinctly are in a hostile attitude to one another. What he desires is that they should authoritatively recognise one another's substantial agreement in Christian faith, and one another's right to think differently on matters which are not of the essence of the common faith; a peace which should be consistent with independence, but which would put an end to the perpetual evidences of jealousy and defiance, and would make it as natural as it is now strange for Christians of one Church to seek and to admit the communion of another. He wants such a peace among Churches as there is among States; such a good understanding and forbearance in the religious organisation of Christendom as there is in the political. Adopting the well-known words of De Maistre, he thinks that the Church of England holds a specially advantageous position for the work of mediation and reconcilement. De Maistre's words have often been quoted, but they are worth quoting again, coming as they do from one who certainly bore no love for what is English:—

Si jamais les Chrétiens se rapprochent, comme tout les y invite, il semble que la motion doit partir de l'Église de l'Angleterre. Le Presbytérianisme fut une œuvre exagérée. Nous sommes trop éloignés des sectateurs d'un culte trop peu substantiel; il n'y a pas moyen de nous entendre; mais l'Église Anglicane, qui nous touche d'une main, touche de l'autre ceux que nous ne pouvons toucher; et quoique, sous un certain point de vue, elle soit en butte aux coups des deux partis, et qu'elle présente le spectacle un peu ridicule d'un révolté qui prêche l'obéissance, cependant elle est très précieuse sous d'autres aspects, et peut être considérée comme une de ces intermèdes chimiques, capable d'approcher des élémens inassociables de leur nature.

Dr. Pusey has something of the same sort in his mind in such statements as the following :—

The Church of England preserves the entire faith, as our Lord left it with His Apostles, to evangelise the world. She believes all that the undivided Church believed, as of faith. Why should not the Church be again united in that faith which she held before a miserable quarrel first caused her disunion? Pious Roman Catholics, too, have felt that the Churches are mutually weakened, that faith and morals and life are alike injured in each by these mutual divisions. . . . The organic reunion of Christendom, and of the Protestant bodies, too, has been held to be possible, even by the Ultramontanes of the Roman Church. Cardinal Wiseman quoted, nearly a quarter of a century ago, the expressions of the " profound and pious Möhler." . . . And now God seems again to be awakening the yearning to be visibly one. . . . The authorities of the great Russian Church (we hear, as sounds floating on the breeze) look favourably on the wish for restored communion. Our position gives us an advantage towards her also ; because, while we are widespread enough to be no object of contempt, there can be no dread on either side of any interference with the self-government of each. . . . We have no ground to fear in regard to her, lest she should force back upon us that vast practical system, still prevalent in the Western

Church, which was one occasion, and is the justification, of our isolated condition. We had nothing to do with the great schism of the East and West. Convinced that (as the Council of Florence states) the Greek and Latin Fathers, though using different language, meant the same as to the Procession of God the Holy Ghost, we should have nothing to ask of her except Communion. . . . A plan which should embrace the Greek Church, also, would facilitate what English Catholics most desire, authoritative explanations. Cardinal Wiseman, in his memorable letter to Lord Shrewsbury, laid down as a principle, "We must explain to the uttermost." The Church of England and the Council of Trent have long seemed to me at cross purposes. In some cases, at least, the Council of Trent proposed the *minimum* of which it would accept, but left a *maximum* far beyond the letter of the Council, to be thereafter, as it was before, the practical system of the Church. The Church of England, in her Articles, protested against that *maximum*, the practical system which she saw around her; but in many cases she laid down no doctrine at all on the subject upon which she protested. She made negative statements to show against what she protested, but set down no positive statement to explain what, on the same subject, she accepted. . . . It may be that, on any such negotiations, she might offer such explanations of the Thirty-nine Articles as the Roman and Greek Churches would accept, such as are suggested by Bossuet, or by the *Commonitorium* of Dupin ; or, according to the precedent of the Council of Florence, the Thirty-nine Articles and the Council of Trent (which was so largely directed against errors of Luther) might pass away and be merged in the Eighth General Council of the once more united Christendom.

Such a pacification, perhaps, if it could be accomplished, would be an improvement on our irrational state of chronic prejudice and warfare, that normal condition with which in spiritual matters we seem to be content, though in temporal matters we look upon it as the proof of barbarism. Yet it seems strange that as Dr. Pusey put his thoughts into words his pen did not drop from his hand, and his mind recoil aghast at the array of hopeless difficulties which the mere mention of such a scheme instantly summons up. The problem is but partially considered when he keeps in view only the ancient ecclesiastical organisations, and leaves out of account, in sketching the reconstitution of Christendom, that vast and stirring body of religious life which has its sphere without them. But, confining ourselves to the limits within which he contemplates the possibilities of reconciliation, what is the process to which he trusts for bringing it about? When he comes to a definite question, he naturally enough treats the matter as one between the English Church and the Roman, and it seems as if his one idea of what is requisite to pave the way for reconciliation, and sufficient to bring it about, is a comparison and adjustment on each side of the theological statements of authoritative formularies. The first thing to observe of this is that it is a very narrow basis on which to rest so large and eventful a scheme.

The mere diplomatic balancing and harmonising of complicated and obscure refinements of thought and expression on subjects of the deepest popular interest does not sound hopeful in our times. It was according to the habit of mind of former days; it is said that, from the decay of theological knowledge, we are incapable of it now; but it is certain we should be impatient of it, where issues such as these are to hang on it. A man must misinterpret the dominant tendencies of thought in our times if he can bring himself to think that anything in the quarrel between England and Rome can really depend on nicely finding the points where the Thirty-nine Articles and the Canons of Trent touch, without striking one another. Dr. Pusey appeals to former instances in which people seemed for a time hopeful of success in this way. But the whole weight of precedents in their results is against him. Compromises and explanations always in the end came to nothing, even when people were more ready to believe in them than we are now. He lays stress especially on the negotiation between Wake and Dupin. Like all the rest, it utterly failed and collapsed at once as soon as it showed the faintest tendency to pass from a private correspondence into anything of public import. It is, no doubt, curious and instructive. It shows on Wake's part great dignity and good sense, combined with a moderate and conciliatory spirit. It shows how little Roman peculiarities *need* mean when people wish to make them mean the least. Dupin appears even to have been willing to drop the term "transubstantiation" if Wake would accept in name seven sacraments, instead of two. He was willing to allow, as was also Dr. Doyle with other Roman authorities of the days previous to Catholic Emancipation, that the points of agreement were numerous, and the points on which there was hesitation few, and these not the most important. But it must be remembered that as a precedent the correspondence is entirely beside the point in discussing questions relating to the Roman Church, and the union of Western Christendom. In as far as it was anything, it was a negotiation on both sides against the Roman Church. It was an attempt to see, not whether a union could be brought about between the English and Latin Churches, but whether, in a quarrel between the French Church, or rather between the Sorbonne and the Pope, a separate alliance against him might not be arranged between the two Western Churches. It may be a question whether a Reformation such as the Sorbonnist doctors imagined, under patrons like the Regent and Dubois, would have been worth the long triumph which the Roman controversialists would have drawn from the close imitation which they would at once have seen in it of what happened under Henry VIII. But it is to little purpose, and hardly fair, to appeal to the correspondence as an instance of the way in which Roman divines have been willing to meet us half-way. In a matter affecting the claims of

Rome it is no use to cite a discredited authority like Dupin.

There seems to be another obvious objection to Dr. Pusey's idea of mutual explanations. It is difficult to imagine that those which he suggests would be given on the English side, or, if they were, that they would be allowed or reciprocated on the Roman. He would restrict the force of the English Articles, which are popularly taken to condemn Romanism in a lump, to well-known practical excesses and corruptions growing out of the exaggeration and misapplication of doctrines which, in themselves, are much older than Romanism, and belong to the times of Athanasius and Augustine, and the four great Councils. This is, in reality, taken in connection with the history and other circumstances of the English Church, a perfectly natural principle of interpretation, familiar to every student of history and exact theology, and as much required and made use of by every strongly marked school of thinking in the English Church as by the disciples of Andrewes and Bull. When stated some time back, in rather a naked and startling form, it caused a great outcry; but this outcry must be felt even by some of those who were foremost in it, with the comment afforded by subsequent events, to have been in itself, whatever may have been the circumstances which provoked it, ludicrously exaggerated and one-sided. The particular interpretations suggested were of various worth and validity, but, on the whole, neither better nor worse than many which had long passed current and are still accepted in entire good faith; while the general object aimed at in putting them forth was the perfectly legitimate one of asserting a standing-room for a particular class of opinions, which on other grounds have ample right to claim their place in the comprehensive system of the English Church. Dr. Pusey uses the same principle also with varying degrees of fairness and success; and in the same way he would wish to see in the Canons of Trent a meaning restricted mainly to the definition of old doctrines which St. Augustine might have taught or allowed. But it seems to have escaped him that the matter on which he is engaged is one in which the more popular views must sway everything. The objection to Dr. Pusey's explanations is not that they are illegitimate, for they are as fair subjects of theological argument as any other; but that they would not be accepted by the great body of those in whose behalf he supposes them put forward. It is one thing for him to claim his right to them for himself; it is quite another to take them as a basis for a supposed attempt at pacification and compromise, involving those who do not in the least agree with him. He forgets who are to be satisfied, before any one could venture to speak with authority on the English side of the question in the way which he suggests; and it is equally plain that he misconceives the general spirit and feeling of the Roman side. His explanations would be thrown back in his face as absurdly insufficient; and if Dr. Pusey had more sense of the ludicrous he would see that most people on all sides require an effort to keep their gravity when they are asked to think of the Roman Church "making explanations." The instinctive and only natural attitude of the Roman mind is to expect unconditional submission from those who are clearly wrong to those who are clearly right. Except under the pressure of circumstances no thought of pacification enters it; no thought of union with any one who does not come in a posture of humiliation and admission of wrong which no English Churchman could assume, and which no one ought to suggest. It has never been the way on the Roman side, except under the stress of a temporary emergency, to extenuate Protestant heresies, much less to admit that Roman language wanted clearing up or modifying. Dupin had a quarrel with the Pope, and was looking out for help. Dr. Doyle was thinking of Roman Catholic Emancipation; and when Cardinal Wiseman talked of "explaining to the uttermost" he had in view a particular state of things which soon passed away, and thus saved him all necessity of explaining. "Bossuet," says Dr. Pusey, "would, we believe, have listened to us"; the terms on which he wishes to see the Church united, Bossuet, he hopes, would have sanctioned; and he asks, "Will those who think like Bossuet aid towards reunion?" We are afraid that he would have found that Bossuet, when not himself contending with the Pope, was inexorable. We suspect that, after all, even Bossuet played with the subject out of compliment to Leibnitz. Dr. Pusey seems to write about ideal Churches, but a union or reconciliation must be between real ones, as they are.

But, as has been remarked before, Dr. Pusey's views or hopes appear to undergo a modification as his work goes on. He does not end in quite the same mind as he was in when he begins. He is, it must be said, loose in his way of writing, and there is a want all through of gathering up and bringing to a point what he means to urge, which is embarrassing to a reader. He began with the contemplation of theological statements, and arguments on the strict letter of ancient articles and canons. But he passed on to the region of the books of devotion that represent the living belief and feeling fostered by the modern Roman Catholic system; and before the work was brought to an end he found himself confronted with the famous Encyclical of last year, and with the comments of the Roman Catholic school, which undertakes with most confidence and appearance of authority to tell us what it means. The aspects of the subject change; and, as it appears to us very naturally, his feelings are not unaffected by the change as it passes before him. The effect on a mind desirous of peace and hopeful about reconciliation, of considering the abstract language of formularies, is very different from that produced by coming face to face to what is, in fact, believed and acted upon in the living system.

He based his idea of the union of Christendom on the distinction between what is authoritative and what is popular. He can hardly have helped feeling at last, that of the two the popular system is the more real and the more powerful, the one which in all practical issues would carry the day, the one with which those who speak of union must expect to have to reckon. If in the one he persuaded himself to think that he could discern the chance of coming to an understanding, what he has shown us of the other must have convinced himself, as it will certainly convince most of his readers, that there is no such hope. The most instructive part of his work is that in which, earnestly desiring union, he makes it evident that all thought of it is impossible.

He enters very fully into the way in which certain Roman Catholic writers speculate and conclude as to what ought to be thought and said of the Blessed Virgin. We are all accustomed to hear a good deal about Roman Catholic exaggeration on this subject; but Dr. Pusey's account can hardly be read without new wonder and amazement, as a picture—we do not say of religious feeling, on which we are not here presuming to pass judgment—but of a manner of thinking and argument. For all is based on argument; all hangs together with at least a show of consecutiveness and completeness. The tendency is all one way, one of perpetual advance, of continual discoveries of something greater and bolder to say. From the single consideration of what was fitting and "congruous" to the Mother of our Lord, a whole system has grown up and expanded to proportions which, to those who are not under its influence, appear simply inconceivable and incredible. Inference has been piled upon inference, deduction has been drawn out from deduction, each growing more astounding than its predecessor. There seems to be a rivalry of hardihood among these writers; each appears to try to outdo those who have written before him in the daring ingenuity with which he claims for the Virgin a more Divine title, and in the nearness of his approach to the fine line which divides the highest devotion from acknowledged blasphemy. The only way of describing generally what it all results in is by saying that what the general sense of Christians has considered for centuries to be the special and incommunicable prerogatives of the Saviour of mankind are now, one after another, with emulous eagerness, claimed, sometimes even with something that marks superiority, for His Mother. "It seems," says Dr. Pusey, "to be part of this system to parallel the Blessed Virgin throughout with her Divine Son, so that every prerogative which belonged to Him by nature or office should in some measure be imputed to her." And his pages bear out to the letter this statement. When she is proved in deliberate dogmatic language, duly guarded by appropriate distinctions, to be, what she is frequently called, our "Co-Redemptress," it might be thought that the zeal of her devotees had reached its limit; but they have advanced one step further, and laid down that she, too, is present, and is received in the sacrament of the Eucharist; they have not only maintained her "co-presence" there, but defined the manner of her presence; and we are told further by Dr. Faber that "to St. Ignatius was shown at mass the very part of the Host which had once belonged to Mary." Apart from the religious judgment on such speculations, there is something absolutely bewildering, like the imaginations of a sick dream, in this audacious extravagance of dogmatism, unfolding itself inexhaustibly into ever stranger and more startling conclusions. But they are the speculations of pious, earnest, intelligent men. Whatever may be said of each particular mode of speaking, they manifestly represent, on the whole, the direction which religious feeling and belief are taking, and taking with great strength, in the Roman communion. They indicate that more and more the subject of them is becoming the governing idea in a very definite and practical manner of regarding the Divine dispensations and man's relation to things unseen.

This, if anything, was meant by the famous dogmatic decree about the Immaculate Conception. The dogma is itself an opinion which any one might hold, if he thinks that there are materials in the world from which to form an opinion about it. In itself there is not much to object to it, except its ground—which is absolutely nothing, not even a tradition, not even a misinterpretation of a dislocated text, nothing but the merest inferences from suppositions about a matter of which we know nothing — and its end, which is to give a new stimulus to a devotion which wanted none. It is the mode of establishing it, and the system of which it is the central feature, which make it so important. And all this is not enough. A popular and accomplished Roman Catholic writer, the late Dr. Faber, is not satisfied with the zeal which he finds on the subject. He looks forward to the speedy coming of a great age of the Church which is to be the "Age of Mary," and declares that what his co-religionists need is an "immense increase of devotion to our Blessed Lady." In fear that he should be thought to have spoken loosely, he adds, "But, remember, nothing short of an *immense* one." "Here in England," he complains, "Mary is not half enough preached." "Thousands of souls perish because she is withheld from them." And, "What God is *pressing* for, if we are to believe the revelations of the saints, is a greater, a wider, a stronger, *quite another devotion*" to her. Here we see the evidences of a real, living, energetic system of belief. Dr. Pusey points them out, and observes also on the dangers to all belief of such a highly strained and really baseless system. But even here he is haunted by thoughts of "explanations." "An authoritative explanation," he says, "such as might be satisfactory to the English Church, might hereafter be of benefit to the Roman also." What can possibly be the worth of any explanations, even if they could be had, against a broad, irresistible, growing popular tendency, such as he has so fully described? Is it not plain that with such a gulf between us, widening every day, they must go their ways and we must go ours?

Of course the foundation of this wonderful system of belief is remarked upon by Dr. Pusey. It could only be possible on the supposition of a controlling and authorising infallibility. It is less certain that Christianity is true than that the ideas and language of the Bull about the Immaculate Conception were unknown to the writers of the New Testament. Yet there is one ground on which they may be believed to belong to the same religion of which the beginnings are found in the New Testament; but one ground only. That ground is the supposition—in opposition to the old idea of a revelation delivered once for all, and coming down to us with due attestation from its original ministers and witnesses—that revelation has been from the first, and is still without interruption going on, not only guarding the original communication, but substantially and largely extending it. St. Paul's doctrines of grace were unknown to the Mosaic times, but the continuous thread of a revelation going on with equal anthority is held to connect two religious systems, apparently so unlike. So is the contrast explained between early Christian teaching and modern Roman theology. A power, varying in intensity but the same in essence, reaches from the days of the Apostles to those of Pius IX.;

a power of declaring to men, in all things needful for them to know, the Mind and Will of God; a power commissioned and qualified to declare it with a plenitude of authority which excludes doubt and dispenses with the necessity of proof. Such a power is believed to reside, not only in the body of the Church, in its episcopate, in its councils, but in the person of the Pope, by those who appear to represent with most authority the present belief of their communion.

One of the saddest parts of modern controversy [says Dr. Pusey] is the thought how much is owing to forged writings; to what extent the prevailing system as to the Blessed Virgin came in upon the authority of writings which Roman Catholic critics now own to have been wrongly ascribed to the great Fathers whose names they bear; to what extent the present relation of Rome to the Eastern Church and to ourselves is owing to the forged Decretals. . . . The forgery of the Decretals, after they had passed for true during eight centuries, was owned by all, even in the Church of Rome. But the system built upon the forgery abides still.

On this foundation rest the prerogatives out of which the claim of infallibility has grown. But, whatever be its foundation, there is now no hesitation in carrying it forward to its most eventful consequences. Dr. Pusey, on whose thoughts of union it forces itself with painful significance, shows us how on this point, too, the energetic disposition to push everything to extremes is manifest. The infallibility which satisfied Bellarmine appears not to satisfy Pius IX., and certainly does not satisfy those who most claim to understand and explain his acts. The Pontificate of Pius IX. has been an active one in the promulgation of authoritative documents; he appeals himself, in the Syllabus accompanying his Encyclical, to as many as thirty-two, touching not merely on matters of faith, but on the various questions, social and political, of the time. These are now said by his champions to be infallible utterances. The old distinctions between matters of faith and morality necessary to salvation, and other matters touching the general good of the Church, its discipline and safety, is, not without a considerable show of logical consistency, thrown aside. If the Pope is infallible at all, it is as reasonable to believe that he is infallible about a practical matter of importance to the Church, like his "civil princedom," as about the exact balance of theological propositions in the Jansenist controversy. He is infallible in all the statements and decisions of the Encyclical. He is infallible in matters of fact and things unconnected with former revelation. He is infallible, when speaking of matters relating to the good of the Church, even in informal communications addressed, not to the whole Church, but to individuals. There are phrases which, even when their meaning is implied, people ordinarily shrink from using; and when they bring themselves to use them they show to what lengths they go. Such infallibility can, in reality, only mean direct revelation ; but most people would avoid bringing it directly into juxtaposition with what is understood among Christians as the "Word of God." But this is not the feeling among the modern interpreters of the Pope's infallibility.

The doctrine of Papal infallibility [Dr. Pusey observes] laid down by Bellarmine is declared in the Encyclical of last year to be inadequate. Pius IX. distinctly rejects as " contrary to the Catholic dogma of the full power divinely given to the Roman Pontiff by the Lord Christ Himself, of feeding, ruling, and governing the Universal Church, the audacity of those who, not enduring sound doctrine, contend that, without (deadly) sin, and without any loss of Catholic profession, assent and obedience may be withheld from those judgments and decrees of the Apostolic See, whose object is declared to regard the general good of the Church, its rights and discipline, provided that that object does not touch upon dogmas of faith and morals." And this "assent" to every utterance of the Pope is required to all his "judgments," which "determine concerning truth and falsehood," and that under pain of mortal sin. " Cardinal Patrizi, writing," says the *Dublin Review*, "to the Catholics of Pius IX.'s own diocese, by his express sanction, and under his very eye, claims for the Encyclical, and, consequently, for every like expression of the Pope's mind, to be *the very Word of God*, to be received on pain of forfeiting heaven." (Italics of the *Dublin Review*.)

After this it can hardly be said that Dr. Pusey

overstates the effect of the claim when he says :—

The present Ultramontanes have apparently changed the old Ultramontane doctrine of the inerrancy of the Pope, *i.e.* that of his preservation from error, into that of Divine perpetual inspiration. We have, according to them, a perpetual revelation from God, disclosing new truths, as infallibly as if St. Peter or St. Paul or St. John were yet on this earth.

Nor are the consequences slow in following. According to an able and authoritative representative of modern Roman Catholic doctrine in the *Dublin Review*, " the Church's whole doctrine on the Pope's civil princedom, as regards its methodical expression, has been commenced, matured, and perfected by Pius IX." And this doctrine, involving the Divine right of the temporal power, has the seal of infallibility. It is not surprising, then, that another prominent Roman Catholic writer should describe the neutrality and non-intervention of the English Government as being "essentially a denial of the Divine institution of the Church," and as making that Government "the most Anti-Christian power in the world."

"Archbishop Manning," says Dr. Pusey—

two years ago, had so made the belief in the personal Infallibility of the Pope *on matters not directly relating to faith and morals* part of his Creed, that he made the temporal princedom of the Pope also a part of that Creed, and maintained that "non-intervention in the question of the temporal power of the Pope is essentially a denial of the divine institution of the Church." . . . He declares that "the English Government, in proclaiming this principle of non-intervention [in the Roman question] assumes an attitude towards Christianity and the Church, and towards the Christian society, which gives it at this moment the melancholy pre-eminence of being the most Anti-Catholic, and therefore, if not in its intentions, certainly in its influences and results, the most Anti-Christian power in the world."

This is too much even for Dr. Pusey's habitual gravity, and he cannot refrain from an unwonted expression of gentle irony—"Happy condition of the world, when mere neutrality makes a civil power the most Anti-Christian in it!"

But here we have the real state of the case. While he is speculating on the possibilities of reunion, down comes the Encyclical, with its train of pretensions and consequences. While he is cautiously examining the language of formularies by the rules of a learned theology, the living belief is growing and asserting itself loudly to a perpetual revelation; and we have Dr. Faber proclaiming the "advent of the Age of Mary," and Archbishop Manning branding the English Government as "the most Anti-Christian in the world" for being neutral in the defence of the temporal power. Dr. Pusey is striving to place some reliance on the more moderate language of great French divines, like Bossuet, more than 150 years ago; but the language of the distinguished ecclesiastic who actually fills the first place in the Roman communion in England, is that the "dogmatic Bull of the Immaculate Conception, and the Encyclical of last year, will, as he believes, mark an epoch in the reconstitution of the Christian order of the world."

Nor is there really any pretence for saying that these views are the unauthorised exaggerations of an advanced party. They are the views of the Pope himself. They are the views of all who claim to speak with authority, and to represent the legitimate and the prevailing belief. The sympathy and assent of every right-thinking man are taken for granted without rebuke or protest. It is hard to see what mark of general sanction they want. They may not actually be the views of the majority; but views which no one can contradict without the charge of disloyalty and trimming are manifestly those which have present possession of the ground. Doubtless there are numbers who have their own opinion as to the soundness of the fashionable doctrines, and the wisdom of pushing everything to extremes. In the very curious extracts which Dr. Pusey has given from the answers from the Bishops of the Roman Catholic world when consulted previous to the Bull of the Immaculate Conception, not only is there great variety of sentiment shown, but the counsels of moderation and good sense vary for the most part with the reputed cultivation and learning of the different parts of the Episcopate. The Bishops of Italy and Spain, for the most part, were eager in their demands that the dogma should be made an article of faith; those of France, Germany, and the United States, by equally marked majorities, hesitated, dissuaded, or were silent. But nothing could show more strikingly the force of the current than the nature of the resistance to it. For among the Bishops who most objected to the proposed article of faith there does not appear to be one who, as a matter of fact, doubted the doctrine as true in itself. They objected on grounds entirely apart from the question of its acknowledged reception, which most of them ostentatiously proclaimed. They objected on grounds of possible scandals or controversial embarrassments, or because they doubted about making a new article of faith at all, or because the reasons for this one were insufficient, or on the curious plea that their people might be startled and shaken by finding that what they had always devoutly believed was not yet, and had still to be made, a formal article of faith. But a certain amount of opposition there undoubtedly was; and as clear is it that the opposition was overborne and swept away, and has left scarcely a trace behind it. With no more notice of the objections than if they had never been invited or made, the Pope pronounced his decree; and, as Dr. Pusey says, all this body of earnest and, in many cases, grave remonstrances became a matter of simply historical interest. The Pope undoubtedly showed that he understood the sentiment and spirit of his communion when he ventured to propose the new article; ventured to elicit whatever objections were felt to it; and ventured, supremely ignoring them, to decree it. This, and not some assumed or imagined system, is the real Roman Church; and what explanations can bring about union between it and the rest of Christendom?

Can there, then, be any use in asking the question seriously whether reconciliation is to be thought of? Here is an *Eirenicon* by one who, within the limits of what he believes to be true and right, heartily wishes it; who is willing to concede a great deal more than most English theologians, probably, would be willing to concede; and what does it come to? Dr. Pusey begins with considerations in conformity with the title of his work. He ends with the Encyclical, and all the decisive proof which it supplies of the impossibility of pacification. The effect of what he himself advances is in curious contrast with his wishes and intention. In the way suggested by Dr. Pusey there is no hope, and, unless something more practical can be proposed, it would be well to realise distinctly that there is none. But though there is always risk in dwelling on what is impracticable, we should not like to say that the consideration of this great question was useless, even when for the present it seems to lead to nothing. In our narrow grooves of sect and party and communion, it is wholesome to be taken out into a larger range of thought, a wider view of possibilities, a more extended circle of sympathies. A more disheartening subject of contemplation than that of the unity of Christendom it is not easy to conceive; but a man can hardly think about it seriously without learning to be more forbearing, more distrustful of loud assertions and narrow claims, more capable of entering into the ideas of others, more apt to believe that he may not have all truth to himself. And though we cannot believe that there is anything to be done or hoped for at the present moment, it is well to notice that discontent with the narrow views inherited from ancient quarrels and a disposition to take a larger and more generous view of the divisions of Christendom are not only found among Protestants. In spite of the general and tyrannous pressure of opinion, there are Roman Catholic writers both in England and in Germany who can discuss the great question with a frankness, a modesty, a boldness, which would do honour to any controversialist, and in a very far larger and more truth-loving spirit than anything that is to be met with in Bossuet and his contemporaries. Some people may think that they are only more prudent and cautious advocates of a bad cause. But this is a very unworthy way of regarding them. Where there is manifestly moderation, self-restraint, honesty, and a desire to be accurate and to be fair, it is injurious to our own character as candid men not to see in them a promising sign for the future. These things take a long time to produce their effects in making people understand one another; but they will do so in the end. And we may hope that in the time to come their influence in every generation will be an increasing one. Reason manifestly gains as time goes on; and the quarrels of Christendom may, perhaps, at last yield to the subtle and vague, yet undeniable power which has made men wiser than they used to be in regard to the interests of this world.

XIX

DÖLLINGER ON THE REUNION OF CHRISTENDOM[1]

IF mankind were able to learn in anything like proportion to their experience, they would have learned by this time, what they certainly have not learned, that, though it is easy to break, it is very difficult to mend. If there is an organic law of the Christian society to be traced in the New Testament, it is the law of unity. On each several occasion which has in the course of centuries led to a breach of that unity, those who must be supposed to have felt themselves bound in conscience to accept division and separation in order to maintain truth and right probably thought that the necessity under which they seemed to act would be but temporary; that the corruptions or oppression against which they protested would in time disappear with their upholders, and that when the tyranny was overpast, and the error

[1] *Lectures on the Reunion of the Churches.* By J. J. I. von Döllinger, D.D. Translated, with a Preface, by H. Nutcombe Oxenham. *Saturday Review*, 8th March 1873.

fully exposed, unity would return with returning reason and sober judgment. It is curious to speculate how many of these disruptions would have been risked if those responsible for them had been able to look forward, and to see that the tyranny might pass and the error be cleared up or surrendered, but that the rent would be incurable. It might have been thought beforehand so obvious and natural that, when the heat of a controversy or a quarrel had died away with the progress of time, the strong forces in Christianity tending to peace and union would resume their paramount influence; that broken ties would be knit together again; that good feeling and calm sense, to say nothing of Christian charity, would easily arrange differences; that sects and minorities would run their course, and then be re-absorbed in the large public body from which they split off. But we know that, though nations may make peace, Churches are irreconcilable. In the whole course of Church history it is hard to find a single clear instance of genuine voluntary reunion between separated bodies. Order and liberty, unity and truth, an honest conscience and peace, may be adjusted to one another, and may long coexist in a religious community; but once let the tension of their rival influences overcome its cohesion, once let the real or alleged claims of liberty, truth, and conscience require secession, and we may safely prophesy that, whatever becomes of the separated fractions, an amputated limb will grow again before their division is healed. One or both may perish, or may pass into something different ; but it is most unlikely that they will ever, as bodies, come together once more.

And yet it is impossible to conceive anything more monstrous than this impossibility of reconciliation between Christian bodies which has hitherto been found to be almost the rule in Church history. All the noblest and best minds in all the divisions of Christendom rebel against it, and earnestly protest against erecting the formidable fact into a necessary condition of religious society. There can be no doubt that it is one of those cases where it is as right not to yield to the discouragement of countless failures as it is right for the martyr to maintain his convictions of the unseen truth, and the certainty of its triumph, with the world against him and death before him. When, then, a divine like Dr. Döllinger, seconded by a disciple who is so worthy to represent him as Mr. Oxenham, invites our thought to the prospects of the "Reunion of the Churches," we listen with the keenest interest and the deepest respect. If only because they are bolder and more hopeful than the mass of us, they command our attention. If attempts in the same direction have hitherto failed, adequate reasons can be assigned in each case for the failure ; it does not follow that they must always fail. The time may not have been ripe for them ; the idea, like many other ideas which have at last found their way into practical life, may need great changes in men's thought and knowledge and circumstances before it can be realised. At any rate it is one which, if it is to be realised, must be kept prominently before the minds of Christians; which, even if we are not to see it realised, we need to have kept before us as a measure of our shortcomings. Dr. Döllinger has claims on attention such as very few men possess. He has few equals in his knowledge of the causes which have led to the divisions of the Church, and which keep those divisions alive. Few Protestants have understood the case of Catholics and sympathised with them as he, alone among Catholics of his eminence, has understood and sympathised with Protestants and Greeks. And, next, anxious as he is for reunion and sanguine of its possibility, he is so resolute and unflinching in his loyalty to truth that, when acquiescence in fraud and falsehood was the alternative, he deliberately chose to countenance by a fresh example the policy of separation. Truth is with him above the unity—the unity apparently unbroken and impregnable—of the most imposing portion of Christendom. The only reunion he will think of is one based on definite and positive avowals of truth; of that which ignores differences, and hides them under ambiguities and compromises, he will have none. It may seem idle to think of reunion on such terms; but at least they are the only fair and reasonable terms, the only terms on which a man of serious convictions could think of it; and on these terms, undaunted by the actual appearance of the world, Dr. Döllinger bids us not despair of reunion. The "Nestor of Catholic theology," speaking [so Mr. Oxenham writes] from a profound acquaintance with the past history of the Church, and an extensive familiarity with the present condition of both Catholic and Protestant society, he declares that union to be at once a supreme necessity of the Christian commonwealth and a perfectly practicable achievement. It is not the voice of a youthful zealot, or a dreaming mystic, or a fiery reformer, which addresses us, but a venerable priest full of years and of honours, cautious by temperament, and of a nation preeminent for its critical acumen, conservative and Catholic to the backbone in his instincts and habits, who sums up in these weighty words the concentrated convictions of a lifetime.

What is there, then, in the circumstances of the time to induce a man like Dr. Döllinger to think that this union of Christendom, hitherto attempted in vain, is now "a perfectly practicable achievement"? We ask the question with the most sincere wish to agree with him, and with the fullest recognition of the calmness and candour with which he surveys the scene. The favouring circumstances which present themselves to his mind seem to be mainly these. In the first place, the events of the last few years have paved the way for a reconciliation between the two greatest bodies of Christendom—the Latin Church of the West, and the chief representative of Oriental Christianity, the Russian Church. It is clear that he thinks that the proverb must come true of the Papal system, that when things are at the worst, they must soon mend. The Vatican decree is the climax of that intolerable tyranny long exercised by the Jesuit party in the name of the Pope; and the result of it must be a general reaction and revolt in the Latin Church against this tyranny, which shall place the Papacy in its true constitutional position, a position in accordance with the genuine tradition of the ancient Church. With a Latin Church which has got rid of the irresponsible despotism established in the Roman Curia, supported by the inflexible policy of the Jesuits, and consecrated by the Vatican decree, the greatest and most serious hindrance to union with the Eastern Church will have been removed; the two great bodies are at bottom agreed in doctrine, and the real bar to reconciliation is the usurped power of the Popes. Another sign is the increased spirit of sympathy in the English Church towards the great traditional Churches both of West and East from which she has so long kept aloof—a sympathy developed directly from the doctrinal and historical position of the English Church, which, in spite of the strong Protestant temper dominant in England, has never let go her hold on Christian antiquity, and whose most learned divines and most consistent schools have always laid the greatest stress on this unbroken connection. Lastly, in the new circumstances of Germany Dr. Döllinger sees a great source of encouragement. Everything has told of late to disengage Catholic Germany from Rome; and what tends to disengage German Catholics from Rome turns their thoughts towards reconciliation with their Protestant countrymen, who were driven reluctantly into separation by precisely the same policy of insolent fraud and imposture which has just now so profoundly shocked the conscience and intellect of devout and learned Catholics. And since Dr. Döllinger's Lectures were published the attitude and claims of the Roman Court have turned a religious quarrel into a political one, and have brought the Pope face to face with the new German Empire, as the secret enemy of German unity and the intriguer against its peace. We know what such a feeling has brought about in former times; our own times are hardly likely to be more patient. And whatever weakens the attraction of Germany to Rome is an opening and advantage towards a unity which shall be independent of it—a unity which, however much men desire it, they will not accept coupled with the condition of submission to Rome.

Dr. Döllinger looks to Germany as the most hopeful source and guide of this movement :—

At the beginning of any eirenic movement, its opponents will outnumber its friends and helpers. But we may count on the sympathy, if not the active help, of those who have at heart the greatness and unity of Germany, and who believe that the political union is but half the work and requires an ecclesiastical union of all its tribes as the completion, fulfilment, and crowning of the edifice. In Germany the two religions are constantly becoming more and more intermingled, and the artificial devices for keeping them apart are more and more felt to be disturbing and hindering influences, superseded by the movement and needs of the present, and are being gradually put aside. . . .

I have found it the almost universal conviction in foreign countries that it is the special mission of Germany to take the lead in this world-wide question, and give to the movement its form, measure, and direction. We are the heart of Europe, richer in theologians than all other lands; and the linguistic knowledge indispensable for this task exists with us in a higher degree than anywhere else. What can, what ought to be done? A negotiation between Churches through plenipotentiaries accredited on either side promises no result; the mere proposal or attempt would now, after July 18, 1870, be a folly. The right instruments would be found in men, both of the clergy and laity, who would unite for common action, first in Germany, untrammelled by instructions, and simply following their own mind and judgment. They would soon draw others to them in rapidly increasing numbers, by the magnetic power of a work so pure and pleasing to God, and would thus be brought into communication with like-minded men in other countries. *The basis of their consultations would be Holy Scripture, with the three Oecumenical Creeds, interpreted by the still undivided Church of the early centuries.* Thus would an international society of the noblest and most beneficial kind be formed, and what began as a snowball might well become an irresistible avalanche.

If Germany were the world, or if the world were like Germany, these expectations might appear better grounded. But large elements have been left out of the calculation. If the Eastern Church were attracted, what about the Latin populations? What about Italy, Spain, and Ultramontane France? What about the strong anti-Catholic element in the English Church? What about the 126 sects of English Nonconformists, fiercely insular, fiercely suspicious of Popery, or of anything which their ignorance or their instinct confounds with Popery? What about the land of triumphant sectarianism, the United States? Do they give much promise of coming into a scheme of reunion like this? The writer and the translator of these interesting lectures will seem to most persons to be too sanguine in speaking of the union which they long for and urge on Christians as a "perfectly practicable achievement." "Why," asks Mr. Oxenham, "is reunion considered an 'idle dream'?" "*Simply because we choose to make it so.*" But who are the "we" with whom it rests? Not himself and those who sympathise with him, but all the Churches, and sects, and parties, and single minds and souls, with all their separate convictions, and traditions, and prejudices, and interests, all over the Christian world. And who is to make all these infinitely differing views and habits and inherited opinions converge to the point where variations may be adjusted and agreement may become possible? who is to attract to any common ground, even for discussion and deliberation, bodies and individuals so remote in distance, and still more remote in ideas and sympathies?

And yet it is no useless task to which Dr. Döllinger

has devoted himself. He seems to us more of a mere pioneer than he conceives himself to be; but it is enough even for a writer of his position and ability to be but a pioneer in the cause which so interests him. Before any such result as he contemplates can be even approximately reached, there must be a long —a very long and doubtful—work of breaking up the ground. Evidently the public mind is still absolutely unprepared even to take in the conception of such a reconciliation as he has in view. The disintegration of what still holds together, the destruction of what is established—this it can understand; but the fusing into a stable cohesion elements which have long been kept apart, the reconstruction of Christendom on larger and nobler principles than have yet ruled in it —this we are yet a long way from regarding as a thing of practical interest. All that can be said is, that there is more chance of gaining a hearing for words of truth and soberness about such questions than there was when Calixtus and Sancta Clara, and Leibnitz and Molanus, and Wake and Dupin ventured to feel their way towards counsels of peace. If many differences have since their days become consolidated and hardened by time, if extreme opinions have become more extreme, yet there is a wider and better-informed public opinion than they had, and one less embarrassed by political considerations, to listen to and judge of reasonable and serious arguments.

For the sake of generations to come it is well to familiarise our own generation with the two great points of truth on which Dr. Döllinger in his Lectures and Mr. Oxenham in his eloquent preface insist. One is the monstrous anomaly of the existing state of division of the Christian Church; an anomaly which, familiar as it has become to us as an existing fact, no prescription can ever legitimate, no excuse can ever palliate as a fatal violation of the very idea of Christianity, and which is obviously and confessedly the poisonous influence for which there is no antidote, sapping its strength and arresting its advance. The other point is the extravagant and absurd insignificance of the greater part of the causes of separation and disunion. To each particular separated body the points of doctrine which keep it separate seem, of course, to be of paramount and supreme importance; but they are likely to appear so to none but its own partisans.

There are two subjects on which to differ is necessarily to find it impossible to unite with any truth and reality in religious association. To differ about the object of worship, and to differ about the source and guarantee of religious truth, must be and ought to be, as long as they last, fatal bars to union. It never can be taken as a matter of indifference whether we refuse worship and all that goes with worship to one who is entitled to it, or whether we give worship to one who is but a creature. And, again, it cannot be a matter of indifference whether or not we believe that there is in the world, in the flesh like ourselves and speaking human words, a living oracle of divine truth, who may be consulted on all the difficulties and dangers of thought and life, and whose voice is certainly and without fail equivalent to the answer of God Himself. Between divergent convictions on these two fundamental conditions of religious belief there can be no compromise; and no religious community could, without losing that which made it religious, embrace them together.

But, besides these two points, it is difficult to name a third, absolutely and *in limine* fatal to an honest attempt to reunite a shattered Christendom. Certain it is that many grave points of difference which in former times have been thought insuperable obstacles to union have sunk more and more into differences of aspect or point of view, perfectly compatible with sincere co-operation and a large measure of sympathy. Dr. Döllinger enumerates a number of questions on which great changes have come either over the Catholic or the Protestant mind, where these questions have been reviewed and examined with competent knowledge, and on a higher level than that of urgent and keen controversy. The Lutheran article of justification is still of interest to numbers, and will still be of interest as long as St. Augustine is studied and human experience remains the same; but it has not the factitious supremacy which it once had, as the article of a standing or falling Church. Questions about the efficacy and administration of the sacraments, about church discipline, such as celibacy and the self-devoted life, about our relations to the other world, such as the intermediate state, the invocation of saints and prayers for the departed, are all questions on which the deepest and most legitimate interest is felt, and on which the right or the wrong is of the greatest consequence; but they are questions which are more and more recognised as having two sides, and admitting of being looked at from varied points of view. There is a wide margin relating to them within which members of the same Church might fairly differ. How the lines are to be traced which shall comprehend these differences, Dr. Döllinger does not adequately show us. But it is no small service that he renders to Christendom when he reminds us, not only as a learned man, but as a sincere Catholic, how much wider these lines of comprehension ought to be than any of those with which use and custom have made us familiar.

XX

BREWER'S HENRY VIII.[1]

THE value of Mr. Brewer's Prefaces to the Calendars of State Papers of the first portion of Henry VIII.'s reign has long been recognised. The result of a close and critical attention to the most important collection of original documents relating to the period that exists in England, they rest on a solid base of authentic evidence, beyond anything yet employed by the historians of the time. Some writers, of course, had known and had used this evidence partially; they had selected what seemed to them material and important; but none of them had undertaken the labour and reaped the advantage of going steadily through the whole series of papers, without picking and choosing, and so of gaining, not strong impressions from this or that salient portion, but a combined and well-proportioned view of the effect of the whole. In this way the weight and worth of documents become more capable of determination than when they are appealed to, as they

[1] *The Reign of Henry VIII. from his Accession to the Death of Wolsey.* By the late J. S. Brewer. *Guardian*, 7th May 1884.

continually are in our histories, as final pieces of evidence. We see in a footnote a quotation from a Venetian report or a Spanish despatch; and the fact of its being contemporary evidence imposes upon belief. But as in the case of manuscripts as authorities for a Greek and Latin text, there is a further question as to the character and peculiarities and relationships of each witness quoted. Before we take the word of the Venetian or the Spaniard, we ought to know not only something of the man himself, but the circumstances favourable or unfavourable to his knowing and speaking the truth. And this is what a study, such as Mr. Brewer gave to the documents, brings with it. He follows his letter-writers through a long correspondence, under changing circumstances, which try and reveal their character, their ends, their prepossessions. Knowing how each writer is situated at the moment—whether his attitude, or that of those whom he serves, is hostile or friendly, whether he is likely to be well informed or kept in the dark, whether he shows credulity or suspicion, whether the interests entrusted to him or the influences brought to bear on him affect the character of his evidence—Mr. Brewer not only had the best accessible evidence before him, but he had the opportunity of forming a comparative estimate of the weight of each of his witnesses. And he was not only an accomplished judge of the worth of evidence; he knew how to use it. The Prefaces were masterly surveys not only of English but of European history in the beginning of the sixteenth century. The threads of that history are very tangled. There never was a time perhaps when impudent and cynical bad faith ran riot so gaily in the counsels and plans of kings and statesmen. The opening of archives and State Paper offices has let us see a good deal of it, though by no means the whole; and into this maze Mr. Brewer has pointed the way, with a caution, a shrewdness of insight, and a clearness of exposition which, though no man cared less for the show of originality, made his review of those strange times one full of novelty and surprise.

The book in its present shape has the disadvantage of a posthumous publication. Though divided into chapters, it appears still in its original form, as when its portions were prefixed as separate Prefaces; and it loses something of the finish, the proportion, and the arrangement of a regular history. There are offhand remarks and phrases which pass muster in the careless freedom of what is ostensibly an account of the contents of a calendar, but which would seem out of place if Mr. Brewer had been professedly unfolding the whole story of the time. In a set history Mr. Brewer would probably have left out the comparison of the buildings of the Field of the Cloth of Gold with "the gigantic glass greenhouse, sprawling over half an acre, in its livid and shapeless length"—an outburst of irritation and outraged taste, plainly caused by a recent visit to the Crystal Palace. But, on the other hand, the Prefaces cover the ground very completely, and they have all the freshness, the strong conviction, the direct and forcible language, of a man who has risen straight from having been daily almost face to face with the real actors in the great drama, who has had in his hands the very paper on which they wrote, and who has been allowed to see with his own eyes in their own handwriting the secrets which they so anxiously concealed. The serious student can spare a good deal of literary completeness for the sake of this directness of impression, rendered with such masterly strength of language.

Besides the insight which Mr. Brewer gives of the connection of England with the tortuous politics of the Continent—a survey far the most penetrating and adequate that has yet been given—two important and to some extent novel aspects of the early years of Henry VIII. come out in his pages. One is his view of the real state of English society, and the condition of English opinion, religious and political, in those years which immediately preceded Henry's attempted Reformation. The other is the real position of Wolsey in the political world of his day.

Remembering all that followed, we very naturally read the early years of Henry VIII. from the point of view of the later Reformation. We look for the signs and symptoms of its approach, for the antecedents which made it necessary and inevitable, for the tendencies which so soon and so formidably developed themselves. We look for the indications of dissatisfaction and unrest and impending changes. We make no doubt of the presence of deep-seated and irretrievable corruptions. The King, we are told, when he began to move, had the heart of the nation with him; and we look to see what movements gave notice of the storm which was so soon to burst. Especially we look for two things—the existence of widespread indignation against an ignorant, superstitious, and immoral clergy, and as the consequence, the rapid growth of a popular sympathy with the reforming movements abroad, and a revival of the never extinct spirit of Lollardry in the middle and lower classes. Assuming all this, what followed becomes natural and clear.

But when we come upon the history, as it shows itself in a day-by-day series of contemporary documents, and as it is interpreted from them, the effect is very different. We have the picture of a great and flourishing kingdom, richer and more prosperous than its neighbours, free from the scourge of war within its borders, in strong and powerful hands which have raised it to the rank of a leading power in Europe, and under whose guidance it takes its full share in the politics, the diplomacy, and the quarrels of the Continent. It is an anxious and eventful time, full of vicissitudes, of success and failure; full of obscure movements and intricate antagonisms; but the one great interest which is conspicuously absent is religion. This, all through the time, is taken for granted, as if nothing threatened the old ways, as if men went about their business acting on the faith which they had received from their fathers, and assuming the ancient constitution of Christendom as something beyond dispute. The "new learning" was abroad; Erasmus and Luther were known and read, but their significance was not perceived; one charmed and the other repelled, but simply for their own sake. There was comparatively little fear, and little persecution of heresy. There were quarrels with the Pope and plenty of abuse of him and his people, as there had been for the last five hundred years past. There were evils and dangers in the State; a gulf, widening every day between the rich and the poor—monstrous extravagance and display in the one, desperate misery in the other; it was the result of the growth of national wealth without a corresponding rise of moral sentiment to govern its use. The engrossing by a few both of land and of merchandise, the encroachments by the powerful on the old rights of the poor, the destruction of small holdings to make great farms, the lowering of wages, the severity of legislation against the weak—all these were sources of mischief, perhaps not very remote, but for the time they were patiently submitted to. What was visible to all and felt by all was the immense power and greatness of the Crown. Royalty, consolidated by the austere genius of the first of the Tudors, had blossomed under the second, at the opening of the sixteenth century, into something not yet known in England. The language, indeed, of law about the rights of the Crown had always been large and imposing; but the Tudors and their servants read into it meanings far beyond what it ever had before them. The Tudors were kings and emperors who rivalled in what they claimed and in what they did the despotic monarchs of the Continent, though with a dexterity of accommodation to the traditions of England which was not known and was not needed on the Continent, and which was lost by their successors the Stuarts. The Supremacy of the Crown, which was to be such a tremendous engine in the changes which the future had in store, was, as Mr. Brewer points out, no new thing in England; it was implied in the claims of William the Conqueror and the two first Henrys; it was asserted in the *Praemunire* statutes of the fourteenth and fifteenth centuries. It was in the air when the Tudors came on the scene; they saw all the use that, in spite of laws and charters and statutes, in spite of the boasted rights and liberties of Englishmen, it could be turned to by strong and fearless handling; and silently and as a matter of course they took it for granted and used it. Beyond the limits of the period comprised in these volumes, it was to do work at which the ears of all Christendom should tingle. The first sign of what it meant was seen in the fall of the Duke of Buckingham, described so fully and so pathetically by Mr. Brewer; the next was the fall of Wolsey. But the rise of this tremendous power, and not any questions of religious reformation, is what really comes before the historian who, without too much thinking of what was to follow, attempts to pourtray this period as it really was.

But the point on which Mr. Brewer has put out his

full strength, and on which he has worked with deep
sympathy and conviction, is the character of Wolsey.
The most ill informed and most prejudiced of writers
could not, indeed, fail to recognise the vast place
which Wolsey filled in his day. But he was too distinctly the representative of a cause hopelessly ruined
in England, and too much associated with the popular
views of its characteristic faults and vices, to have ever
attracted sympathy and admiration. The traditional
judgments about him have been taken from biassed
and untrustworthy sources—ill informed and uncritical
chroniclers like Hall, unscrupulous partisans like Foxe
and Tyndale. To their reckless and sometimes malignant statements Mr. Brewer has opposed testimony
which cannot be tampered with—the documents and
the letters of the time. The deep and thorough study
of the vast mass of State Papers belonging to this time
has revealed to him a very different aspect of the man
that Wolsey really was; and it is impossible, we think,
to follow Mr. Brewer's exposition of his view without
being convinced that it is substantially true. Wolsey,
with all his faults, his own special faults, and the faults
which he shared with the men of his time, was the
first great English minister, the first in that line of
strong men, the creation of modern conditions of
political life, to which in after times Sully and Richelieu
and Colbert belonged in France, and the Cecils,
Strafford, and the Pitts belonged in England. We
see in him the beginnings of modern statesmanship.
Genuine and boundless devotion to the greatness of

his country and his king; ability as vast to conceive
and to carry forward that greatness, and to keep up
the never-ceasing and manifold struggle with those
who were bent on overthrowing it; unswerving fidelity
and loyalty to his master and his master's true interests; unresting industry; the power of a strong man
to keep in view great general purposes, and to inspire
vigour and watchfulness into a whole series of admin-
istrative arrangements; the loftiness of a high-aiming
character shown in all personal enterprises and projects—this is what is seen throughout the service of
the great minister. Pride there was, unscrupulousness, imperious contempt for all obstacles to his will;
nothing stopped him from deceiving the deceivers,
and from being faithless to the faithless; it is easy to
find in him traces of all the bad qualities of the
selfish and corrupt intriguers with whom his daily
business brought him into contact or correspondence.
But he had, what they had not, beyond the thought
of personal ambition, a distinct idea of a great public
duty and obligation, which was, to promote by every
means in his power the greatness and the safety of
England, and with that the renown and glory of his
king. When no one else in that age of fierce ambitions, both the loftiest and the meanest, believed in
the capacity of England to be a great nation equal to
the greatest; and while his king, so brilliant at the
outset of his career, so popular and so magnificent, was
wasting his time in jousting and hunting, in dancing
and gaming,—Wolsey did believe in that capacity for

greatness, and took care that the task which he had undertaken to build it up and consolidate it should not suffer from the King's dislike of business. For this he toiled and watched and plotted and counter-plotted against the most remorseless and most slippery foes. For himself, what he desired was to leave behind him the most splendid educational institutions which the world had seen. If ever statesman deserved well of his country in labour and purpose, if ever any man deserved to be called a great Englishman, it was Wolsey. And this is the great contribution that Mr. Brewer, who yet sees and records all his shortcomings, has made to history.

No doubt all that he attempted, or the most of it, came to nought. Not that the currents of movement and change in the time were against him. He had much sympathy with what was wholesome in those tendencies of change, and with fair play might have guided and controlled them. But he was the victim of two merciless and malignant enmities. He was undermined by a greedy and sycophant nobility, savagely envious of his ability and his greatness, too stupid to play the part which he played in the face of the world, too proud to endure mere genius towering over their heads—the Norfolks, and Suffolks, and Boleyns of the idle and self-indulgent Court. He was sacrificed and struck down at last by the almost incredible baseness and ingratitude of the King, whom twenty years of prosperity, the gain of Wolsey's stedfast loyalty, had utterly spoiled and corrupted, and turned from the high and noble prince whom all Europe had once admired, into the shameless adulterer, beginning, in Wolsey's ruin, a career, as yet unknown in England, in which the words and forms of law were used with audacious and cynical deliberation to cover some of the most monstrous cruelties recorded in English history. The divorce, with all its revolting accompaniments of craft and trickery on all sides, was the miserable end, not altogether undeserved, of Wolsey's otherwise splendid ministry. When it made its portentous appearance his downfall was rendered certain; it would have been better for his fame if he had perished earlier, in withstanding it in its very first stages. But the special form and mode which the King's brutal malice chose to give to his overthrow— the *Praemunire* sued out at common law for the exercise of the Legatine authority which he had assumed and exercised by the King's wish, and by his sanction, and for his interests, and the wholesale and immediate ruin which *Praemunire* brought with it— has scarcely a parallel among the worst inventions of tyranny.

In that perfidious and violent age things were done more cruel and more bloody; but there is nothing to be found so base, so full of the sickening and hypocritical meanness of an ostentatiously bluff and outspoken nature, as Henry's treatment of his great minister. Then he seized the power which Wolsey had created for him; and in his hands, which none controlled and none resisted, English history became a byword in Europe for reckless and insolent dealing with the most sacred interests, for all the shame of monstrous caprice, of unbridled selfishness, and of appalling bloodshed.

XXI

MOORE'S LECTURES ON THE REFORMATION [1]

PUBLIC judgment of the English Reformation, its causes, methods, and results, would probably have taken an almost accepted and settled shape, and that a severe if not adverse one, long before this, but for two things. One was the theological requirements of a large and powerful party in the Church, uncongenial in its spirit, leading ideas, and practical life to those of the Church, measured by the Church's devotional and most authoritative theological standards. The other was the temporary popularity of a brilliant *ex parte* case for the extreme proceedings of the Reformers, Mr. Froude's history. The Evangelicals wanted something authoritative to sanction the unecclesiastical and even Puritanical platform of their dogmatic teaching; and they found this amply furnished in the *formulae* of doctrine and the general religious temper

[1] *Lectures and Papers on the History of the Reformation in England and on the Continent.* By Aubrey L. Moore. *Guardian*, 19th November 1890.

of a party whose chiefs had not only taught, but died
for what they taught. This was an advantage of
which the Evangelicals naturally, and with good right,
made the most, loudly, if not always consistently:
they insisted that there must be no going back behind
the Fathers of the Reformation; Cranmer, Ridley,
and Latimer, Hooper and Jewell, were the true
apostles of the modern English Church, the creators
of its spirit, and the spokesmen of its doctrine. And
as the Tractarian movement had alarmed the national
jealousy about Popery—a deeply rooted feeling quite
independent in its origin from the Reformation—the
circumstances of the times helped them; while to
influence not theological partisans but neutral men of
the world, Mr Froude's volumes put the great Tudor
revolution in a light in which it had never been put
before. But for these coincidences the current judgment on the Reformation would by this time have
been that of writers with no strong theological prepossessions, but who judged by the common standard of
right and honesty among men, and who hated the
injustice, the insincerity, the cruelty, and rapine of a
revolution, even if some of the causes which provoked
it were real, and some of its results were beneficial.

But the glamour of Mr. Froude's romance has
somewhat faded; and though there are still some who
see nothing absurd in the assumption that the opinions
and decisions of the Tudor Reformers are the final
law and settlement of a Church which had, after
terrible trials and almost ruin, to be reorganised

afresh in the following century, the time has gone by when it seemed irreverent to criticise the words and deeds of the Reformers, and when it seemed an act of piety to put a good meaning on the most questionable of their words and deeds. We feel at liberty to judge the Reformation as we might judge the French Revolution, or the system of the Papacy, or the proceedings of the Long Parliament. We do not feel ourselves bound to take it *en bloc*, as pure in its origin and unmixed in its blessings. We can venture to examine the motives, the capacity, the learning, the honesty of its chief representatives. We have been freed from a superstitious deference to it; and any school or party will be ill counselled which attempts a revival of that feeling for it. It may become an instrument of ruin. It never will be a bond of peace. It is no longer safe to view it as it was viewed at one time, as almost a second revelation. Our authorities about it are no longer Foxe's untrustworthy stories, but the letters and records of the men themselves and their contemporaries; and our guides and interpreters are no longer Burnet and Merle D'Aubigné, or even Hallam and Macaulay, but writers of the severe and judicial temper of Bishop Stubbs and Dr. Brewer.

It was in this spirit that Mr. Aubrey Moore studied the history of the Reformation, on which he lectured at Oxford as Dr. Bright's assistant; and this volume, edited by his friend, Mr. Coolidge, of Magdalen College, is, unfortunately, all that remains of these lectures. He probably intended to make a finished work on the subject on which he was lecturing; but the time never came, and we have here a certain number of lectures and papers more or less completely written out, and with them a collection of notes and heads of lectures in the briefest shape, eked out by fragmentary memoranda jotted down by pupils at his lectures. Yet, incomplete as the volume is, and a manifestly inadequate representation of Mr. Aubrey Moore's vigorous and comprehensive mind, the book may be made of great use as a text-book both for lecturer and student, and the finished papers in it, some of which have already appeared in the form of reviews, show the mastery which he had over the facts of character and thought in that perplexing time which we call the sixteenth century, and show also with what power and vividness he could put his views before an assemblage of pupils.

In the English Reformation he distinguishes, as others have done, two stages; but he dwells with adequate force on the all-important differences between them. The acts of Henry VIII., putting aside their motives and methods, were of a kind familiar to the great kings of those days, in their continual wrangling with the Popes. Francis I., when the Pope was obstinate, threatened a Gallican Council. Charles V., in the same case, had always hanging over his refractory spiritual superior a national council of the German nation. Even Philip II. could not bear everything from Rome, and sometimes talked strange language for so devout a Catholic. The difference was that the scene shifted more rapidly abroad, that Henry had a definite personal object, and was doggedly resolute about it, and that he had the nation, Bishops and clergy, Peers and Commons, at his back, in their deep hatred, a feeling not of yesterday, of the arrogance and extortion of the Roman Court. Foreign interference and greed, long practised in fearless security at Rome, and borne, not without much bad language, by a much-enduring clergy and laity in England, ended in a sullen disgust, not yet with the Roman creed, but with Roman practical ways. So when Henry stood up to the Pope, and asserted the independence of the English kingdom and the English Church, though he put his claim in terms which implied a new submission to himself, even Fisher, in the first and less violent form of the claim, could accept it; and the other Bishops, like Gardiner, made no difficulty about it. For the independence which Henry claimed, he claimed not as the author of a new form of religion, but as the representative of the ancient and existing Church, which he was to protect and reform, but not to create anew. And though his changes—as was inevitable with a man like Henry, more like an Asiatic Sultan, or the Ottoman Mahmouds and Solimans and Selims, in his sensuality, his fanaticism, his caprice, and his cruelty, than like any other Western king— were tremendous and far reaching, yet to the end the independence of the English Crown and Church was the ruling and paramount consideration, and the continuity of the Church was never so much as touched by his measures. In truth, as Mr. Moore points out, the English ideas of the relation of the kingdom and Church to Rome, and of the obedience due to the Pope, had, from the days of William the Conqueror, been much looser than those which prevailed on the Continent, where rulers and people were in closer and more constant contact with the Popes, and where the study of the canon law was a perpetual reminder of their claims.

The second stage was widely different. At the death of Henry power passed from an irresistible despot into the hands of rival oligarchical cabals of selfish and unprincipled schemers, the Seymours and Dudleys, who were, perhaps, the basest and most worthless politicians who ever had made themselves masters of the fortunes of a great nation. Public plunder, for themselves and for the partisans who were to strengthen their power, became the real object of these new rulers of England; while a crowd of foreigners, and Englishmen who by living abroad had become as estranged as foreigners, and who brought back the peevish bitterness of their own quarrels abroad, were called in, to devise a new form of government and teaching for English religion. With these men the guiding principle was to bring about a complete break with the old English Church. It could not be done at once, for they did not quite know their own minds as to what was to replace it, and the temper of the nation would not have endured a sudden change. But they had their foreign masters on the Continent, who, in the midst of their own theological disputes, condescended to lay down the law for their English friends, who consulted them so deferentially; and the advice of these masters was prudent but steady advance in the ways of Zurich and Geneva. Their special object of criticism and attack was the Prayer-book; and in the humble and feeble apologies for it we may see how ready their friends in England were to alter and give it up, if they dared. The objection to the surplice and Hooper's obstinacy against the "relic of the Amorites" were really meant to force on the question as to when the break with the past should be declared, when the denial of continuity and the fresh start of English State religion should be publicly notified. The hesitations of Cranmer—the most bewildered and vacillating of public men, who knew so much, and yet too much ever to make up his mind for good—humane and considerate by nature, yet who had lent himself to some of Henry's worst acts, and could consent to the burning of an anabaptist—put off the day, so impatiently waited for by the Reformed teachers abroad and by à Lasco and John Knox at home, when England should dutifully follow in the path of the Swiss and German Churches. Happily, though within so little, that day never came; and Edward's death left the English Church miserably maltreated and in serious danger, but still a body in which its continuous life had not been extinguished. But it was only the death of Edward that prevented the Privy Council and their divines from breaking at last with the Church of St. Augustine, and taking out new commissions from the Popes of Switzerland, not less infallible and intolerant than their antagonist at Rome.

But the Marian period and the Spanish match followed, and that, by adding another evil memory to the old dislike of Rome, left things still in confusion. Mr. Moore notices how many of the worst things of those days were "un-English." Henry's idea of kingship was "un-English"; it was even beyond Italian tyranny; it was Asiatic and barbarian. The ways and ideas of the foreigners who were the forefathers of Puritanism, and were so warmly received and well provided for in England, the Peter Martyrs, and Bucers, and à Lascos, were utterly "un-English"; their pedantry, their positiveness, their airs of superior wisdom and religion, as if they had come to teach the ignorant and guide the blind, did not suit English ideas. Mr. Moore remarks on this character in the Marian persecution :—

The four years, 1555-1558, include the most un-English period of English history. . . . Everything tends to throw the blame not on the Church, but on the State. The Bishops were notoriously backward in executing the law. . . . The strong Spanish influence of Philip and his inquisitors explains the fires of Smithfield. Philip's sentiments are not a question of doubt, and his familiars, Alphonsus da Castro, and the Dominicans, Pedro di Soto and Juan di Villagarcia, may be judged by their views and actions in Spain. The persecutions can in no way be made intelligible to Englishmen except on the assumption of strong foreign influence.

The Elizabethan settlement and the foreign Reformation are sketched by the same firm and discriminating hand. We may call attention especially to the striking account of Zwingli, a paper which shows how a strong and just critic may be separated by the deepest gulf from the spirit and teaching of the object of his criticism, and yet be able to give a more intelligible, and, therefore, a more generous and interesting representation of it than the strongest partisan.

XXII

A FRAGMENT ON ELIZABETH [1]

THE movement which we call the Reformation of the sixteenth century was really a great revolution. It was not merely a great and permanent change in all the ideas and habits of life; beyond that it was a great catastrophe, violent and irresistible, like an epidemic or an earthquake. It was revolutionary in its objects, in its spirit, in its methods. There is only one parallel to it in the history of modern Europe, and that is the revolution which began at the close of the eighteenth century. By revolution, I mean a great political and social convulsion, in which all the foundations of life, hitherto deemed secure, even amid the conflicts of parties and the changes of power, have been unexpectedly overthrown; all the leading assumptions

[1] The fragment which follows, and which bears the date of May 1889, was written as the opening chapter to a volume on Queen Elizabeth which the Dean had undertaken to contribute to Mr. Morley's series of English Statesmen. Nothing beyond this chapter was written, but, incomplete though it is, it has seemed worth while to add it to the other historical sketches in the volume.

under which men have ordinarily passed their lives and followed their business, have been violently and successfully broken down. Whatever reasons there may have been for so vast a change, whatever benefits may have followed in its train, a revolution is in its own nature subversive, destructive, cruel, unreasonable. The ordinary laws of the game in the political trials of strength, the ordinary restraints that men submit to, even in their ambition or their quarrels, are trampled down with scorn. Action begets reaction, and a revolution induces in its opponents a temper as fierce, as unscrupulous, as unsparing, as its own. The building-up may come afterwards; meanwhile, it is a burst of enthusiasm in the direction of hatred and ruin; and with watchwords which inflame, but of which it has never dreamed of fathoming the meaning, it plunges two or three generations into confusion and anarchy, without foresight, or care to provide an outlet. It is Elizabeth's great claim to statesmanship that she was able, during her lifetime, and for some time after, to keep the formidable heritage of revolution, bequeathed to her by the members of her house who had preceded her, from bursting all bounds, and wrecking in its fury the peace and hopes of her realm.

The political conditions of her time were difficult and dangerous; but, serious as were her political difficulties, they cannot be said to have been greater than have been confronted and surmounted by others who have had to guard the fortunes of England. Elizabeth's new and special trial was the revolutionary break-up and confusion of religious ideas in England and all round her. No such revolt had yet happened in the history of Christendom as that which followed Luther's defiance of the Pope at Wittenberg. It was a revolt against ideas which had long held possession of the minds of Christians; but it was still more a revolt against authority—authority hitherto regarded as supreme, and venerated as the highest and most sacred thing known on earth. And in proportion to its hitherto matchless and unapproachable greatness, was the completeness of the defiance hurled against it; in proportion to the reverence and sanctity which had hitherto encompassed it, were the savage scorn and mockery of the new revolters. Venerable with an authority supposed to come directly from the Redeemer, it had long claimed without contradiction the allegiance and obedience of every Christian soul, of his thoughts and convictions as well as of his outward acts; it was now rejected as an imposture, and denounced as the greatest source on earth of error and sin. It had challenged a place in the economy of grace only short of God; it was now held up to execration as the Antichrist, the Man of Sin. And this great revolt proceeded on its victorious path with a lighter heart, because it was able to set up against the authority which it dethroned a counter authority which was acknowledged by all as sacred, and which was put forward by the revolters as infallible and all-sufficient. No Catholic could challenge the authority of the Bible; in the Bible the Reformers had found the reality of which they had destroyed the counterfeit—a source of truth without alloy or doubt, a law and a judge without appeal, a foundation of doctrine clear and certain, where an answer could be found for every question by the unlearned as well as by the learned. That the Bible was open to varying interpretations, that teachers of great name and considerable schools and parties among the Reformers deduced from its texts very different systems of theology, did not arrest the confidence of an age which believed itself to have found, in divine knowledge as much as in new kingdoms and continents, what other ages had failed to discover. In an astonishing manner, unlike anything before or since, the subject of religion, with its questions, its debates, and its practical consequences, took possession of the minds of men. It governed political action, it dictated and it destroyed alliances, it kindled wars, it was the talk of the market-place and the secret of the council-chamber. No man doubted that he and his friends were in full possession of the truth. The revolution had brought its usual fruits in immense divergence of opinion, growing more extreme in exclusions and more passionate in zeal as time went on. On all sides was debate, uncompromising positiveness, stern condemnation. But all sides dogmatised as being sure that they knew the mind and will of God; and all sides waged their war, on paper or in the field, in the name of God, and in support of His evident cause.

Amid this turmoil of religious strife Elizabeth's life was passed. The strife began before she was born, and it had almost reached its height when she died. It was ever on the surface of every question she had to deal with, and every resolution she had to take. There was much of political growth, much of social and intellectual development, much of commercial expansion, going on beneath it. Influences as powerful, and even more far-reaching in the long run, were at work at the same time; but for the present they were in the background, and they had for the most part to ally themselves to the name of religion to gain due attention. What was apparent, what men professed to be interested in and to take sides about, what seemed to be the supreme object of their hopes and fears, their delight or their abhorrence, were the conflicting principles and assertions and practical habits of rival religious systems. Amid these turbulent and perilous elements Elizabeth had to find her way, to mediate, to balance, to reconcile, to bridle, if necessary to crush without scruple or mercy; and meanwhile to lay solidly the foundations of a modern State. The forces which she had to control and direct were not those which try the power of ordinary rulers. They were far more unmanageable than those which usually are in play in the political game. For they drew their strength from what is far stronger than even passion, ambition, or expediency; they had their roots in the domain of conscience, conviction, and faith. On all sides these great names—which admit of no accommodation, which pardon no compromise, which demand self-sacrifice—were invoked in real earnest. Elizabeth had to rule a people never very tractable at the easiest of times, but in her day restless after the agitation of the most tremendous revolution they had yet heard of, and on both sides made obstinate and impracticable by the persuasion that interests far higher than anything worldly were at stake; and that in a novel way which admitted of no questioning, the will of God had been disclosed to them, and His cause committed to their hands.

Elizabeth came to the throne, a young woman of twenty-five, at a moment of great disaster and difficulty. Calais, "the chief jewel of the realm," had just been lost—a cherished trophy of ancient triumphs, and an important place of arms in the perpetual quarrel between England and France. The resources of the country had been drained for the benefit of foreigners. Finance was in utter confusion. And the English soldier had fallen behind the soldier of the continent in his arms and the skill to use them; and except for his undiminished spirit of valour was held in little account. And at home the nation was sore and deeply angry at Mary's unhappy reign, and at the insane and heartless cruelties which she had made part of her religion. On all sides there was discouragement, uncertainty, exasperation. The reigns of Edward and of Mary had introduced, or at least had deepened, a new division, destined to last for centuries, and certainly not yet effaced; separating and estranging great bodies of opinion in English society —those who clung to the older traditions of religion, and those who hated and abhorred them, and claimed the adherence of all true and honest Christians to changes which were equivalent to a new religion. And between these classes of men there was the most hopeless distrust, and on both sides a fierce vindictiveness. All the elements of mischief abounded. The prospect was gloomy and formidable; but the new Queen showed no signs of fear or trouble. Elizabeth had on her side the deep reverence of Englishmen for the royal name, her own youth and wit and gaiety of mood, and, as some thought, personal beauty, and the consciousness of a temper as fearless, as resolute, as inflexible, as that of her father. She was sure that with these things she could win the hearts of her subjects; after so many years of failure and distress she brought them the hope of a brighter time; and with this confidence in their loyalty, and her own power to rule them, she quietly took her place, for which she had long prepared herself, and faced what was to come.

What came was serious enough. She had to choose between peace or war with France and Scotland, and ultimately between peace or war with

Spain. Her legal title to the Crown was strangely irregular; it depended on the arbitrary will of a father who had declared her illegitimate, and had never in words recalled his declaration. The Crown once worn, it was said, cured all defect of title. But she had to meet the claim of a rival Queen, a claim which many of her subjects thought better than her own, and which was backed by the power and ambition of the great House of Guise. She had to choose how she would deal with the proffered friendship, and more than friendship, of Philip II., to whom in Mary's reign she probably had owed her life—a friendship which she knew could only be had on very difficult and definite terms, perilous to accept, yet certain to turn to deadly enmity if refused. She had to claim her rank in the proud and jealous Courts of the continent without fear or shrinking, though they looked on her as the illegitimate daughter of a heretical and dishonoured mother. But beyond all these political difficulties was the question of religion. It seemed as if in this she must at once take her side without hesitation or mistake. The daughter of Anne Boleyn, she had always lived with those who sympathised with the new teaching; and under Mary she had been exposed to insult and extreme danger for her supposed opinions. And it was naturally expected on both sides that as the days of Mary were gone, the days of Edward VI. would come back. They expected her to respond by immediate and unequivocal measures to the eagerness of the winning side. But her measures were neither immediate nor unequivocal; neither in this nor in her political resolutions would she allow herself to be hurried. On one point only she left no room for doubt. She made it clear at once that she meant to use to the full, in carrying out what she judged necessary or desirable for the good and tranquillity of the realm, the powers gathered up in the royal prerogative by Henry VIII. She let it be seen indeed by a number of slight but significant indications which way her leanings went in the great conflict of religion—which way she ultimately meant to go in asserting her independence. Out of a host of councillors of opposite opinions she chose for her special adviser, William Cecil, who, though he had conformed under Mary, as Elizabeth herself had, was known to be deeply hostile to all the Roman claims. She allowed certain portions of the service to be said in English. She forbade the Elevation of the Host. But she sternly forbade all premature and unauthorised changes. She did not mean to have her hand forced by either party. She would have no wild preachers; the old ceremonies were to go on for the present, and were observed at her coronation. She herself set an example of devotion, and would allow none of the customary irreverence of the Protestant zealots in her presence. And she took pains to appear fair to the weaker side by admitting at once a large minority of them to her council, though any violent language or appearance of resistance was visited by immediate imprisonment. All sides were to learn to wait her time and her pleasure. And she was determined that her steps should be unforced and deliberate.

She was not singular among the princes or the people of her time in thinking that it was her business, indeed her chief business, to settle what was the best religion for her subjects. The belief prevailed in Germany and in Geneva, as well as in France and Spain; and it prevailed, at least it was taken for granted, in England. It was acted upon by Philip II. It had been acted upon by Mary as well as by Henry VIII. and Edward VI. Elizabeth came to the throne inheriting from her father this belief; and from the first she never doubted that to fulfil this duty adequately, in the face of all difficulties, and at the sacrifice of her own personal opinions and tastes, was the highest work of her royal office. But she took warning from what had gone before, and what she herself had seen. Haste, rashness, violence, one-sided extremes, had been the common marks of the forms of religious policy—except in their revolutionary character, so different—of her father, brother, and sister. She was determined to be as masterful as any of them, and to have her way—the way she chose to go in—as effectually, in the face of the resistance which she knew she must reckon with. But she came after great failures; and the experience she had thus gained, and her own larger temper and intelligence showed her that whatever in religion was now, after all that had happened, to take hold of the

English mind, however strong and clear it might be in point of independence of foreign interference, must have its roots in the past, in the history of the realm, and in the common convictions and sanctities of Christendom ; and that to violate them might attract a few daring speculators or satisfy a few fanatics, but must alienate the multitudes and the sober and quiet spirits who loved to worship in the churches and at the altars where their fathers had worshipped, and round which their fathers were buried ; and who could not bear to think that they were separated in any important degree from what their fathers believed and hoped. It was her object to maintain the continuity of the Church, to secure for it a fixed and stable character, which it had lost in the storms of the late reigns ; and to get it to speak and minister in a way which should command the assent of calm and reasonable believers. That her idea could be only imperfectly worked out, that her policy issued in results which could easily be assailed as illogical, anomalous, imperfect, did not greatly disturb her. Her own interest in religion, though serious, was probably not very deep. She dealt with the whole matter as a statesman would ; and she knew enough to know that a statesman must often be content with something much short of what he aims at.

With no waste of time and with resolute purpose, but without impatience or hurry, her domestic and foreign policy went on side by side. The country had to be recovered from its false position ; a need-

less war with France had to be brought to an end
even with the real, though disguised, surrender of
Calais; Philip II.'s offer of his hand and protection
was courteously but firmly declined—if she married
she would willingly marry him, but she meant to reign
and die a maiden Queen. An eye had to be kept
on what was the real danger of the moment, the
movements of the French Dauphiness, and the
establishment of French power in Scotland. The
defences of the country, the levies, the ships, and the
armaments, which had been allowed to decay, had
to be put in order. And, as a matter of course, a
new Parliament was called. Its first statute was a
recognition of the ancient supreme jurisdiction of the
Crown against all foreign interference; its visitatorial
power over everything, and a refusal of the Marian
statutes on religion. But Elizabeth's shrewdness
showed itself in almost ostentatiously refusing Henry's
favourite title of "Head of the Church." The Act
of Uniformity in the use of the English Prayer-Book,
Edward's Prayer-Book, with some significant altera-
tions, followed. She would not have her legitimacy
canvassed or asserted by Act of Parliament as Mary
had done; it was taken for granted in making it
treason to deny the Queen's title. And Mary's
restitutions of Church property were set aside,
and all such property was united once more to
the Crown. A protest from the Lower House
of Convocation in favour of the ancient doctrines
had no effect. And by way of accustoming the

public mind to the notion that the changes from
what been established under Mary were not the mere
result of arbitrary will, but were the inevitable lessons
of instructed reason dealing with the history of the
Christian Church, a sort of theological tournament
was appointed at Westminster, at which, as might
have been expected, the Roman Catholic champions
were declared by the Queen's officer, who presided,
Sir Nicholas Bacon, to have been signally worsted.
There was a good deal of plain speaking on the part
of the Roman Catholic leaders in Parliament; but
the majority was now against them, and the answer
to their strong language was sometimes a summary
order for imprisonment. But though it was quite
clear that all Mary's work was to be undone, and
her men replaced by others, and that opposition,
especially on the part of the Bishops, involved for
them disgrace or arrest, there were no signs of sanguinary reprisals. The outward form of ecclesiastical
government remained. Death, which had swept off
a large number of the old Bishops—among them
Pole and Gardiner—saved the Government the appearance of wholesale deprivations. She kept her
ambassador at Rome till the fierce Caraffa Pope, Paul
IV., with insults and threats, refused any longer to
recognise him or his mistress. Finally, with as much
careful observance of ancient forms and rules as was
possible in such a revolutionary time, and with not
more violence done to them than had been occasionally done in troubled times in the election of a Pope,

the see of Canterbury, vacant since Pole's death, was filled up, and Matthew Parker, learned, cautious, sensible, and in full sympathy with Elizabeth's policy, continued the great line of English Primates. The other vacant sees were duly filled up, and the outward order of the Church appeared as it had been in the first days of Edward VI.

But the beginnings of Edward VI.'s reign had been violently disturbed, and greatly changed as it went on. The ecclesiastical leaders of his time felt the want of some authority behind them, and turned for countenance and support to the reformers of Geneva, Zurich, and Bâle. An eager correspondence began. The counsels of the Swiss were given with magisterial condescension and decision, and were received in England with submissive deference. The hesitations, the inconsistencies, the clinging to old usage on the part of the islanders, excited the mild contempt of the thoroughgoing theorists of the school of Calvin and Zwingli, who were in their sweep of generalisation and trenchant logic very much what continental thinkers are to Englishmen now. It was coming to this, that English ecclesiastical affairs were to be directed by rescripts from Switzerland as formerly by briefs from Rome. How far this subservience would have been carried it is impossible to forecast; it was put an end to by Edward's death. But the changes in Mary's time had scattered a great number of the enthusiasts of the foreign school over the continent, and naturally they found their way to the Calvinistic centres on the Rhine and in Switzerland. There, during Mary's reign, they worked out systems of doctrine and platforms of discipline under the eye of their foreign guides. There too came, as usual, the division between the extreme men and the moderates, the impatient and the cautious, the irreconcilables and the temporisers and opportunists. It was a division which extended over the whole field of religious differences in Europe; and it led among the English "exiles" to disputes and quarrels which brought down upon them the interference of the local authorities to compel the strangers to keep the peace. At Mary's death the refugees flocked back, naturally hopeful, naturally resentful, naturally eager to begin the good work for which they had been preparing themselves abroad. They were in touch more or less with the public men of the reforming party, who saw in the "exiles" at once an indispensable source of strength, and also—from their violence and recklessness, which offended and alarmed the Queen—a grave embarrassment. She herself saw in them a religion which she disliked, and a menace to her prerogative. And though she was obliged to put up with the sympathy which her chief servants, Cecil, Leicester, Knollys, Walsingham, Essex, showed to these disciples of the foreign schools, she herself revolted from their arrogance and narrowness, and discerned that they were even more dangerous than the Romanists to that larger and more comprehensive Church system on which she had set her heart. For they were allies whose demands increased in extent and peremptoriness, and who would be turned into implacable enemies and disloyal subjects as soon as they found that the Queen would not concede changes which they believed to be according to the will and commands of God.

END OF VOL. I

www.ingramcontent.com/pod-product-compliance
Lightning Source LLC
Chambersburg PA
CBHW020543300426
44111CB00008B/774